THE WAKE OF THE WHALE

THE

WAKE

OF THE

WHALE

*Hunter Societies in the
Caribbean and North Atlantic*

RUSSELL FIELDING

Harvard University Press

*Cambridge, Massachusetts
London, England
2018*

Publication of this book is supported, in part, by a grant from
Furthermore: a program of the J. M. Kaplan Fund.

Library of Congress Cataloging-in-Publication Data
Names: Fielding, Russell, 1977– author.
Title: The wake of the whale : hunter societies in the Caribbean and
    North Atlantic / Russell Fielding.
Description: Cambridge, Massachusetts : Harvard University Press, 2018.
Identifiers: LCCN 2018009236 | ISBN 9780674986374 (alk. paper)
Subjects: LCSH: Whaling—Saint Vincent and the Grenadines. |
    Whaling—Faroe Islands. | Whaling—Environmental aspects. |
    Whaling—Health aspects. | Hunting and gathering societies—Saint Vincent
    and the Grenadines. | Hunting and gathering societies—Faroe Islands. |
    Marine resources conservation—Saint Vincent and the Grenadines. |
    Marine resources conservation—Faroe Islands.
Classification: LCC SH382.2 .F54 2018 | DDC 639.2/8—dc23
LC record available at https://lccn.loc.gov/2018009236

For Diane
l,h

Contents

THE WAKE OF THE WHALE

INTRODUCTION

———

The Sea Bean

If you were a young Faroese boy living in the village of Nólsoy during the late sixteenth century, the scale of your world would be defined by the beaches and sea cliffs that ring your small North Atlantic is-land, also named Nólsoy. An island with one village; the village's name is the island's name. That's the scale. Too young to row, to fish, or to sign aboard a merchant vessel from the Danish trade monopoly, you would watch as your father occasionally rowed across the strait to sell the puffins that your older brothers had caught on the mountain or the wool that he had sheared from your family's flock of sheep.

This settlement across the water, at the time a village of barely more than a hundred, is called Tórshavn—literally "Thor's harbor," a safe haven for the Norse god of thunder and lightning. Despite its diminutive size, Tórshavn would long serve as both the internal cultural hub and the entrepôt for commerce from abroad to the Faroe Islands. One French traveler to the Faroes would later call Tórshavn "le Paris de l'archipel," equating its importance within the archipelago to that of his own beloved French capital.[1] Tórshavn achieved this status due to the significance of a small peninsula jutting into the harbor that, since the Vikings first settled here in the ninth century, has been used as a meeting place, a space for discussion among village chiefs and landowners, a location where differences are resolved. This landform, called Tinganes—meaning "parliament peninsula"—sits obscured by the intervening hills, just out of your view. To a young boy whose childhood universe is constrained by the Nólsoy coastline, Tórshavn may as well have been *le Paris de France.*

Spending your days in the island's hills and beaches, chasing sheep, avoiding the dive-bombing skua birds, you watch for *huldufólk*—half hoping and half dreading catching a glimpse of these hidden people, like elves, who are said to inhabit the rocky places of the North Atlantic. You spend a lot of time on the beach. Since the medieval era, the Faroe Islands have been shackled with a series of colonial trade monopolies that will end only in 1856 when another Nólsoy native, Poul Poulsen (Paul, son of Paul), will fight to establish free commerce and, because of the pride he will bring to the island, come to be known simply as Nólsoyar Páll (Paul from Nólsoy). Under the monopoly, however, there remains one promising, yet unpredictable, way around the law: beachcombing. Denmark may tax everything coming in by ship, but the king has no jurisdiction over the tides.

The shores of the Faroe Islands are regularly littered with all manner of maritime debris. Items washed overboard from ships throughout the Atlantic, some valuable, but most worthless, arrive on Faroese beaches every day, completing their journeys of hundreds, sometimes thousands, of miles. With almost no native forests, the Faroese have long relied on beachcombing for timber, turning driftwood into boats, oars, farming implements, and houses with a skill for carpentry that belies their arboreal poverty.

One day, while walking along the beach, your mind wandering to thoughts of growing up and being able to leave the island, perhaps to see Tórshavn or even Copenhagen, you glimpse an object that at first looks like an ordinary pebble, but its shape and color beg further inquiry. As a wave recedes, you stoop down and pick up the object, turning it over in your hand. Its surface is smooth in a way that resembles no stone you have seen before, and its color is a rich brown, like the oil-darkened wood handle of your father's whaling knife. Its shape is like a swollen heart, or perhaps a kidney. You know these organs well, despite your youth, from helping your father and brothers slaughter sheep. You've never seen a living tree in your life, but your Faroese upbringing is teaching you what's needed to be Faroese—nothing more.

The stone—*is it a stone?*—feels light in your hand, certainly light enough to float on water. You are still standing there, staring at the object when the next wave comes in, upsets your footing, and causes you to lose hold of whatever it is that you found. Frantically, you drop to your knees in the cold Atlantic swash, feeling through the foam until you have found it again. You quickly stuff it into your pocket for safekeeping and trot off toward home.

That evening, as your family gathers around the peat fire, your father smoking his pipe and your mother spinning wool into yarn, you retrieve the object from your pocket and show it to your sister and brothers. You show it to your father, whose eyes widen as he begins a tale that will eventually expand your view of the world far beyond Tórshavn and Copenhagen. *Vitunýra,* he calls your newfound treasure, and tells you, "If you keep it in your pocket, you'll never drown." Your father could not have known it then, but the object you hold in your hand actually has a sterling record of drowning avoidance, for it has made its own oceanic journey from farther away than you could ever imagine.[2]

The seed you now keep in your pocket as a talisman—for it is actually a seed—comes from a tropical plant that grows on the islands of the Caribbean Sea. This plant, identified by botanists as *Entada gigas,* is known by a variety of local names, "monkey-ladder" and "sea bean" among them. The former refers to the length of its pods, over two meters, each containing dozens of seeds like yours. The latter speaks to the seed's propensity to drift long distances at sea and hints at its arrival on the beach at Nólsoy. Sometime, perhaps two or three years ago, a large monkey-ladder grew in the rich volcanic soil of some tropical island across the vast ocean that spreads out from your own island's shores. The pod split open, spilling its seeds onto the ground. Rain washed your seed into a gully, which led to a stream, which carried it to sea. Perhaps some indigenous Carib boatman, paddling his dugout, actually saw your very seed as it drifted farther from the coast. Perhaps his young daughter, about your age, tracked the seed with her eyes as it swirled in the small eddies of her father's paddle strokes. More likely it was a European colonist—the Carib population would already have been decimated by then—who gave your seed only the briefest of glances, for gold does not float. From the coast of this newly conquered island, it wound its way into the flow of that great oceanic river that Benjamin Franklin would first chart in the eighteenth century, based upon his shipboard conversations with merchants and whalers: the Gulf Stream.

The Gulf Stream begins in the warm waters of the Caribbean, moves northward, and nestles against the coastline of Florida from Key West to Jacksonville. It continues on, up the east coast of North America, where it grows ever more distant from land as it gains latitude, carrying its cargo of warm tropical water—and whatever else happens to be brought along by the current. The stream, like most rivers, meanders. At Cape Hatteras it comes as close as twenty kilometers offshore. By Cape Cod it can be more than 150 kilometers out. The Gulf Stream is the reason deep-water, pelagic fish can be found just offshore from the Florida Keys; why New Jersey fishermen catch tropical yellowfin tuna; why Iceland is green and Greenland is icy; and, as this warm current drifts across the cold North Atlantic toward Europe, why palm trees grow in Scotland. Upstate New York and the French Riviera sit at nearly the same latitude. Where would you rather spend the winter?

The Gulf Stream is also why sea beans wash up on Faroese shores with enough frequency to have worked their way into the local folklore. Over the years, as you ask around, you occasionally encounter another person who has found a vitunýra. In some odd coincidence of current patterns and shoreline shapes, more have washed up on your home island, Nólsoy, than on any of the other sixteen inhabited islands in the archipelago. You've carried yours in your pocket since the day you found it. You grow up and become a sailor. Seafaring takes you well beyond Nólsoy's harbor, into Tórshavn, across to Copenhagen, to the green fields of Iceland and the ice-bound shores of Greenland. You have worked aboard a fishing ship, a wooden schooner owned by a Dane and piloted by a Basque, taking cod in the Denmark Strait. You've taken your place along the gunwale of a small wooden dory as part of a flotilla, rowing like mad to drive a pod of fleeing pilot whales into a fjord of a neighboring island. You've never drowned. It must be working.

The endpoints of the course followed by your sea bean serve as the settings for this book. These faraway places, the North Atlantic and the southern Caribbean, are connected in more ways than might immediately be obvious. The similarity that I focus on here, and which I have studied for the past decade, is the use of small cetaceans—a category that includes whales, dolphins, and porpoises—as a source of food for human consumption. The main target species in each location is the pilot whale. Residents of the Faroe Islands and St. Vincent & the Grenadines, an archipelagic country in the southern Caribbean, hunt and consume basically the same whales, "cousin" species of the genus *Globicephala.* The Vincentians hunt whales in a way that is familiar to anyone who has read *Moby-Dick:* they venture out to sea in small boats, harpoon individual whales, and tow them back to the shore. The Faroese, on the other hand, whale in a most unusual way. Using flotillas of several dozen boats, they drive entire pods of whales ashore and kill them with specially designed lances. Each of these artisanal whaling operations takes hundreds of small cetaceans every year for food.

Artisanal whaling is a term used to distinguish the forms of whaling practiced in the Faroe Islands, St. Vincent, and other places around the world from commercial whaling, which involves large fleets from Japan, Iceland, and Norway, hunting large whales from massive and technologically advanced factory ships. Artisanal whaling is also distinct from *aboriginal subsistence whaling*, which is a technical term used by the International Whaling Commission to designate operations that have been given an exemption from the worldwide moratorium on commercial whaling of protected species, owing to their provision of food to meet the needs—either nutritional or cultural—of recognized aboriginal groups. Randall Reeves, a prominent marine mammal scholar, has characterized artisanal whaling as being centered around "localized family-based operations" and involving "a substantial investment of manual labour . . . traditional skills, and techniques." These are not necessarily non-commercial operations, though. Reeves continues to explain that in artisanal whaling operations, while "products are generally consumed at the household or village level," surpluses can also be sold in "local or regional markets."[3]

The term *whaling operation* also requires explaining. Following the landmark "taxonomy of world whaling" created by Reeves and another marine mammal scientist, Tim Smith, I will use the term to refer to a specific group of people taking cetaceans at a specific time and place.[4] Scientists often use the term *take* instead of *hunt* or *catch* when discussing whaling. The reason for this is that some forms of whaling don't involve actual hunting or catching; we'll discuss the diverse methods later. The global history of whaling is broad and interconnected, with many discrete operations. The bold idea that a human could take a whale—kill it and manage to deliver its carcass to shore—has arisen independently many times throughout history. Techniques and technologies of whaling have also been shared and diffused from one culture to another. While neither the Faroese nor the Vincentians invented whaling, or even the methods of whaling they currently employ, together these distant and disparate operations represent relicts of what was once a much more common way to produce food and resources.

Why, when whaling operations have ceased in many of the places throughout the Atlantic and around the world where they once existed, have those based in the Faroe Islands and St. Vincent continued? What is it about the histories, geographies, cultures, economies, and cuisines of these vastly different places that maintains their use of the pilot whale as a food source? How have the Vincentians and Faroese managed to maintain seemingly sustainable take levels, despite significant increases in both human population and available technology? And how will they deal with emerging environmental crises that scientists are just beginning to understand?

To answer these questions, I knew I would need to conduct a broad and interdisciplinary study of the cultures, conflicts, and conservation strategies that occur in each of these places. I decided to spend a lot of time in both St. Vincent and the Faroe Islands. I made some short visits but also lived in each for months at a time. I went back year after year, not merely as an observer but rather as a participant-observer: trying, as much as possible, to understand what life—of which whaling was just a part—is like there. During my travels, I sought to understand what has allowed whaling to continue in these two places. I was especially interested to learn how each group had managed independently to maintain an apparently sustainable use of the whales, especially in the days before the science of conservation biology, before the techniques of genetic analysis and satellite tracking, and before the advent of the modern environmentalist movement.

Whaling has occurred in St. Vincent for more than a century and in the Faroes for much longer, maybe a millennium.[5] Before anyone had ever heard the slogan "Save the whales," the Vincentians and the Faroese knew that their next meal might depend upon saving some of the whales for later. While they lacked the scientific language to explain the concepts of local extinctions, the importance of robust genetic diversity, and the patterns of regional migration in a population of large marine predators, these early whalers, separated by an ocean, developed their own locally appropriate methods of conservation. These methods became hidden, embedded within the culture, and were not seen as overtly existing for the purpose of conservation. Because of this hiddenness, these "culturally embedded conservation strategies," as I call them, were rarely questioned; they evolved through the generations, and—in what is perhaps most interesting to conservationists today—like the magic of the sea bean, they seem to have worked . . . so far.

Today, whales are sighted off the Faroes almost every year, mostly in the summer, and some portion of them are driven ashore, killed, processed, and consumed. Caribbean whalers in small, hand-built vessels set out almost every day from the one whaling village on St. Vincent to take small cetaceans for food and small-scale local trade. Relying primarily on their culturally embedded conservation strategies, each society has kept its traditions, adapting to changing conditions when necessary, and seems to have reached an equilibrium with its local cetacean populations. How have both whaling cultures maintained this balance? Why have others throughout history failed to do so? What lessons can we—the overwhelming majority of us who do not think of whales as food—learn from their successes, challenges, and failures? What can we apply to our own interactions with the natural environment and use of its resources? And, perhaps most important, what happens to these traditional practices in the face of massive and rapid global environmental change?

Both the Vincentians and the Faroese now find themselves confronting an environmental threat, the scale and nature of which may be more than their culturally embedded conservation strategies can handle. Industrial pollutants, particularly mercury emitted from the world's coal-fired power plants, but other toxic substances as well, are deposited in the ocean through precipitation or runoff and sink to the bottom, where they are ingested by microscopic organisms living in the benthic, or sea-floor, environment. From there, these pollutants work their way up the marine food web and, through the process known as biomagnification, are concentrated most highly in the bodies of top marine predators: sharks, large fish, and marine mammals including the whales and dolphins that the Faroese and Vincentians hunt for food. Humans who consume these animals take their place at the top of the food web and expose themselves to the highest concentrations of all. The Gulf Stream, along with the entire system of global ocean currents, distributes the pollutants around the world, so mercury emitted in China, India, Europe, or the United States can end its journey in the flesh of a pilot whale harpooned off St. Vincent or driven onto a Faroese beach.

Additionally, as new technologies facilitate instantaneous global communication, more and more people are becoming aware of these whaling operations without necessarily understanding the cultural and historical contexts in which they occur. Bloody photographs are circulated through both traditional and social media, provoking disgust and anger—often at the expense of comprehension—among their viewers. Protests have erupted, more so in the Faroe Islands than in the Caribbean, and calls to stop the practice of artisanal whaling through legislation, treaties, boycotts, or simply by force reverberate across the internet.

Can knowledge and understanding travel across an ocean of cultural diversity, charting a course like that of a sea bean? Would greater understanding on both sides of the whaling debate temper the controversy? Does education hold the answer to the issue of mercury contamination and other forms of global environmental degradation? Or are the problems too far gone and the Vincentians and Faroese should simply abandon whales and dolphins as a traditional food source? What is the future for the people of the Faroe Islands and St. Vincent, who rely on cetaceans for their livelihood, their cultural identity, and—in some cases—their next meal? It would be hard to answer these questions in a straight line. There is no one set of scientific data that can definitively address the complex ethical, ecological, cultural, and health issues related to whaling. To study a topic like this, we must follow a meandering intellectual current, winding like the Gulf Stream as it flows from St. Vincent to the Faroe Islands.

It is with humble understanding of the variety of intense human emotions that can be stirred during a fair and inclusive discussion of whaling that I begin this book. Nearly thirty years ago, Finn Lynge, a Greenlandic sociologist and policymaker, advised against attempting to minimize the emotional element of the whaling debate and instead advocated welcoming it into the conversation.[6] Lynge's advice still seems difficult to apply today. Science and emotion are uneasy partners in inquiry. My approach here is similar to that with which Ernest Hemingway opened his treatise on bullfighting, *Death in the Afternoon:* "I suppose, from a modern moral point of view, that is, a Christian point of view, the whole bullfight is indefensible; there is certainly much cruelty, there is always danger, either sought or unlooked for, and there is always death, and I should not try to defend it now, only to tell honestly the things I have found true about it. To do this I must be altogether frank, or try to be, and if those who read this decide with disgust that it is written by some one who lacks their, the readers', fineness of feeling I can only plead that this may be true. But whoever reads this can only truly make such a judgment when he, or she, has seen the things that are spoken of and knows truly what their reactions would be."[7] In the same vein, the late neurosurgeon Paul Kalanithi wrote in his memoir that "direct experience of life-and-death questions [is] essential to generating substantial moral opinions about them."[8] Neither of these statements diminishes the role of judgment—what Kalanithi calls "moral opinion." There is a place for it, even in academic, scientific research. Rather, it's an ordering: experience first, opinion second. All too often—with whaling, sure, but with countless other issues in life as well—we form our opinions without the benefit of experience.

I have "seen the things that are spoken of" here and have had "direct experience" with the whales and whaling communities about which I write. Thus, meeting both Hemingway's and Kalanithi's requirements, I feel that it's right to have formed "substantial moral opinions" about the questions of whaling—though perhaps, to be honest, still with a foreign observer's never-complete understanding.

We'll get there, to my own opinions, for whatever they're worth. Before then, the majority of this book is about the experience of research, the data and memories that this experience created, and, as much as possible, a compilation and critique of the most relevant literature—the science and stories of others who were as intrigued by these hunter societies as I am.

I must be, in Hemingway's words, "altogether frank," and so I will present not only empirical findings but also subjective reflections on what it was like to do this research. I'll introduce the characters I met and tell stories about the adventures and misadventures that led to the understanding I now have of Faroese and Vincentian whaling. Some of the narrative and images may be disturbing, especially to readers who—like me—love the natural world in general, the ocean more specifically, and whales and dolphins with an affection most particular of all. For these sensitive readers, I have included the occasional non-whaling-related story—not only to offer a break from the hunt, but to present a humanizing view of the Faroese and Vincentian people. Yes, they kill whales. But that isn't all they do. With that one glaring exception—which, I acknowledge, may be insurmountable to some readers—the lives of those with whom I spent time in their whaling communities looked a lot like my own, once the façades of language, ethnicity, economics, and geography were breached.

In fact, my own hands are not clean. The participatory nature of the fieldwork that led to this book required that I be present to assist in the process of whaling in both locations. To one who equates whaling with murder, I was an accomplice. To the whalers themselves, I was merely an assistant, at best a semi-inept sharer in the labor, at worst a body in the way. In both field sites, more than once, I traveled uncomfortably back to my lodgings after whaling, dried blood and salt residue staining my skin, the smell of the butchery lingering around me, wafting from my clothes and from my hair. I never personally killed a whale, although at times I wanted to. Not for the macabre experience, like some big-game trophy hunter, but to put a suffering cetacean out of its misery when the process of dying—coldly measured by my stopwatch during the time-to-death portion of my research—seemed to drag on forever.

From the perspective of the whalers, I was also a beneficiary of their labor. Early in the research planning process I decided that I would eat the food that whaling produced. This decision was a triumph of curiosity over apprehension but also yielded a practical outcome. By eating whale meat and blubber with the people I would meet in the Faroe Islands and St. Vincent I was able to connect with them in a way that abstention would have made difficult. Of course, by eating whale meat I also gave up my pretense of objectivity—if any such thing ever actually existed in academic research.

Because I cannot lay claim to objectivity, I don't set out to argue for the rightness or wrongness of whaling in the Faroe Islands and St. Vincent. Rather, as an academic geographer and environmental scientist, my goal is to understand and learn from and about our diverse uses of the natural environment. I apply the techniques of my discipline, borrowing heavily from the repertoires of the anthropologist and the ethnographer. Whaling is but one example of the complex interdependent relationship between humans and what we call "nature." It's neither the most important nor the most ubiquitous example of this relationship but one that ignites passions—in favor or against—far beyond the scope of its actual practice.

Whales and dolphins are "charismatic megafauna," meaning they are large and have endeared themselves to many people. Most cetaceans are perceived correctly as being intelligent, social, and ecologically important. Their killing is controversial within the cultures of most developed nations. Faroese whaling has attracted protests, boycotts, and direct intervention. The fact that the Vincentians haven't had the same experience speaks more to the obscurity of their whaling activities than to some judicious approval on the world stage. Certainly there is a need for conversations about how—and even whether—Faroese and Vincentian whaling should continue. But the arguments being aired today on social media and reality television about Faroese whaling, while largely excluding Faroese voices, promise little in terms of productive outcomes.

My greatest fear in writing this book is that it will expose the as yet little-known whaling operations of the Caribbean to unjust international opposition, the likes of which the Faroese have grown well accustomed to. I discussed this concern with Samuel Hazelwood, the greatest living whaler in St. Vincent, who allayed my fears with a simple admonition to "just tell the truth. I'm not ashamed of what I do." Samuel, thank you; I've done my best.

At a moment when whaling is a major point of contention between the Faroese and the rest of the world, and when it could become so at any time for the Vincentians, what I write is of course not meant to be the final word on the matter. I only set out—following Hazelwood's instruction and Hemingway's example—to make it true. I write this book to present the reality of whaling as I have come to know it.

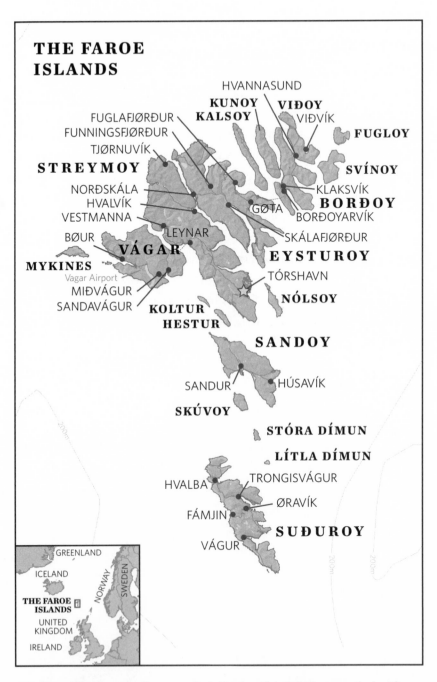

THE FAROE ISLANDS

HVANNASUND
KUNOY **VIÐOY**
KALSOY VIÐVÍK
FUGLAFJØRÐUR
FUNNINGSFJØRÐUR **FUGLOY**
TJØRNUVÍK
STREYMOY **SVÍNOY**
NORÐSKÁLA KLAKSVÍK
HVALVÍK **BORÐOY**
VESTMANNA GØTA
BORÐOYARVÍK
BØUR LEYNAR SKÁLAFJØRÐUR
VÁGAR **EYSTUROY**
MYKINES
Vagar Airport TÓRSHAVN
MIÐVÁGUR **NÓLSOY**
SANDAVÁGUR **KOLTUR**
HESTUR

SANDOY

SANDUR HÚSAVÍK
SKÚVOY

STÓRA DÍMUN

LÍTLA DÍMUN
TRONGISVÁGUR
HVALBA ØRAVÍK
FÁMJIN **SUÐUROY**
VÁGUR

GREENLAND
ICELAND
THE FAROE
ISLANDS
UNITED
KINGDOM
IRELAND
NORWAY SWEDEN

The Faroe Islands, with all approved whaling bays labeled. Cartography by Alison de Graff Ollivierre, Tombolo Maps & Design. *Data sources:* Open Street Map, Umhvørvisstovan, and the University of Minnesota Polar Geospatial Center.

1

—

The Most Exciting
Word in Faroese

Grindaboð. Pronounced "GRIN-da-boa." Try saying it a few times: *GRIN-da-boa. GRIN-da-boa. GRIN-da-boa.* The first time I was on Faroese radio, the interviewer asked me to repeat this word just after he started recording. I first thought that the audio engineer needed to check the sound levels and that maybe he was using this word as the Faroese equivalent of "check one two." Or that maybe he figured it would be funny to hear such a pure, iconic Faroese word pronounced with my American accent. Like an American hearing a British person say, "Howdy, partner." When the interview played later, though, during the twelve o'clock news hour—one of two times per day (the other being six in the evening) when every Faroese conversation pauses, radios are turned up, and listeners look askance at anyone who dares interrupt—I knew the actual reason: it was an attention-grabber. Like "Fire!" in a crowded theater. The American anthropologist Jonathan Wylie has called *grindaboð* "the most exciting word in Faroese."[1] If you want to command the attention of any Faroese person within earshot, say—no, shout—"Grindaboð!"

The word is composed of two parts: *grind,* meaning "a pod of pilot whales," and *boð,* meaning "message." *Grindaboð* literally means "pilot whale message" and is used to announce the message that pilot whales have been sighted and there is going to be a whale drive. The radio interview began with a looped recording of my voice saying—chanting, rather—"Grindaboð! Grindaboð! Grindaboð!" People listened.

In Faroese, *hvalur* means "whale." Because there are many different kinds of whale, the term *grindahvalur* is used to specify the long-finned pilot whale, known to scientists as *Globicephala melas* since first being identified as a unique species by the Scottish physician Thomas Stewart Traill in 1809.[2] The long-finned pilot whale is a small, toothed cetacean, not a large baleen whale. It would more accurately be described as a large species of dolphin; after all, its taxonomic family is *Delphinidae.* The genus *Globicephala* comprises two species: *G. melas* and *G. macrorhynchus,* the long-finned and short-finned pilot whales, respectively. There are morphological differences between the two species, the most obvious of which is the eponymous fin length—up to 30 percent of the body length in *G. melas,* but maxing out at 19 percent in *G. macrorhynchus.*[3] While individual whales of the two species may be difficult to distinguish at sea, the need rarely arises because they inhabit nearly separate ranges. The only pilot whales in Faroese waters are long-finned. In the Caribbean, the only pilot whales are short-finned. Both kinds of pilot whales travel in pods, which are made up of a few dozen to several hundred individuals. Pilot whales of both species are recognized by their jet-black skin and bulbous foreheads. The former characteristic led to one of their common names, blackfish, used throughout the Caribbean and along the eastern coast of North America. The latter feature is the reason Newfoundlanders refer to pilot whales as "potheads." The most common English name, pilot whale, is likely a reference to the whale's behavior: congregating together in large pods and traveling together behind a leader, or pilot.

Pilot whale behavior also likely influenced the development of the Faroese word *grindahvalur.* Kate Sanderson, a literary scholar and expert on the textual history of the Faroe Islands, identified a seventeenth-century geography text that describes a type of whale, of which "many hundreds congregate in a large group and chase each other and that is known as a *Hvalsgrind*," or whale-*grind.*[4] Used in this way, *grind* describes the clustered movement of a pod of whales in a tight formation, based on a related word, *grindast,* used to describe the actions of a group of excited or agitated people. This behavior of congregating in large, dense groups makes the Faroese method of whaling possible. Pilot whales instinctively herd together even to the point of collective endangerment—the whole pod can be driven ashore by a flotilla of boats, the whales then killed on the beach.

Grinning and Grinding

Grind is pronounced with a short-*i* vowel sound, and sounds almost exactly like the English word *grinned* (the past tense of *to grin*). I have heard *grind* pronounced—never by Faroese people—with a long-*i* vowel sound, like the English verb *to grind.* This pronunciation is used mainly by those who don't know better or who wish to connote the harshness or violence associated with the English word *grind,* usually when they are discussing whaling in the context of their opposition to the practice. In English, to grind something is a violent act. One grinds coffee beans, teeth, or tree stumps. The purpose of grinding is to break something down or to destroy it. By intentionally pronouncing the Faroese word *grind* (short *i*) incorrectly, like the English word *grind* (long *i*), the speaker subtly—and often intentionally—imparts the harshness of the English meaning of the word to the Faroese meaning.

The Faroese term for the act of killing pilot whales, *grindadráp,* is not without its own harshness. *Dráp* means "slaughter." *Manndráp* is the Faroese word for "manslaughter." A grindadráp, then, is a slaughter of a pod of pilot whales. The acute accent diphthongs the *a* in Faroese to resemble a softened version of the vowel sound in *cow*. The final syllable of the word is between "drop" and "drowp." Therefore, the pronunciation of *grindadráp* can be sounded out as "GRINNED-a-drowp." Perhaps confusingly, the term *grind* itself can be used for either a pod of pilot whales or a meal of pilot whale meat (which is usually served with *spik,* pilot whale blubber). Considering these two, related meanings of the word *grind,* Jonathan Wylie, the anthropologist, points out that the whole grindadráp can be seen as representing "a progression from one meaning (a school of whales) to the other (meat)."[5] Indeed, a grindadráp begins when a pod of whales is sighted and ends only when they have been driven ashore, slaughtered, and turned into food for human consumption.

The Finder's Fish

For a grindadráp to happen, whales must be sighted. Unlike other hunting situations, it is not customary in the Faroe Islands to go out in search of whales; rather, the whales must come in toward the islands on their own. When the whales approach the islands, unaware of what awaits them, Faroese boats surround them and drive them to the beach, where a great slaughter commences. But to gather enough hands to slaughter a pod of whales the message must go out. The grindaboð has been calling Faroese to their boats and beaches for nearly a thousand years.

Grindadráp are opportunistic events that can be announced at any time, during any part of the year, and are in no way predictable. This hasn't stopped people from trying to predict them. Paging through a Faroese-English dictionary provides a linguistic clue to the supposed signs, or predictors, that a grindadráp is imminent.[6] For example: *grindalokkur,* a type of fly that is said to appear shortly before a pod of pilot whales arrives; *grindamjørki,* a type of dense fog (of which there are many in Faroese meteorology) that supposedly results in pilot whales losing their way and swimming into a fjord; *grindaregn,* a heavy rain that precedes and predicts the coming of a pod of whales; and *grindaprestur,* literally "pilot whale priest," a churchman whose tenure in a particular parish is thought to coincide with frequent whale sightings there. Incidentally, the opposite of *grindaprestur* is *grindatrøll,* not a troll, but an official—in this case, a priest or a politician—whose term sees a lack of whales.[7] In other countries, elected officials worry about events beyond their control such as natural disasters or economic downturns affecting their re-election prospects. In the Faroes, one's approval rating can also be connected to the abundance—or lack—of pilot whales. Despite all these alleged predictors, there isn't much statistical correlation between flies, fog, priests, or rain and the appearance of pilot whales in the fjords of the Faroe Islands.[8] Instead, these superstitions can probably be attributed mostly to *grindahugur*—defined as "the feeling of intense desire to take part in a grindadráp."

Despite the lack of predictors, there is a basic statistical correlation that does show when whale drives are more likely: they happen mainly during the summer. An analysis of more than 400 years of whaling records by Faroese scientists showed a clear increase in the incidence of grindadráp from June to October, peaking in August.[9] More than 64 percent of all recorded grindadráp have occurred in July, August, or September. One reason for this increase in grindadráp occurrence is simply that the weather is more agreeable for marine activity in the Faroe Islands during the summer and early autumn than at other times of the year. The presence of more people on the water increases the chances of sighting a pod of whales. Could the whales themselves also be more common in Faroese waters during the warmer months? It's hard to say because not much is known about the whales' movements throughout the year. While they don't migrate in the truest sense of the word—moving from a winter home to a summer home—the whales do travel long distances, most likely in pursuit of their main prey: several species of squid. The routes they take and the influences on these routes are the subject of much ongoing study.

Whatever the cause, pods of whales do frequently swim into the fjords and channels of the Faroe Islands. When a sailor or fisherman—or anyone, for that matter—sees a pod of whales, they contact the district *sýslumaður* (SHOOSH-la-maw-er), a police authority whose title is most often translated "sheriff." (When I mentioned this comparison to the sýslumaður of the district that includes Tórshavn, he laughed and asked how he would look wearing a "gold star and a big white cowboy hat.") Upon hearing of the sighting, the sýslumaður contacts one or more of the district *grindaformenn*—whaling foremen (sing. *grindaformann*)—to discuss whether or not to pursue the whales, and if so, into which bay they should be driven. The Tórshavn sýslumaður called the district foremen his "prolonged arm" in the regulation of the grindadráp. Faroese law states that each whaling bay must have four grindaformenn. Given their whaling experience and nautical knowledge, these foremen are the most qualified to decide how to best handle a particular pod of whales given particular oceanic, weather, and economic conditions. Any of a number of variables could lead to a grindadráp being aborted. Uncooperative ocean currents, difficult whales, darkness, or the abundance of meat and blubber already in storage throughout the district have all been reasons that whale drives were called off. If conditions are right, though, and the meat is needed, the sýslumaður, in consultation with the grindaformenn, declares that the grindadráp will be attempted and states which bay will be the target of the drive. The grindaboð, the pilot whale message, is quickly sent out.

A recently controversial Faroese law *required* everyone—making no distinction between Faroese citizens and foreigners, including tourists—to report all pilot whale sightings to the authorities. While this law was basically unenforceable (How would the authorities know if someone had actually seen pilot whales and identified them as such?), it exemplified the seriousness with which the Faroese approach the possibility of a grindadráp. Although the law had long been part of the pilot whaling regulations, it recently made the news in conjunction with anti-grindadráp protests conducted by the Sea Shepherd Conservation Society. In some international media it was branded "the Sea Shepherd law," as it was seen as being used to prosecute members of that organization for their opposition to the grindadráp. The law, in fact, covered a range of uncooperative activities with regard to the grindadráp, from merely failing to report the sighting of pilot whales to actively interrupting or interfering with the drive or the slaughter. The Faroese government has since revised the law to clarify its intent, stating that it is "highly unlikely that an ordinary tourist who has sighted pilot whales will be punished for not reporting this."[10] This clarification refers to the general principle that grindadráp are regulated events, over which the Faroese government is sovereign, and indicates that the primary targets of the law are those who would take "the law into their own hands or . . . interfere illegally in a whale drive" and not those who merely opted out—either by conviction or through ignorance—of the grindaboð process.[11]

In the old days, boat crews who sighted pilot whales would raise a sweater or some other piece of clothing up the mast—the accepted sign that whales were in the area. Today, of course, mobile phones or marine radios are the standard means to communicate the sighting. Compliance with "the Sea Shepherd law" comes with an incentive: after a successful grindadráp, the person who was recorded as having first reported sighting the pod of whales is given the largest whale of the pod in its entirety. This whale, known as the *finningarfiskur*, literally the "finder's fish," is much too large for any one person or even a family to use. The finder, then, is able to give gifts of meat and blubber or to trade for other needed things.

Whales are most often sighted from sea. Captains, sailors, and passengers aboard fishing boats, ferries, container vessels, and pleasure craft have all been awarded finder's fish. One does not have to be Faroese to qualify. For this reason, I feel compelled to remain on the deck during all ferry travel in the Faroes, no matter the weather, in hopes that I'll be the finder. There are so many people in the Faroe

Islands to whom I owe debts of gratitude for the help they've offered me in my work there and the most culturally appropriate gift I can think of would be a share from the finningarfiskur, should I ever receive it. This hasn't happened yet, but I'll keep up my watch.

Pods of whales have also been spotted from shore and from the air. The Faroese government subsidizes a helicopter service to better connect its citizens living on the more remote islands—those not connected by bridge or undersea tunnel to the rest of the archipelago. People flying and being flown in this helicopter occasionally benefit from their elevated vantage by being the first to see a pod of whales below. Joen Remmer, a pilot for the Faroese national airline, Atlantic Airways, told me that he once radioed in a sighting as he was flying passengers to Denmark on a commercial flight—only to be told that someone on a boat had already seen and reported that pod.

Historically, the possibility of a grindadráp has taken priority over any other activity. While this shows signs of changing, especially in modern and affluent Tórshavn, historical anecdotes abound of churches being emptied mid-sermon, barbers and their clients running—one aproned and the other half-shaven—from the shop to the whaling beach, and even of a surgeon leaving his patient open on the table when word of the impending grindadráp arrived. (Lawrence Millman, in his travelogue *Last Places,* recounts a more extreme version of the last tale, which has the patient rising from the table and joining the doctor at the beach!)[12] Today the grindaboð is usually delivered electronically via text message or social media, though in the past elaborate systems of runners, rowers, shouters, and smoke signals were used to carry the news from village to village and island to island.[13]

Things are slowly changing in the Faroe Islands with regard to the urgency of the grindaboð. I recall sitting with friends in a Tórshavn sushi restaurant one Friday evening in 2009 when the call came in. I stood up in this crowded eatery and repeated loudly into my phone, "Grindaboð? Where?" "Where?" (*hvar* in Faroese) is usually the first question asked after the announcement arrives. A few diners looked up at me. Most barely paused as they slurped their miso soup. I noticed one middle-aged man who, wiping the corners of his mouth, appeared ready to stand up, until he caught the disapproving look on his dining companion's face. "Stay put" may sound different but it looks the same in any language. I apologized to my friends for the premature departure, grabbed a handful of edamame for the road, and ran out to catch a ride to the whaling beach.

When I arrived at Gøta the whales had already been killed—it was a small pod, only twenty-three whales. But you wouldn't have known it from the scene by the waterside. The quay was abuzz with activity: children tentatively poking the rubbery flesh of the steaming whale carcasses, the sýslumaður's assistants measuring and numbering the whales, people milling about in this impromptu cause for socializing. For centuries in the Faroe Islands, grindadráp were the most exciting thing going. The monotony of village life could be broken at a moment's notice with the arrival of a grindaboð. Your evening's plans could suddenly change from watching the peat fire and knitting to meeting a couple hundred friends and neighbors to procure meat for the next four months. It was a chance to fulfill both social and nutritional obligations. On many occasions the grindaboð came just in time, announcing the arrival of food during a period of extreme need.

In the past, grindadráp began with anticipation, followed by intensely hard work, and ended with singing, dancing, drinking, and feasting—often until the next morning. Things could sometimes get rowdy. One sýslumaður, or sheriff, told me that in recent years the aftermath of a grindadráp, when the meat was being divided and emotions were lubricated with adrenaline (and often alcohol), was the only time he carried his service revolver. Even amid the post-grindadráp chaos, however, he never wore a white hat and gold star.

The revelry is largely absent from modern grindadráp. The scene I witnessed in Gøta is typical for the Faroes today: enthusiasm, community participation and interest, and excitement at the prospect of obtaining the free food that the activity produces, but not the

A crowd gathered around whales killed in Gøta

instant doubling of a village's population with the influx of grindadráp participants, observers, and beneficiaries. There is rarely any dancing or singing. With transportation made considerably easier by the modern Faroese road system, there's no need to stay all night in the village where the grindadráp took place. You can go home, warm up and clean off, and still be back in time to get your share of meat and blubber. This is a change in style more than in substance. Where the real substantial change is happening is in the sushi restaurants—and karaoke bars and coffee shops and theaters—frequented by the more urbanized Tórshavn residents. A grindadráp now has competition. Instead of the only question being "Hvar?" the recipient of a grindaboð in Tórshavn now asks, "Is the football match still on? How far away is the whaling beach? What time am I likely to get home if I go?" and, in some cases, "Who's going to eat all that whale meat and blubber anyway?"

The urban-rural divide is increasing in the Faroes. People from the villages shorten the name Tórshavn to Havn. (The word sounds like the English *hound* without the *d*. It just means "harbor.") *Havn* is often accompanied by a subtle rolling of the eyes or preceded by a quick, dismissive burst of air from the nostrils. The dismissiveness goes both ways. The Faroese word *bygdasligt,* pronounced "BIG-dis-lair" and based on the word for "village," *bygd,* is used in something of an affectionately derogatory manner to denote anything rustic, traditional, or backward. I first heard this word when David Geyti, a Faroese friend, and I were waiting in his car on a two-lane country road, which was being blocked by two vehicles facing opposite directions, stopped so the drivers could chat. The driver facing us looked, smiled, and went right back to his conversation. "This is so bygdasligt!" complained David, who is from Tórshavn. During the impromptu linguistic discussion that then took place, as we had nothing else to do but wait, David and I decided that the closest English equivalent was the non-word *redneckish.* It's redneckish to block traffic. People from Havn [eye roll] have places to be.

There is a small but growing view in the Faroe Islands that the grindadráp is somewhat bygdasligt. Most Faroese would certainly not like to see the practice end, but they don't necessarily prioritize it the way they used to. This feeling is stronger in Tórshavn than in the rural villages. Today the patient Millman wrote of would likely stay on the operating table and might even avoid strenuous activities like the grindadráp until completely recovered from his surgery. Additionally, since meat and blubber are usually divided freely among the residents of the community where a grindadráp has occurred, there is almost always more to go around in the villages than in Tórshavn, owing to the comparatively large population in the capital: Tórshavn's metropolitan area is home to more than 40 percent of the Faroese population. For all but the largest grindadráp in Tórshavn, only a portion of residents are able to get a share, the rest being content to know that their names have moved up on the alphabetized priority list for next time.

A Dreadful Sight

My earliest exposure to the idea of the grindadráp came during my first solo overseas trip: a month-long backpacking adventure through Iceland in 2001. I made a slow circuit of the country using a hop-on, hop-off ticket with the national bus line, carrying a tent, a sleeping bag, and a copy of *The Sagas of the Icelanders* in my pack.[14] Near the end of the trip, I passed through a small town, Ólafsvík, on Iceland's Snæfellsnes peninsula, just in time for a cultural festival called Færeyskir Dagar, or Faroese Days. It was here that I first heard stories of the Faroe Islands in general and the grindadráp in particular. The Faroe Islands sounded like Iceland before tourists arrived. I began to wonder if future travels in the north might eventually lead me there.

After returning from Iceland, I began reading everything I could find about the grindadráp. I learned that across the ocean, Vincentian whalers were hunting pilot whales too. I wondered how their operation might compare with that of the Faroese. With this, my research topic fell into place. I would make a comparison: the cultures and ecologies of Faroese and Vincentian pilot whaling. All I lacked was the money to make it happen.

Finding funding for academic research is a complicated matter. The British explorer Douglas Botting wrote, regarding his time conducting overseas fieldwork as a student at Oxford, that researchers are "like the tramps who wander the countryside and offer to dig gardens or chop wood in return for a loaf of bread or a cup of tea."[15] Botting added that these exchanges, ideally arrangements by which "interested scientific bodies will contribute towards their expenses in return for the scientific data and specimens they aim to collect," are "of mutual advantage and not at all unethical."[16] I agree with Botting's researcher-as-tramp metaphor but would add the caveat that actual tramps need only survive and get from place to place; researchers must also find enough meaningful data to justify their rambling in terms of academic output. Because of this we often stretch the funds we receive to maximize time in the field, even if that comes at the expense of comfort, nutrition, and occasionally safety.

I was—and continue to be—fortunate in that grants from funding organizations usually come in when needed. But not always. When the funding isn't there, the researcher has to be both creative and frugal.

In 2009, midway through my longest research trip to the Faroe Islands, I found myself running out of kroner. It seemed likely to be my last time in the field for this portion of the study. Because of this, I resorted to doing everything I could to stretch the money I had. Bjarki Dalsgarð, a Faroese friend who worked at a Tórshavn grocery store, had been leaving crates of vegetables, bread, and sometimes meat outside by the store's garbage container for me every Saturday at closing time. Supermarkets in the Faroe Islands import nearly all their inventory by ship from Denmark and have to place an order every week. They don't know what they'll need very far in advance, so there is often the problem of what to do with last week's leftover stock when the new shipment arrives on Sunday. Hungry foreign researcher? Problem solved. This provided my food, but there was still the problem of a restricted cash flow. I needed money to pay for bus fares, tunnel tolls, and supplies.

At graduate school in Louisiana I had taught capoeira, the Brazilian martial art / dance, for a few years. Why not give it a try in Tórshavn? Although I lacked a Faroese work visa, I was able to convince the owner of a local fitness center to give me the space to offer a class. He generously split the course fees one-third for the gym, two-thirds for me. I only had a few students, but the commission I drew allowed me to stay in the country long enough to finish the year's research. To this day I think it's still the only time capoeira has been taught in the Faroe Islands.

In 2010, I became a professor, first at the University of Denver and then at my current institution, the University of the South, in Sewanee, Tennessee. In addition to conducting research abroad I'm now able to bring students to my field sites for classes. This allows me to see familiar places through new eyes, to guide students through the same adventures of discovery that I've had, and to revisit my field sites without all the uncertainties of food, lodging, and transportation.

A memorable grindaboð, for me, came during a 2012 field course on environmental geography that I taught in the Faroes for the University of Denver. The events unfolded as I sat in a small café on the remote island of Mykines with my teaching assistant and ten American students, warming up after a long, windy hike to the lighthouse at the western end of the island. Our ferry back to Vágar would depart in about an hour, and from there we would drive back to our guesthouse in Tórshavn. Vágar is the westernmost island with road connections to the rest of the archipelago. Mykines is further west.

My phone vibrated with a text message from Høgni Arnbjarnarson, a biologist in Tórshavn. Whales had been sighted about ten kilometers north of the Faroes and there was a chance that they could be driven in. "*Takk.* Keep me posted," I wrote back, not yet expecting the sighting to lead to anything. About fifteen minutes later, another text from Høgni arrived, sounding more certain. Boats were beginning to gather in a northern harbor. Five minutes after that, texts and phone calls began pouring in from friends and colleagues across the Faroes and even from one Faroese friend living in Norway. Rumors of a grindaboð can travel far and fast in the era of cellular networks and the internet. All I knew so far was that the whales had been sighted offshore and that boats had left the harbors to meet them. If wind and ocean conditions stayed favorable, the boat captains would steer their flotilla to the seaward side of the pod of whales and attempt to herd the animals together in preparation for driving. The drive would aim toward one of the approved whaling beaches on the Faroes' northern shores. Høgni thought Tjørnuvík seemed most likely. I told my students to gather their things and move down to the dock.

We had to wait for about an hour. The anthropologist Jonathan Wylie accurately described the feeling my students and I shared as we stood at the shore, watching for a ferry and thinking of a pod of whales: "Awaiting a *grind* today, one feels as never otherwise—except in winter storms, and then for different reasons—how isolated the Faroes are, how immense is the sea, and how broad the fjords between one island and the next. It is easy to appreciate how hopefully a *grind* must have been awaited in the days when a *grindadráp* meant a better chance of surviving the winter."[17]

The ferry arrived on schedule—by no means a given in this weather-dependent place. Windblown and wave-tossed Mykines is no Switzerland, the land of on-time public transport; ferries and helicopters here are sometimes delayed for days. Wylie's winter isolation is felt on Mykines more than nearly anywhere else in the Faroes. Our day, though, was fine. We arrived at Vágar without delay. Tracing our driving route on the road map, from the parking lot of the ferry terminal to our guesthouse in Tórshavn, I found a roundabout with one exit heading north toward Tjørnuvík and the other south toward the capital. This would be our decision point. If the grindaboð was issued by the time we reached the roundabout, we would go north. If not, home. As we loaded into the van I handed my phone to the student riding in the front seat and started the long drive back with the instruction to read me any text message that came in. The roundabout was within sight when the grindaboð arrived: "get 2 tjørnuvík!" We passed up the Tórshavn exit and headed north.

Tjørnuvík stands behind a beach at the base of a long and deep fjord facing north-northeast. If you were to sail straight out of Tjørnuvík's fjord, you wouldn't hit land until Svalbard, a Norwegian archipelago far above the Arctic Circle. If you missed Svalbard, you would come ashore in northern Alaska after crossing the Arctic Ocean. Like most of the landscapes in the Faroe Islands, the area surrounding Tjørnuvík is intensely beautiful, described in some travel literature as resembling a layer cake—presumably more appetizing under the vanilla icing of winter's snowcap unless you prefer your cake green.[18] And green dominates the Faroes. While the archipelago is nearly devoid of trees, fields of grasses, both wild and cultivated, carpet the tops of the islands, right up to the very cliff edges, which drop precipitously into the sea. Unlike their neighbor Iceland, which, volcanically speaking, is still very much active, the structure of the Faroe Islands is old basalt, built up during periods of volcanism that predate human history, later dissected and smoothed by glaciers, resulting in a land of rolling hills, long fjords, narrow inter-island straits, and steep sea cliffs. The road to Tjørnuvík perches like a sure-footed sheep, of which the Faroes have many, on the edge of one of these long, cliff-fringed fjords.

After driving over mountains and rounding bays, the road bent around a final headland and the village came into view. Until this point the grindadráp had been, to us, merely hypothetical. The final turn put our van parallel to the flotilla of boats, which had just entered the fjord. We got our first visual proof that the grindadráp was happening. The students were bouncing in their seats, leaning toward the passenger-side windows to watch the event. We drove toward the village as the boats drove the pilot whales toward the beach. Dozens of jet-black dorsal fins broke the surface in a froth just ahead of the boats, which followed in the wake of the whales, steadily but at a fixed distance. The whale drive seemed achingly slow. Traffic was slow too, as drivers craned to see the whales while attempting to stay on the road. As the improbable race toward Tjørnuvík continued we realized we would make it in time. Our van reached the base of the fjord and the village. We quickly abandoned the vehicle and set out on foot for the beach, where a line of anxious men, and a few women, stood shoulder to shoulder behind the most seaward berm. Some of these shore-based whalers wore jeans and traditional densely woven brown sweaters with buttons on the left shoulder. Others wore work clothes, sports clothes, or wetsuits. The attire seemed to indicate how much time each participant had taken to prepare for the event.

Some apparently had rushed over immediately from whatever they had been doing before.

The boats, holding a semicircle formation just behind the whales, were perhaps a hundred meters offshore and approaching steadily. Anticipation filled the village. Five or six men in yellow safety vests marked GRINDAMAÐUR (pilot whale man) marched back and forth in front of those gathered on the beach, repeating orders. A few photographers jockeyed for perches on high points or village balconies. Students dispersed. Some sought good positions to observe; others joined the cadre of whalers standing on the beach. A few hung back near the village, where they would be able to turn away and avoid the sight if necessary.

As the boats approached we heard hands slapping hulls, wrenches and other tools tapping rails, and low, staccato shouts in Faroese. We watched passengers riding forward in boats toss stones into the water, aiming just behind the whales' flukes. All of this was intended to keep the whales moving straight ahead. At about forty meters offshore the boats began to speed up. The whales sped up in response, fleeing from the boats, and soon began to strand in the shallow water. Now in addition to dorsal fins we saw flukes rising above water. Some whales tried to turn back but the boats were there. The whales were trapped. A few turned their bodies vertically and raised their heads above the surface, spyhopping. The pod dispersed as much as possible within the confined area in which it found itself. Tjørnuvík's beach is framed by rocky cliffs on both sides. Some whales turned sharply to the left or the right, in an effort to avoid beaching, and raked their bellies against the sharp undersea rocks.

A vested man gave a signal and, with a shout, the whalers on the beach ran into the surf. Most were part of two-person teams carrying large metal hooks tied to long, thick ropes. When the first man reached the first stranded whale, he raised the hook and drove it down into the blowhole. Immediately, six or seven others, chest-deep in the cold sea, took hold of his rope and began hauling the whale—still very much alive and fighting the whole way—toward the beach. When the whale's head rested on the sand a man withdrew a knife from a wooden sheath tied around his waist and sawed into its flesh. The blood came immediately. Great spurts, truly thicker than water, erupted as the whale went into its final spasm—the knife having just severed its spinal cord. The process was both quick and complex. The whale thrashed its fluke and arched its back high above the man's head, revealing its massive size. Its blood soon mingled with the blood of other whales simultaneously being killed. The seawater turned red. As each whale died, men hauled its carcass farther onto the beach, then turned, dispersed, and joined other teams hauling or killing other whales. The process was methodical and, after the whalers' initial shouts as they entered the water, quieter than I would have expected.

Throughout the killing, I found my attention constantly drawn to the waves as they crashed thigh-high, one after another, onto the beach. At this very beach a few years earlier, I had ridden these waves together with a few members of the budding Faroese surfing community. Owing to Tjørnuvík's exposure, the waves here can get massive. On that day, I had noticed that the large amount of kelp fragments in the water gave the waves a green hue. Today the waves were red. Seeing these color-wheel opposites in the same water brought to mind the indifference of the ocean. Whether surfing or whaling, waving or drowning, the activities of human beings in the vast sea play out at a scale much finer than that of the waves themselves. The green kelp was replaced with red blood, which itself would be diluted some hours after the grindadráp had ended. We would not witness the aftermath of this grindadráp, but I knew what the next several hours would entail. The authorities would assign portions of the whales to each person on the list of recipients. Villagers would strip the whale carcasses of their meat and blubber, and a few volunteers would haul the unusable remains out to deeper water. Then Tjørnuvík would return to its quiet existence. Waves would keep crashing onto this beach, methodical and determined, indifferent to whatever they wash over.

I paused to locate each of my students. Most were milling about the shoreline taking photos. Two had joined rope teams and were standing knee-deep in bloody water, hauling whales as though they were Faroese. Another pair had disappeared into the streets of Tjørnuvík, seeking diversion from the events at the beach. When I noticed that these students had gone off to avoid watching the whales being killed I was reminded of the words of the eighteenth-century Faroese poet Venceslaus U. Hammershaimb, who remarked in reference to the grindadráp, "Yes, this is a slaughter, which is a dreadful sight for whomever stands on the shore peacefully watching."[19] I thought of the incongruity of *peacefully* watching a slaughter, of the rarity in today's world of this sort of activity happening in public.

The world is consuming more meat than ever before and, at the same time, becoming less connected to the origin of its food supply. We have reached an era that historian Richard Bulliet calls "postdomesticity." In *Hunters, Herders, and Hamburgers,* Bulliet's long-view account of the changing relationships between humans and the animals upon which we depend for meat and other needs, he defines this era as a time in which, first, "people live far away, both physically and psychologically, from the animals that produce the food, fiber, and hides they depend on, and they never witness the births, sexual congress, and slaughter of these animals. . . . Second, a postdomestic society emerging from domestic antecedents continues to consume animal products in abundance, but psychologically, its members experience feelings of guilt, shame, and disgust when they think (as seldom as possible) about the industrial processes by which animals are rendered into products and about how those products come to market."[20]

The Faroe Islands are as connected to the world market as any remote island country can be. In Faroese supermarkets one finds animal- and vegetable-based food products both produced locally and sourced from around the world. Restaurants in Tórshavn tend toward Scandinavian cuisine, but pizza, hamburgers, and sushi can all be found. The capital features, as international travelers have come to expect, both an Irish pub and a Chinese restaurant. Despite these conveniences of globalization, the Faroese remain staunchly un-postdomestic through practices such as fishing, sheep rearing, fowling, and of course the grindadráp. In October, when sheep are slaughtered, blood literally runs in the streets, draining through pipes leading from household abattoirs into the gutters of some small Faroese towns and out to sea—making one wonder whether the infrastructure was originally built to handle rain or blood. The continued practice of such visceral and ancient food production methods in an otherwise modern, wealthy, and developed European nation stands out as incongruous.

Grindadráp records date back to the sixteenth century. Most researchers believe that the practice itself is much older.[21] For most of its history, foreigners have observed the grindadráp and commented on it in their writings without judging its morality. Beginning in the mid-1980s, however, animal welfare organizations in Europe and North America began to initiate anti-whaling protests that sometimes threatened boycotts against Faroese products—mainly seafood. Since that time, the level of international attention to the grindadráp has risen and fallen. The advent of social media and reality television seems to have fostered an increase during the current decade, with examples ranging from chain emails and viral social media posts to direct interventionist campaigns by environmental action organizations.

About an hour after the grindadráp began in Tjørnuvík, the fiftieth and final whale lay dead on the beach. There was nothing special about the number fifty; it was simply the last whale of the pod. A grindadráp ideally takes the entire pod of whales, letting none escape. This standard is based on pilot whale behavior, not human greed. Sometimes when the Faroese have tried to split a pod of whales, driving some ashore and letting the others go, those not driven ashore have stranded on another beach. The herding instinct of pilot whales is strong. If the entire pod is likely to end up on shore anyway, Faroese reasoning goes, it's best to have them all in one place so nothing goes to waste.

Compared to other grindadráp, this was by no means a large slaughter. But my students were tired and hungry. Those who had participated in the hauling of whales were wet with seawater and blood. Those who had taken to Tjørnuvík's back alleys and deserted streets were glad that the whole event was over. We spent the drive to Tórshavn in silent meditation, each of us individually processing the experience. Back at the guesthouse, after a quickly prepared pasta dinner, we left the dishes on the table and engaged in a fruitful discussion about the events of the afternoon. Impressions varied among the twelve of us, but all agreed that we had witnessed something ancient, intensely cultural, and multilayered to the point that a quick summary or description would risk oversimplification.

I think one reason the grindadráp inspires such dread among those who, like my students, stand on the shore peacefully watching is that it forces postdomestic people to confront the reality of their own subsistence. The foreignness of whales as the food source—as opposed to cattle, swine, or fowl—surely plays a part in the discomfort of this confrontation, but I doubt many American university students, or most other people from developed nations for that matter, have witnessed the killing and butchering of any animal. As we sat around the table, discussing and reflecting upon what we had seen, the details of species, culture, and geographic setting faded into the foreground and the basic truth remained: this is what humans do to make food.

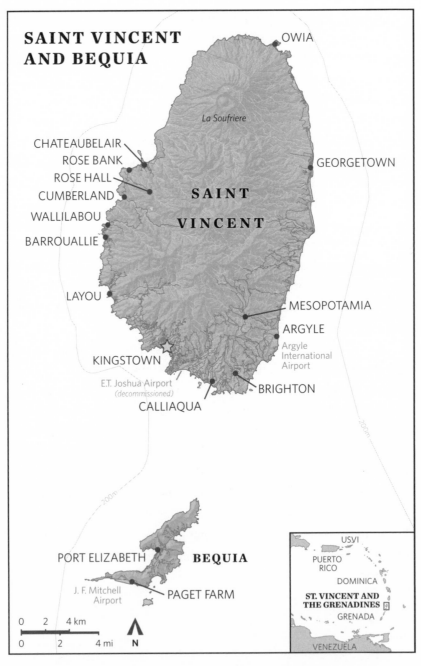

SAINT VINCENT
AND BEQUIA

OWIA

La Soufriere

CHATEAUBELAIR
ROSE BANK
ROSE HALL
CUMBERLAND
WALLILABOU
BARROUALLIE

GEORGETOWN

SAINT
VINCENT

LAYOU

MESOPOTAMIA
ARGYLE
Argyle
International
Airport

KINGSTOWN

E.T. Joshua Airport
(decommissioned)

BRIGHTON

CALLIAQUA

PORT ELIZABETH

BEQUIA

J. F. Mitchell
Airport

PAGET FARM

USVI
PUERTO
RICO
DOMINICA
ST. VINCENT AND
THE GRENADINES
GRENADA
VENEZUELA

0   2   4 km
0   2   4 mi   N

The islands of St. Vincent and Bequia. Cartography by Alison de Graff Ollivierre,
Tombolo Maps & Design. *Data sources:* St. Vincent & the Grenadines Physical
Planning Unit and The Nature Conservancy.

2

———

Oil and History on a Caribbean Beach

The whaling village of Barrouallie—the name rhymes with *merrily*—
was once the capital of St. Vincent & the Grenadines. It's now the
capital of Caribbean whaling. Barrouallie's black sand beach faces due
west. A rocky promontory called Bottle-and-Glass forms the beach's
northern limit; a sea cliff bounds it to the south. Eastward toward
St. Vincent's volcanic center, Barrouallie's streets and houses stretch
inland, uphill until the topography becomes too steep to build upon.
Within these geographical boundaries and slopes, everything in
Barrouallie eventually ends up on the beach. That's exactly where I
went the first time I visited the village in 2008. Colorful boats were
drawn up onto the shore, which was backed by trees bearing breadfruit, plum, wax apple, and mango. These, along with broad-leafed
Indian almond trees, cast shade for the dozen or so men sipping rum
on benches or leaning against beached fishing boats. A few were
cleaning fish, and one old man sat on the sand repairing a fishing
net that he held stretched on his lap with his toes. Women sat on

Fixing the net

overturned buckets feeding babies; a few stood by bamboo racks, hanging thin sheets of dark red meat to dry in the sun.

From the direction of these women and their work I noticed a familiar scent, carried by the sea breeze, one that stood out from the other Caribbean smells of charcoal fires, overripe fruit, the dust of volcanic soil, diesel smoke, and the sea. This familiar scent was deep, full, and pungent. It commanded attention but lay mellow in the background—impossible to ignore but difficult to locate with any precision. It seemed to be everywhere, the kind of smell that threatens to permeate your clothes and parasitize you, overwhelming your identity. If it were a texture instead of an odor, it would be soft, thick, greasy, and warm. It would be the sensation, during an oil change, of reaching into a filling drip pan under your car to retrieve a dropped drain plug, or of lying on the bare mattress of a waterbed, heated above body temperature and slathered in cooking oil. It was a smell that, five years before, I never would have thought I could identify so accurately. It was the smell of pilot whale meat.

Within the first half hour of my first day in Barrouallie, my mind was instantly awash with memories, for as Steinbeck reminded us in *East of Eden*'s opening geographical paean to the Salinas Valley, "the memory of odors is very rich."[1] This scent, here, deep in the Eastern Caribbean, called to mind the field seasons I'd already spent in the Faroe Islands. Steep and green, across an ocean from where I then stood, the Faroes might seem worlds away from St. Vincent & the Grenadines. Geographically, there are not many similarities between the two archipelagos, but here on this tropical beach I'd found one: the same scent, carried on a much different wind.

Whale meat smells like oil and history. It is a scent that once was common throughout the world's oceans but now is found on only a few peripheral islands and remote coastlines. Whaling became a controversial subject during the mid-twentieth century, owing primarily to the efficiency of technologies used during the heyday of commercial whaling that greatly advantaged whalers over whales. Humans became so effective at finding and killing whales that some populations of the most intensely hunted species still have not recovered despite decades of policy directed at their conservation. Although the oily scent of whale meat might be the same whether the whaling is commercial or artisanal, the methods, cultures, and philosophies of whaling in St. Vincent and the Faroe Islands have little in common with the operation of an industrial whaling ship.

When I started conducting fieldwork in St. Vincent in 2008, I had already spent two field seasons in the Faroe Islands without seeing a whale drive. *That's all right,* I told myself. *They're unpredictable. I'm getting the real Faroese experience by waiting for the whales to be sighted. Doesn't every Faroese person have in the back of their mind at all times the thought that maybe a grindaboð will come today?* Dorete Bloch, the lead scientist in studies of North Atlantic pilot whales at the time, had extended me the invitation to live in a small bedroom above her office, research, and library complex in Tórshavn. There I spent my mornings drinking thick Scandinavian coffee with the members of Dorete's scientific staff, slicing cheese with a wire, and learning a lot about daily life. As they passed around pages of the two daily local newspapers, which I would take in turn but could not read, they would cast back and forth in their speech from Faroese to English for my benefit. The knowledge they passed on to me was informal, unorganized in a learn-by-living kind of way. I learned that when it's your birthday in the Faroe Islands *you* bring the cake to your friends and not the other way around. When my birthday arrived that August, I was sure to have a box of pastries ready for my colleagues. I went along with the marine biologists to collect specimens from the docks whenever fishermen had pulled up something interesting in their nets. I went out to conduct interviews and came back to discuss what I had learned. In a general way, I conducted my fieldwork.

Dorete Bloch, standing in front of the *grind*-mobile

For the first season, and then for the second, the whales never came in, at least not while I was in the country.

The closest I got to a grindadráp—at least for the first two field seasons—was when I accompanied a team of biologists on a mission to drive in a pod of Atlantic white-sided dolphins. We piled into the red Citroën van with the black pilot whale silhouettes painted on the sides—affectionately known as the *grind*-mobile—and drove off to the beach nearest where the dolphins had been spotted. A small team in rubber-sided boats drove them into shallow water. This drive wouldn't end in a slaughter, though; the whole exercise was for research. When the dolphins were close enough to shore, we waded out, caught them by hand, and attached small satellite tags to track their movements. Then, in what must have seemed like madness to any old-time pilot whalers watching from shore, we walked the dolphins back into deep water and used the boats to drive them back to sea. The spatial data collected from the satellite tags helped the biologists understand dolphin movement but brought me no closer to my goal of understanding the grindadráp.

When I came home from these first couple of research trips I felt like a war reporter who hadn't been to the front lines. I did my best to answer the inevitable questions: What's it like? How do they do it? Why do they do it? Is it necessary? Is it bloody? Is it wrong? But I hadn't seen it myself. To fully answer the questions my friends and colleagues back home would ask—and that I would pose in my research— needed to see whales being driven ashore and killed, and I would return to the Faroes again and again until it happened.

My first visit to St. Vincent was different. I had already been in contact with Vincent Reid—a local author, historian, engineer, singer, and polymath, named for the island of his birth—by email after reading some of his work on the culture, as expressed through folklore and song, of Vincentian whaling. He was the first person I looked up after arriving in Kingstown. We hit it off immediately and Vincent took me to Barrouallie, St. Vincent's only whaling village, to

The author, helping biologists place satellite tags on the dorsal fins of dolphins.
Photo © Høgni Arnbjarnarson

meet Samuel Hazelwood, the de facto leader of the Vincentian black-fish, or pilot whale, operation.

The operation targeting pilot whales in Barrouallie has long served as something of an understudy to the more famous whaling operation based on the nearby Grenadine island of Bequia, pronounced BECK-way, that targets humpback whales. Bequia whaling has inspired books, magazine articles, documentary films, and music—including one song by the local calypsonian J. Gool that extols Athneal Ollivierre, the late, charismatic leader of Bequian whaling: "Athneal, he was the greatest whalerman / He had nerves of steel and a powerful right arm." If Athneal Ollivierre was the greatest whalerman, Samuel Hazelwood is the greatest blackfish man. Quiet and pensive, Samuel lacks the flamboyant showmanship that Athneal exhibited. Indeed, Samuel is the opposite of flamboyant. During carnival season, while the rest of St. Vincent revels in soca music and street parties, Samuel spends most of every day at sea, listening instead to the sound of the wind, the hum of the boat's motor, and the lap of the waves. At home, he prefers soft country music or the hymns sung at church. His boat regularly takes twice as many whales as all other Barrouallie whalers combined.

Samuel is, of course, aware that his is a controversial occupation. This controversy is confusing to him, though, as it betrays what he sees as a moral inconsistency among whaling's opponents. One day, when the seas were too rough for whaling, Samuel and I sat in the shade next to his workshop in Barrouallie and he asked me, "Why are people so concerned about these mammals' suffering when human beings are suffering so much and they don't care? Places like Africa, where people are dying and we have to give account to God for that and [not for] these animals without a soul, who die and that's it?"

Samuel Hazelwood

I had to confess that I couldn't adequately answer Samuel's question. The vast majority of anti-whaling activists are not misanthropic. They do care about the suffering of human beings. Those with whom I've spoken—especially Paul Watson of the Sea Shepherd Conservation Society—are wonderful people. In 2005, I carried on a back-and-forth email conversation with Watson while he was at sea, sailing to Australia from his home in Washington State. He mentioned that his ship would stop over for a few days at Pitcairn Island, the famous and remote home of the descendants of the *Bounty* mutineers.

I was a Fulbright scholar at the Institute of Island Studies in Prince Edward Island, Canada, then, and I knew that my island studies colleagues would be interested to learn more about everyday life on Pitcairn, which was—and still is—a remote and seldom-visited island. Paul Watson agreed to go ashore with some of his crewmembers to ask questions from a list that my colleagues and I had written and report back to us on the results. He didn't have to do this. It had nothing to do with marine conservation and, owing to the sensitive nature of some of the questions we posed, could have actually soured his relationship with the islanders. Instead, Watson's charm prevailed and he produced for us a four-page report, which, in addition to addressing our areas of interest, branched into the history, religion, economy, and biodiversity of the island. In it Watson concluded, "Overall, I found the Pitcairn Islanders to be the friendliest people I have encountered anywhere. It was a pleasure to meet them and spend a day with them." I got the impression that he has probably said the same thing about many small coastal communities around the world.

My goal in meeting with Samuel was to get on board his boat. I wanted to observe Vincentian whaling firsthand, to experience it as Samuel and his crew do. Vincent vouched for me. My reliability, erudition, and seaworthiness seemed to be the foremost concerns in Samuel's mind. They negotiated the terms during a long discussion, made up mostly of short, staccato phrases and questions spoken in Vincentian Creole, punctuated by stretches of uncomfortable, mulling silence. In the end, Samuel agreed to let me join his whaling crew for a three-month term. I would receive no pay but would work for food in the form of fresh tuna or mahi mahi that we caught with a line trolling behind the boat as we whaled. Within twenty-four hours of meeting Samuel, thanks mainly to Vincent's support, I found myself aboard a small wooden boat, out of sight of land, in hot pursuit of a small pod of dolphins.

Usually the crew consisted of Samuel at the harpoon, myself in the center, and Papas in the stern. "Papas" is of course a nickname. I assumed it derived from his occupation: Papas hunted whales and dolphins for a living, and *papas*—Creole for "porpoise"—is a term used for most cetaceans smaller than a pilot whale (ironically, no true porpoises are found in the Caribbean). I mentioned this assumption to Papas one day and was quickly corrected: "No, no. I got the name when I was a kid. When I was little I was always swimming in the sea. Like a papas. That, and I was slippery and hard to hold on to." Sometimes Samuel would stay on shore and send me out with Papas as the harpooner and Limb at the stern. Limb is long and skinny— like a limb.

Vincentians don't wait for the whales to come in as the Faroese do. They go out themselves and bring the whales back. A standard Vincentian whaling boat carries three people: the harpooner, the sternman, and the centerman. The harpooner's role is that of captain. He stands at the bow, watches for whales and dolphins, and directs the sternman where to steer. My task was simple. I was to take the place of the centerman, to do his job, and to stay out of the way. The man who had to stay on shore so that I could go out got paid a reduced salary. I sat on the center seat row of the boat and handed things back and forth between the harpooner and the sternman. When a whale or dolphin was harpooned, as I was soon to find out, I was to help haul it in, cut the harpoon out of its flesh, straighten the harpoon, and give it to the harpooner for the next shot. I knew all of this from my reading and from the quick briefing—if you can call it that—that I received on the dock just before setting out.

A Careful Disorderliness

From the five-inch-long, knifepoint-sharp, toggling harpoon heads to the twenty-one-foot whaling boats themselves, nearly all of the equipment that Vincentian whalers use is locally designed and built. On days with rough seas, I would often visit Samuel in his workshop, essentially just a tarpaulin suspended over a patch of ground in a vacant Barrouallie lot, to watch him turn scrap metal and lumber into the tools—some authors have called them "weapons"—of the whaling business. The most iconic of these tools is the harpoon.

There are two types of harpoon in use among Vincentian whalers: the hand harpoon and the gun harpoon. These differ primarily in length and, of course, in method of use. Hand harpoons are about three meters in total length and are thrown by hand; gun harpoons are about one meter long and are fired from a modified shotgun mounted at the bow of the whaleboat. The harpoon gun is the distinguishing characteristic of whaleboats. It is what sets them apart from fishing boats, but in practice, the whalers use the hand harpoons more often. "More accurate, if you know how to handle it," Samuel says of the hand harpoon.

There are three main parts to a harpoon of either type: the head (locally called a *gill*), the foreshaft, and the main shaft. Starting with scraps of steel salvaged from discarded machinery, a blacksmith cuts a rough wedge shape that will become the harpoon's gill. He sharpens this wedge to a point and mounts it to the harpoon foreshaft through a central pivot hole with a rivet. Before each use, the harpooner ties the gill loosely with a string to keep it straight until it enters the whale. The purpose of the toggling gill is similar to that of the barb of a fishhook—once the harpoon enters the whale, the gill pivots ninety degrees and provides resistance against slipping back out.

The harpoon foreshaft is built from scrap steel rods, cut to a length of about a half meter, heated, and pounded flat on one end to fit into a channel cut in the gill. The other end of the steel foreshaft joins

A harpoon on the deck of a whaling boat

the wooden main shaft by way of a small metal cup built from scrap steel pipe. These cups are the "murderous chalices" from which Melville's Captain Ahab commanded his harpooners to "drink and swear, ye men that man the deathful whaleboat's bow—Death to Moby-Dick!"[2] The similarity between Yankee whaling during Melville's day and modern Caribbean whaling is no anachronism. While technological and cultural changes have certainly occurred in both Caribbean and Faroese whaling, much of the basic equipment in use by Vincentian whalers today remains the same as what was used two or three hundred years ago on the famous whaling ships that sailed from New England. Referencing Athneal Ollivierre, the late leader of Bequian humpback whaling, the journalist Sebastian

Junger reported in *Outside* magazine that you could "take the guys from Melville's *Moby-Dick* and put them in Athneal's boat, and they'd know exactly what to do."[3]

The main shaft of the harpoon has the diameter of the middle of a baseball bat. It's cut to the appropriate length, depending on whether it will be used for a gun harpoon or a hand harpoon. The blacksmith pounds the foreshaft cup onto the main shaft. If the harpoon is to be thrown by hand, the only remaining step is to attach a length of nylon rope to the foreshaft so the harpoon can be retrieved after a miss, or so that the whale can be tethered to the boat after a strike.

Harpoon heads at various stages of completion

The final step in building a gun harpoon is to cut a rubber disk from a discarded tire and to nail it to the base of the main shaft. This acts to dampen the impact of the shotgun's explosive force against the base of the shaft. Before the rubber disk was introduced, harpoon shafts often splintered when fired. A steel ring is placed around the base of the gun harpoon's main shaft to further prevent splintering. Despite their meticulous construction and quality materials, harpoons rarely last longer than two years owing to their constant exposure to the elements and heavy usage. A new harpoon sells for 200 Eastern Caribbean dollars (US$75); boat owners can reduce their costs by learning the skills needed to make their own harpoons rather than constantly hiring the services of someone else.

All active whaling boats in Barrouallie follow the same basic design. Samuel Hazelwood's boat is a typical example. The *Sea Hunter* is twenty-one feet long and six feet broad at the beam. It was built in Barrouallie in 1993 from imported cedar and is powered by a 65-horsepower Yamaha outboard engine. The boat has four rows of seats and a deck built over the foremost section. Upon a smaller, higher deck in the bow is mounted a five-legged swiveling gun stand. The gun attaches to the post via a circular plate and U-shaped cradle that pivots horizontally and vertically. Adding to the harpoon's range of motion is the coordination between the harpooner and the sternman to point the bow of the boat—and thus the gun—toward the target.

The harpoon gun itself is a modified shotgun. Samuel has removed the barrel and replaced it with a wider steel pipe. Two steel straps hold this pipe to a specially designed forestock carved from a stout piece of lumber. A bolt passes through this forestock, linking the gun to the gun mount. Once the gun is mounted, the harpooner loads it with a cartridge from which he has removed the shot and added a half measure of extra powder. He then loads the harpoon by working its main shaft into the barrel of the gun. Mounted on its stand and loaded with a harpoon, with a firing range of up to a hundred meters, this homemade harpoon gun is the Caribbean whaler's most technologically advanced tool.

Beaching the whaling boat.
Photo © Andy Fielding

Below the gun stand, the harpooner keeps a ball of nylon rope. After loading a harpoon, he ties the end of the harpoon's line to one end of this rope and passes the other end to the sternman. Every Vincentian whaling boat has a block of wood shaped like a giant doorknob mounted to the seat immediately in front of the sternman. This is the loggerhead. When a whale or dolphin is harpooned, the sternman turns the line once or twice around the loggerhead to provide friction. Otherwise the line might run out, allowing the whale to escape and leaving the men on board with nothing but rope-burned hands and a feeling of loss.

Caribbean whaling boats are full of other items that may or may not become necessary during the day's activities. Here is a full inventory of everything that is brought along on a typical whaling voyage: four 18-gallon fuel tanks; three 1-gallon water jugs; three watertight buckets—one for each crewmember—containing lunches, mobile

Papas, winding a line around the loggerhead,
with a whale harpooned on the other end

phones, GPS units, and other personal items; two cutlasses (a charmingly anachronistic term for machetes, used throughout much of the
English-speaking Caribbean); one siphon hose for filling the gas
tank from the reserve tanks; five or six large plastic buoys to attach
to harpoon lines; two dull and rusty knives; one flat-head screwdriver,
one of the boat's two proper tools; one hammer, the other tool; hand-
lines for fishing; two raincoats (for three whalers, mind you); one
box of shotgun shells; one modified shotgun; seven hand harpoons;
twelve gun harpoons; one gaff hook; two lances, essentially hand harpoons with the gills sheared off and the foreshafts sharpened; two

bailing buckets; four bamboo poles; many 45-meter lengths of nylon rope; one steel rod about a meter long for clearing the gun barrel; one wooden club for stunning fish; and two flashlights, battery condition unknown.

It is interesting to note items that are not included on the list: life preservers, first-aid supplies, marine radios, extensive tool kits, extra engines, engine parts, or oars. I recall more than once being adrift, out of sight of land, with a dead engine while the whalers tested the limits of hammer-and-screwdriver utility to get the boat moving again. It is a tribute to the mechanical resourcefulness endemic to the Caribbean region that we were always able to return to port under our boat's own power. Cuban mechanics are deservedly famous for keeping their midcentury American automobiles running, usually without access to proper replacement parts. While it certainly is impressive to see, for example, a 1950s-era Bel Air plying the streets of La Habana Vieja with an engine transplanted from a Lada and a fuel pump from a Soviet tractor, these Vincentian whalers achieve equal outcomes in their boats, all while bobbing offshore, out of sight of land, and without any replacement parts whatsoever.

The gear is not arranged methodically; it is placed haphazardly in the boat and must be quickly rearranged when whales or dolphins are brought on board. This jumble, and especially the way that the Vincentian whalers made it work, reminded me of Melville's statement, regarding whaling, that "there are some enterprises in which a careful disorderliness is the true method."[4] The worst are the buoys. These basketball-sized rubber balls roll around in the boat and always seem to be underfoot. They are used when the whalers find so many whales or dolphins that they don't have time to haul each one in before harpooning the next. In this case, they will attach a buoy to the line and let it go overboard. After harpooning a half dozen or so animals, the whalers motor around following the buoys, collecting their injured catch. Often when a whale or dolphin is harpooned it swims quickly away from the boat, causing the line attached to the harpoon to zip out. Anything tangled in the line is pulled overboard, and crew-members must often hop about the boat quickly to avoid getting tangled themselves.

My First Take

The spray from a distant blowhole, catching and refracting the sun-light and falling like prisms back to the surface of the sea. An ephemeral dorsal fin rising, then slipping back beneath again before you're sure you even really saw it. A fluke. The smooth-skinned flash of a breaching dolphin. A flock of feeding seabirds. A ripple, but only the right kind of ripple. Whalers rely almost entirely on visual clues to find their targets. Sunlight and a clear view, without fog, are essential to a successful day of whaling. So while their fishing counterparts set out well before dawn, content to sit under a dark sky and cast their lines, their nets, into a dark sea, Barrouallie whalers wait until a full hour, or even two, has passed since sunrise.

Eight o'clock in the morning on my first day of Vincentian whaling: in my roll-top drybag I had packed a peanut-butter-and-guava-jelly sandwich (a compromise between the Caribbean and my childhood), two liters of water, lots of sunscreen, a waterproof camera, and a GPS. We set out from the dock at Barrouallie, heading due west. Within half an hour we were surrounded by a pod of dolphins. Marine biologists advise their assistants on sighting surveys that a snapshot of surfacing dolphins usually shows 10 percent of the total pod. That is to say, 90 percent of a pod of dolphins is underwater at any given moment. Given that formula, there were easily five hundred dolphins surrounding the boat.

"Skipjack papas," said Papas, in Creole.

"Fraser's dolphins," Samuel translated, standing at the bow with a hand on the harpoon gun. He had been to fisheries colleges in Japan and Canada and could have told me the dolphins' scientific name (*Lagenodelphis hosei*) too, if I had asked.

Samuel would explain to me later that the Fraser's dolphins we saw are part of a resident pod that stays near the west coast of St. Vincent and will actually lead his boat to other whales or dolphins. This seemed unbelievable until I remembered that fishermen in Brazil use wild bottlenose dolphins to round mullet into their nets and that, in the early twentieth century, there was a small Australian whaling village called Eden where killer whales—orca—would lead whalers to humpbacks.[5] Several orca would swim into the cove near the village and slap their tails on the water to get the whalers' attention. After hearing the tail-slapping the whalers would set sail, following the orca, and would usually find a humpback surrounded by other orca like a wayward ewe being circled and nipped by border collies. A tradition arose that the whalers, after killing the humpback, would let it sink, tied to a buoy, and come back for it the next day. Each time when the whalers returned—and this went on for years—the orca would have eaten the whale's tongue: compensation for their services. With those stories in mind I readily understood why Samuel was not taking up the harpoon despite the abundant Fraser's dolphins. Samuel likes to avoid taking too many of these because they serve him in this scouting role, like an aquatic version of the Judas horse in the American West. Sometimes though, after a day of unsuccessful whaling, especially if the Fraser's dolphins haven't been particularly helpful, he'll harpoon a few of them on his way home. Anything is better than returning to Barrouallie with an empty boat.

This day was hardly done, so there was no need to worry yet about finishing empty. We motored through the Fraser's dolphins and out into the open sea. Postcards from the Caribbean usually show palms swaying over white-sand beaches, shallow electric-blue water inviting knee-deep wading with rolled-up pant legs. While the Grenadines do boast this kind of scenery—and without nearly the abundance of tourists seen on some other Caribbean islands—St. Vincent does not. Nearly all the beaches are composed of black sand and the undersea topography drops off steeply. Within a few boat lengths of the dock you cannot see the bottom. The water becomes dark. Several miles offshore, you might as well be in the North Atlantic. St. Vincent, and the waters offshore, can even feel like the North Atlantic. Aside from the regular experiences with overzealous use of air-conditioning, I've only been cold twice in the Caribbean, both on St. Vincent. One was as my brother Andy and I stood atop La Soufrière, the island's volcano, waiting for the cloud cover to part and shivering in the fog. The other was on board Samuel's whaling boat, running home in a squall with the sun obscured behind an extension of the clouds that La Soufrière had created.

But this first day of whaling was sunny. While the water was still dark and the island had disappeared, first within a cloud and then over the horizon, the sun shone bright and hot. Samuel unwound a handline from a broken wooden shingle stowed at his feet. A small, bobbly jig was tied at its tip. He tossed the lure overboard and jammed the shingle into the gap between the inner and outer planks of the gunwale. Later, when I would analyze Samuel's whaling and financial records, I would see that the tuna, mahi mahi, and mackerel caught on this trolling line sometimes made the difference between a day's profit and loss when whales and dolphins were scarce.

A solitary dorsal fin broke the water. When boaters from the United States see dorsal fins in the ocean we instinctively think of sharks; I blame Peter Benchley. In reality, though, dolphins break the surface much more regularly. This dorsal fin was definitely a dolphin—an Americano, as any Vincentian whaler immediately would have called it; a Risso's dolphin, as Samuel would translate for me. (*Grampus griseus,* he no doubt knew.) The dolphin was our target. With a quick series of hand signals that I would later learn to interpret, Samuel silently instructed Papas to position the vessel exactly as he wanted it. He readied the harpoon gun. The first harpoon had been loaded in the barrel since before casting off from the dock that morning, but Samuel took a few seconds to clear the area around the line coiled at his feet. The boat was bobbing on the waves, the engine was idling, and the dolphin was rising once every ten seconds or so. It would take a few cycles of bobbing and breathing before the boat and the dolphin were aligned. The moment this happened Samuel squeezed the trigger, letting fly his projectile like a comet followed by a tail of nylon twine and surrounded by a cloud of blasted gunpowder. I was expecting a pop, but still the sound startled me. Almost instantly there was a splash about thirty meters from the bow, followed by furious splashing. The line pulled tight. The harpoon was secure.

Papas quickly wrapped the loggerhead and held on to the loose end of the line. Samuel climbed down from his perch and took ahold of the line as well. They both started pulling. "Hal!" shouted Papas.

Hal? What? Am I supposed to be doing something? I wondered.

"Hal!" He became more insistent. *Hal. Haul. Haul!* I gripped the line in my hands and leaned back. It took the three of us giving everything we had to get the Risso's dolphin close to the boat.

The dolphin's fluke was still working, pulling hard against us. Its skin was mottled shades of gray with prominent white scars running the length of its body. According to marine biologists, these scars are the result of encounters with squid—the main prey of the Risso's dolphin—or the process of "raking," by which one dolphin scrapes another with its teeth. Considering that some scars were round and located on the head and others were linear, with multiple parallel lines, each of which was spaced about the same distance from its neighbor as the gaps between a Risso's teeth, it's likely that this particular Risso's dolphin carried scars both from squid and from other dolphins.

The dolphin beat against the boat's hull with its tail. Fearing that the harpoon might tear out, Samuel raised another harpoon above his head and drove it in for added security. The animal stopped fighting. The second harpoon had killed, or gravely wounded, the dolphin and it was time to haul it on board. In a coordinated effort, the three of us put our feet against the gunwale, took hold of the rope as near the harpoon as we could, and leaned back, pushing with our legs. The tail came up first. Samuel grabbed it and we leveraged the dolphin up and into the boat. I slipped and landed face-to-face with its lifeless, toothy grin. We'd gotten one. That Risso's would be our only catch of the day. It's a bigger species than most other dolphins

Samuel Hazelwood and Papas, hauling a Risso's dolphin aboard

that Samuel would take—though much smaller than a pilot whale—so the day was a success. We motored back to Barrouallie as I scooped seawater with my hand to wash my skin, my clothes, my bag. Everything was covered in blood. I rode back to my lodgings in a crowded public van, took a long shower to try to wash the scent and memory off my skin, and went to sleep that night with conflicting feelings: I knew Samuel and his crew had provided food for their community and income for their households, but I mourned the dolphin's death.

Flesh, Teeth, and Fear Itself

During my fieldwork I did not live in Barrouallie. Instead, I rented a small apartment connected to a family's home in the village of Brighton. To get to Barrouallie each morning I walked nearly a kilometer to the highway and rode a van, or public minibus, to

Kingstown, walked across the capital, and caught another van to Barrouallie. In St. Vincent, vans are a way of life. These small, multi-passenger Japanese vehicles are meant to hold fifteen but are usually not considered full until at least twenty passengers are on board. There's always room for one more. Each van has a name painted across its hood and its own personality. In addition to their drivers, vans also employ "conductors" to ride in the second row, opening the large sliding door for passengers, calling out the name of the route at stops, and collecting the fares. Vans known for fast driving and loud soca music are called "hot vans." I learned to avoid these. There are few preset stops along the Vincentian van routes. Rather, when passengers see their destination approaching, they call out "Bus stop!" to request a stop. If the driver doesn't hear a passenger in the back row, those in middle rows will often relay the message forward. This sense of community begins at the start of the ride. It's customary, when entering an already occupied van, to greet all the other passengers before sitting down and holding on for the ride.

Just as van riding took some getting used to, over time I came to understand the subtle culture of Vincentian whaling. One example was the intimate and mysterious conversation that occurs between the harpooner and the sternman using only hand gestures and boat movements. The sternman sits just in front of a roaring outboard motor and could only hope to hear the harpooner if the latter took his eyes off the target, turned back, and shouted. In the final moments of the hunt, when it's important for the harpooner to observe the animal constantly to see where it last rose for a breath so he can predict its next surfacing, he cannot afford to turn around and give the sternman verbal instructions. These instructions are essential, though, because the harpooner can be placed in the correct position to make the harpoon strike only through the sternman's precise, fine-scale navigation. The system of communicating through hand signals must have evolved to overcome this conflict.

Most whaling days included some downtime. Usually after about four hours, we were tired and hungry. This was especially true if we

Samuel Hazelwood in the bow, directing the sternman where to go

hadn't yet caught—or even sighted—any whales or dolphins. I often compare whaling to playing goalie on a soccer team: it's either boring or terrifying, but rarely anything in between. An eight-hour day of whaling might include seven hours of motoring around, seeing nothing but ocean swells and the horizon, and one cumulative hour of actually pursuing, harpooning, and hauling whales.

By about midday, if the morning had been slow, the sternman would cut the engine, the harpooner would descend from his perch, and we would all pull our lunches out from our waterproof containers. After eating we would normally take a nap, stretched out across the three benches in the boat, heads and feet resting on the gunwales. One memorable day, when I was out with Papas as harpooner and Limb at the stern, we were suddenly awakened from a nap by the un-mistakable sound of a cetacean exhaling from its blowhole. It was close! We sat up simultaneously and saw a large beaked whale lolling on the surface barely an arm's length from the port side of the boat. "*Grampus!*" Limb shouted, using the local name for the species. Papas leapt to his feet and took up a hand harpoon. The whale dove. Our heads swung like pendulums from one side of the boat to the other, hoping to see it surface again, but it was gone. Beaked whales are known for their deep dives, and this one would not surface again while we maintained our watch. The near-miss, though, was motivation for the rest of the day's hunt.

Another near-miss stands out in my field notes. Midafternoon, and we had been out whaling all day without a single sighting. We had passed through the ring of Fraser's dolphins earlier but their breaches were laconic; they weren't leading us anywhere. Far out of sight of land, we motored around randomly while Papas and Samuel grew increasingly frustrated with the day. Samuel, true to form, never gave up his post. His position at the bow, gripping the harpoon gun with one hand and shading his eyes with the other, never altered. But his glances became more furtive. His quick back-and-forth told me that he was desperate to not return home without a catch. But where were the blackfish? Where were the dolphins?

"Whitefish," Samuel said—killer whales, orca. "They chase away all the papas and the blackfish." According to local belief, if there are killer whales—called "whitefish" because of their white undersides— anywhere in the area, all other marine mammals flee, leaving a sea around St. Vincent with nothing to take, except the whitefish themselves. The orca is the ocean's largest species of dolphin, a predatory cetacean known for cooperative hunting strategies and for feeding on much larger whales. Some people refer to them as sea wolves. One marine ecologist has called them "the top, top predator."[6] The whale's scientific name, *Orcinus orca,* hints at its mythical origin in the underworld, the realm of the god Orcus: a Roman equivalent to Hades. The orca's more common name, "killer whale," indicates its status as perhaps the last cetacean to still invoke some level of fear among humans.

In the earliest recorded interactions between humans and whales, fear was the primary human emotion felt during such encounters. Examples abound. Ancient maps show whales, dragons, and sea monsters—all equally terrifying—inhabiting unknown seas.[7] "Here be dragons" might have sounded just as dreadful if it had been "here be whales." The same Hebrew word is in various versions of the Bible translated as *whale, dragon, serpent,* or *sea monster.*[8] The ancient world seems not to have distinguished much between whales and monsters. There was a belief that the spray from whales' blowholes was poisonous. It certainly doesn't smell good. Perhaps it helped the persistence of the whaling industry to have stories such as that of the whaleship *Essex:* it was rammed by a sperm whale, and its crew was forced into cannibalistic drifting following the destruction of their ship. To petition for an animal's protection, humans must feel some amount of sympathy for it. With their ship-ramming tendencies and poisonous breath, whales were largely seen as enemies to people long before they were seen as friends. Sympathy with all whales came late—for orca, perhaps, latest of all.

The first-century CE Roman naturalist Pliny the Elder, in his *Naturalis Historia,* describes an orca that had stranded alive in Ostia harbor, at the mouth of the Tiber in Rome. The whale, which according to Pliny "cannot be properly depicted or described except as an enormous mass of flesh armed with savage teeth," was put to death with spears by a cohort of soldiers led personally by Emperor Claudius.[9] The whole event, Pliny tells his reader, was conducted as a spectacle for the Roman people gathered along the shoreline— something of a seaside adaptation of the gladiatorial events that would later be held in the nearby Colosseum, the famous arena completed soon after Pliny's death.

In a twentieth-century parallel to Pliny's account, the shooting of a pod of more than a hundred orca for target practice by members of the United States Air Force stationed in Iceland was described in detail, unproblematically, in a late 1950s *Time* magazine article.[10] The pilots simply flew over the ocean, firing live ammunition at whales and allowing their carcasses to sink to the bottom. In what bears the suspicious marks of plagiarism from Pliny's account, written nineteen centuries before, the *Time* author refers to the killer whales as "savage sea cannibals up to 30 feet long with teeth like bayonets."[11] Nearly two thousand years and orca are still reduced to simple assemblages of flesh, teeth, and fear itself. Whether by Roman soldiers or American airmen, their killing was not only justified but applauded.

Orca, despite their appellation marking them as killers and long history of fear-inducing interactions with humans, ironically played an important role in the development of the save-the-whales movement.[12] In 1964, for the first time, a live, captive orca was put on public display. This orca—captured off Saturna Island in British Columbia and named Moby Doll—was originally intended to be killed, its skin taxidermied and exhibited. But when the whale survived the harpooning, several shots from a rifle, and the sixteen-hour tow to Vancouver, veterinarians decided to try to save it. The whale lived in captivity for three months, during which time it provided scientists with a subject for research and became something of an international celebrity. After Moby Doll's death, the *Times* of London ran an especially prescient obituary for the whale, which stated, "The widespread publicity—some of it the first positive press ever about killer whales—marked the beginning of an important change in the public attitude toward the species."[13] People began to understand more about whales and, at the same time, began to question the justifiability of whaling.

Today, thanks in part to the public presence of charismatic orca such as Shamu and Willy, people are more familiar with this species— and to some extent, cetaceans in general—than they were before 1964 and Moby Doll. The documentary film *Blackfish,* despite being confusingly titled in light of the Vincentian names for killer whales and pilot whales, seriously questions the orca-borne cost of this awareness and has been credited with spurring the recent decision by SeaWorld to phase out its captive orca program.[14]

Vincentian whalers hunt orca when they can. The meat is similar to that of pilot whales but the blubber is considered inferior. They are a rare catch: I estimate that the entire operation has only taken twenty during the past three years. But Samuel once brought in three killer whales in a single day. What a day that must have been! Killer whales are much larger than pilot whales. Their teeth, while not quite the length of bayonets, are certainly fearsome.

On a shelf in my parents' home in Tampa sits a well-polished orca tooth: a gift from Samuel. I gave an identical tooth to each of my two brothers. Within days of arriving home with the tooth sent with him to Kentucky, my brother Cory called to tell me that it had exploded, spontaneously cracked in two with a report like a gunshot. It may have been a change in atmospheric pressure or humidity that caused the tooth to crack violently, or perhaps it was a chemical reaction with something that Cory had used to clean it. But I like to think Lexington is just too far from the Caribbean and the tooth destroyed itself in that unfamiliar setting. The teeth that stayed in Florida are still whole.

I don't know how Samuel knew that there were orca in the area that day except that there were no other cetaceans to be found. But couldn't there be other reasons? Is this like the classic fisherman, blaming his lack of a catch on the heat, or the wind, or the phase of the moon? Or like the Faroese, hoping for a grindaboð and watching for flies, rain, or fog? How did Samuel know? Even scientific fishermen like to have something to blame for their empty-handedness. The R. J. Dunlap Marine Conservation Program at the University of Miami makes shark-fishing voyages several times each month, usually bringing students from South Florida schools along to see science in action. I've brought my own university classes on board too. To get the data they're after and to make the trip memorable for the students, the Dunlap researchers need to catch sharks. Their method is to set ten lines at a time and wait for bites. If no sharks bite, the researchers, mostly graduate students or professional scholars with PhDs—educated, empirically minded people—will choose a different color plastic spool around which to wind the fishing line: "Maybe green just isn't working today. Let's try blue." While none of the researchers actually believes that the spool color matters, pretending that it does matters to some. Humans don't like randomness. We prefer to feel like we're in control. Barring that, we like to have someone to blame. On a day like this, devoid of whales and dolphins, Samuel blamed the whitefish. I sat back against the gunwale as Papas slowed the engine. He pulled his mobile phone from his waterproof bucket and checked the screen.

Suddenly there was a flurry of words, spoken in quick Vincentian Creole, flying over my head—both literally and figuratively—from the stern to the bow. By this time in my two-site fieldwork I could understand more Faroese than Creole, despite the English roots of the latter language. I caught the word "whitefish" and the name of another whaler. I also heard the phrase "six missed calls." Another boat had found the orca pod. There were too many of them to manage and they'd been calling us, both to help and to share in the bounty. This was a rare attempt at cooperation between Vincentian whaling crews. Normally, each sets out on its own and barely takes notice of other boats, except, in bad weather, by waiting for one another to come into view before heading back to Barrouallie. This invitation to take part in an abundant catch was truly unusual. And we were missing it— Papas's phone ringing silently, insulated in his waterproof bucket. How long had they been calling? Samuel was impatient. Papas stowed his phone and hit the throttle.

As Papas gunned the engine and turned hard left, a rogue wave several feet high approached from the port bow. We hit it as we were accelerating and the wave launched us airborne. I saw Samuel tighten his grip on the harpoon gun and widen his stance. Papas took a quick, deep breath, and I looked straight ahead at the approaching sea surface. The only thought I had time for was, *We're going to dive.* The boat entered the water at an odd angle—*diagonal* is the best way to describe it—and we were awash. I held on to the bench in case the boat broke up; in the absence of life jackets I'll take anything that floats. With my knees underwater and our downward motion barely slowed, I held my breath. And then we popped up.

Samuel's boatbuilding had provided us with a craft that could distribute the force of the impact, staying intact, and could right itself after its jackknife dive off the rogue wave ramp. Papas accelerated again. Samuel pointed out the course. It was as though we hadn't nearly sunk. A day in the life. I grabbed a plastic bleach bottle with its bottom cut out and started bailing.

After a half hour of speeding toward the other boat's position we arrived to find they had lost the pod of orca. "Toward Bequia," someone shouted. We took off, heading south, but the killer whales could have been anywhere by then. Papas dutifully held course as Samuel beckoned him further south and then began triangulating left and right. "How far will you chase them?" I asked. Samuel, never taking his eyes off the horizon, answered determinedly, "All the way to Carriacou"—the southern limit of St. Vincent & the Grenadines' territorial waters. I settled in for the long ride, but Samuel called it off as we rounded Bequia's southern point.

We headed back to St. Vincent and took about seven Fraser's dolphins on the way home. Samuel maintains a hard bargain with these sentinels: they lead us to the target species or he hunts them. That day the Frasers did not keep their end of the deal. We tied up at the Barrouallie pier as the sun was setting—my longest day whaling: eleven hours since we'd set off in the morning.

3

The Stones of Faroe

In some ways, the Faroe Islands appear to be the model environmentalist society. Remote and isolated in the middle of the North Atlantic, about equidistant from Iceland, Scotland, and Norway, the inhabitants of these eighteen small islands are accustomed to self-sufficiency. Hydroelectric and wind power make up 40 percent of local electricity generation annually, on average. The government has set the goal of achieving 100 percent reliance on renewable energy by 2030. After especially windy or rainy periods, when the power company has been able to shut down its diesel generators and rely completely on renewable sources for a week or more, the accomplishment is announced on Faroese radio. People listen and appreciate the news.

The islands are remote, small, and obscure, as the musician Sting indicated in "Why Should I Cry for You?," a song on his 1991 album *The Soul Cages.* In describing his father's distance—both physical and emotional—during his childhood, Sting employed nautical imagery and imagined his father sailing "north, northwest the stones of Faroe."

To a young Newcastle boy pining for his absent father, the Faroes might represent the edge of the known world. Residents of these "stones" have had to learn resourcefulness and self-sufficiency, whether in generating energy or in producing food. Like many small island populations, they embrace positive attention from abroad, no matter how modest.

Long before "green roofs" were popular in North American or European cities, the traditional Faroese home was topped with living turf for durability and insulation. A teenager's summer chores might include mowing not only the lawn but the housetop too—that is, if the sheep haven't been hauled onto the roof to do the work already. Taking in the landscape of a Faroese village gives a viewer the impression that these houses either have just risen from the earth, sporting the sod from their footprints as rooftops, or are ready to drop underground at a moment's notice, grassy roofs melding seamlessly with the ground, hiding the homes away, should the Barbary pirates return to reprise their seventeenth-century slave raids. Former U.S. president Bill Clinton visited the Faroe Islands in 2007 and had quite an impact on the residents of Tórshavn simply by strolling down the main shopping street and greeting the locals. A small café, Handil og Kaffi, where the former president stopped for—and mildly complimented—a cup of coffee, still displays a framed photograph of Clinton above his understated remark: "This coffee is very tasteful." Shortly after Clinton's visit, his presidential library in Arkansas—a building that already featured prominent Scandinavian architectural influences—was refitted to include a grass-covered green roof. While the decision-making process that led to this remodel is unclear, the Faroese are quick to take credit.

In the wry words of an early twentieth-century geographer writing about the Faroes, these "subarctic regions are not altogether desolate wastes."[1] Indeed, marketers of international tourism are currently discovering the Faroes as quite the desirable holiday spot. The Faroes were named the top island destination in a 2007 *National Geographic Traveler* survey, an honor given in part because the natural

Turf-roof houses in Mykines.
Photo © Andy Fielding

environment of the archipelago is "unspoiled . . . and likely to remain so."[2] But any environmentalist hoping to find a green utopia in
the Faroe Islands will not stay long, for—of course—the Faroese are
guilty of whaling, which some consider to be among the most mortal
of environmental sins.

After the grindaboð has been sent out and the shore-based participants have assembled on the beach, the flotilla of boats steers the
pod of whales into a fjord for the final leg of the drive. The sýslumaður regulates the action onshore, which means that once the
participants are in position and have organized their tools, the sýslumaður tries to keep action to a minimum. It is thought that excess
noise or movement on the beach can frighten the whales and make
them difficult to land. Often the participants are told to stay back
some distance from the waterline and must be reminded of this rule

as the whales approach, so eager are they to begin the grindadráp. The sýslumaður can deputize people for this task; these are the *grindamenn* (plural of *grindamaður,* "pilot whale man") my class observed at Tjørnuvík.

A critical time in the process comes as the whales draw close to the shore. The pod must be kept tightly together so whales don't disperse, turn back, or dive. In the past, before the whaling regulations restricted the available tool set to just the hook and knife (now only the hook and spinal lance), a whaler in a forward boat might prick a whale's tail with a spear. This would result in the pricked whale swimming quickly through the pod, toward the beach, and causing something of a panic within the pod. Other whales, perhaps the entire pod, would swim faster too and become stranded further up the beach than they might have otherwise. The Faroese want the whales to strand high on the beach so they don't have to wade into deep water to hook them or drag them as far. Today the spear is prohibited, so to speed the whales' final approach to the beach the boat captains coordinate a surge in the speed of the flotilla during the last meters of the drive. This is a relatively easy process in all but one of the whaling villages. Since motorboats are used to drive whales, the boat captains need only to open their throttles to give the whales their final push toward the beach. In one village, however—Vágur, on Suðuroy—local tradition holds that motorboats may be used to drive whales into the bay from the open sea, but that only wooden rowboats can perform the task of driving the pod onto the beach. These vessels, called *grindabátar,* or "pilot whale boats," are kept in the small, picturesque boathouses that line the north shore of the harbor. Consider the challenge, thrill, and exhaustion involved in rowing behind a pod of pilot whales, not only fast enough to keep up but with enough speed and coordination to actually drive the whales onto the beach.

When the whales begin to strand in the shallow water—or, if the timing is just right, when the whales swimming at the front of the pod are pushed completely ashore by the waves—the shore-based whalers begin their hook-and-rope work. To do so they must enter

the ocean. The Faroe Islands are located at 62° north—the same latitude as southern Greenland. While the climate and sea temperature
of the Faroes benefit significantly from the Gulf Stream, the sea
surface rarely exceeds 11 degrees Celsius, even in late summer, when
grindadráp are most frequent. Kate Sanderson, the literary scholar,
singles out the entrance of fully clothed whalers into the frigid sea as
a major part of the "ambiguity" surrounding the grindadráp, making
the whole event a challenge for the outsider to even comprehend.[3]
She describes a scene in which "men and whales meet at the intersection of the social and the wild at a place where the whales have
been driven partially from their own environment into another . . .
The human participants join the whales in the borderline region, and,
like the whales, they are in their own and an alien environment at the
same time."[4]

Under ordinary circumstances there would be little reason in the
Faroe Islands for a large group of people to wade into the water. This
is not the home of the Polar Plunge. The sight of the shore-based
whalers boldly entering the sea and the sound of their shouting—
combining elements of a war cry and cries of fear (or are war cries
always mixed with fear?)—can be jarring to the observer. And grindadráp often have many observers. Because nearly all whaling beaches
are located at the seaward edge of villages, the public has a degree of
access to the event unlike that seen with nearly any other form of animal slaughter. The slaughter of domestic animals is typically done
indoors with no audience. Most other forms of hunting occur far
from populated areas and are, by nature, solitary pursuits. The grindadráp, by contrast, occurs in full view of anyone who wishes to
observe. This audience can include Faroese locals, foreign observers,
and even anti-whaling activists.

Besides the boats themselves, only two tools are permitted for use
in the grindadráp: the hook and the spinal lance. The hook, called
blástrarongul in Faroese, is shaped like a fishing hook but much bigger.
Hold up your arm, bent acutely at the elbow, like you're comically
"making a muscle." This approximates the size and shape of the

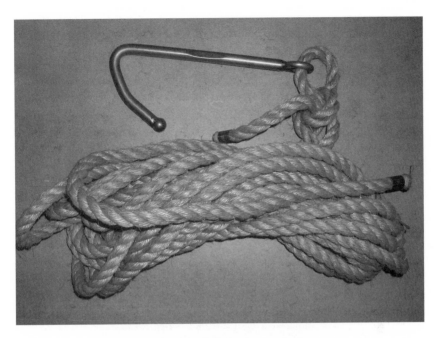

A *blástrarongul,* or blowhole hook, attached to a rope.
Photo by B. Hanusson, used by permission of Justines Olsen

blástrarongul. Attached is a long, thickly woven length of stout rope.
The tip of the hook is blunt, a small metal ball welded where the point
would be. In the past, sharp hooks called *sóknarongulin* (sing.
sóknarongul) were used, but these are currently being phased out,
based on the understanding that blunt hooks cause less suffering in
the whales that are being dragged ashore.

The spinal lance, called *mønustingari,* is a recent invention, almost
a meter in length, with a razor-sharp, double-edged tip, designed and
purpose-built to kill pilot whales. It replaces the *grindaknívur* (pl. *grindaknívar*), or pilot whale knife, which was lauded as the grindadráp's
"most distinguished piece of equipment" and "one of the foremost
Faroese contributions to Nordic artistic craftsmanship."[5] At the
scene of a grindadráp one still sees ornate and beautiful *grindaknívar*
tied to whalers' waists with the *tólvtráðaband,* a colorful cord made
from twelve woolen threads, but their use in killing whales has been

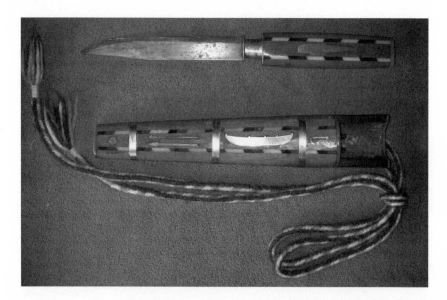

A *grindaknívur,* or pilot whale knife,
along with its sheath and *tólvtráðaband*

forbidden since 2015. Like the change in hooks, the shift from knives
to spinal lances was intended to lessen whales' suffering and to provide for a quicker death.

   To initiate the killing process, a whaler forces the blunt tip of the
hook into the whale's blowhole. A pilot whale has a pair of air sacs on
either side of its blowhole; the blástrarongul was designed to fit into
one or the other of these sacs. When a whale is secured with a hook,
a team of whalers forms along the rope and begins hauling the whale
toward the beach. To haul an average-sized whale requires at least a
half dozen haulers, often more, as the whale is still alive as it is being
pulled ashore and does what it can to resist the whalers' effort.

   When the whale is fully ashore, or in some cases in water shallow
enough to strand, the rope team will hold the living whale secure with
tension on the rope until another whaler can perform the task of the
killing. This is the only part of the grindadráp for which specialized
training is required. Anyone may participate in the driving, hauling,

or butchering, but only licensed "killers" may use the mønustingari in the coup de grâce of the grindadráp. To kill a whale, the whaler places a hand on the whale's body to measure the correct location—one handbreadth behind the blowhole—then grasps the mønustingari with both hands and thrusts it deep into the whale. A pair of Faroese veterinarians designed the tool to pierce the whale's skin, blubber, and muscle, and—if placed correctly—to pass between two vertebrae and into the spinal cord. When the haft lies flat against the whale's skin, meaning that the mønustingari is in as deep as it can go, the whaler rocks the tool back and forth, perpendicular to the whale's spine, severing its spinal cord and arteries. This often produces a violent, back-arching spasm, followed by total paralysis.

When a whaler removes the mønustingari from a whale, a great stream of blood erupts from the wound. Its spinal cord severed, the whale lies motionless on the shore or in the shallows. To quickly exsanguinate the whale, whalers employ the grindaknívur or another "normal" knife to make broad, deep cuts behind the whale's head, often down to the spine. It is the presence of these cuts, made after

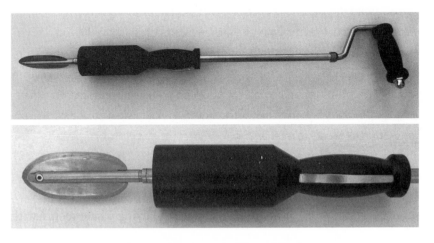

A *mønustingari*, or spinal lance *(above)*,
and a close-up view of the lance's blade *(below)*.
Photo by B. Hanusson, used by permission of Justines Olsen

the whale has been killed, that gives the carcasses their characteristic "nearly decapitated" appearance.[6] It also adds even more blood to the water. Before the killing began, the water already would have begun to take on a slight pink or red hue, owing to the small lacerations and other injuries the whales would have suffered by coming into contact with the rocky or sandy bottom during the final meters of the drive. The voluminous blood flows, added through the use of the mønust-ingari and grindaknívur, accelerate the reddening of the sea by orders of magnitude.

From travelers' accounts to anti-whaling reports to scientific studies, the red sea stands out as the single most memorable sight witnessed during a grindadráp. When you have seen bright red waves rolling onto a gray Faroese beach, you will not forget the image—whether you would like to or not. The Faroese painter Sámal Joensen-Mikines is said to have loved painting scenes of the grindadráp because it provided a rare opportunity to use his red palette, his landscapes ordinarily being dominated by greens, blues, and grays. Nearly every early written observation of a grindadráp mentions the reddening of the waters. "And all the sea is blood!" wrote Anne Morrow Lindbergh, who stopped in the Faroes with her husband and fellow aviator, Charles, as they scouted a transatlantic route.[7]

Although there are only a few grindadráp per year (the long-term average is just over six annually), the scene of any one grindadráp is one of mass slaughter—many whales killed at once. This spectacle, certainly enhanced by the reddening of the water, has served as the subject of many a shocking photograph—a great number of which have been used, with or without their copyright holder's permission, in anti-whaling literature. These images conjure thoughts of biblical plagues or scenes from horror movies in the minds of their viewers. The Faroese acknowledge the difficulty in overcoming this visual effect. "If only the blood was blue," lamented Bjørn Kalsø, then Faroese minister of fisheries, when I interviewed him in 2005. The scene reminds us of both the size and the number of the animals being killed. A grindadráp is a massive operation involving a great number of very large animals. An entire community of humans kills an entire pod of whales. As the nineteenth-century French historian Jules Michelet noted, "The Whale, when wounded, ensanguines the ocean to a great distance; the blood that we have in drops, is lavished upon him in torrents."[8]

The Economy of Mindfulness

While the volume of blood may intuitively hint at suffering and violence, a better and more widely used measure of humane killing methods is the time that it takes for an animal to die.[9] Unsurprisingly, then, one of the major criticisms of whaling in general is that a whale's time-to-death after first being struck by a harpoon (globally, a much more common whaling tool than the mønustingari or blástrarongul) is excessive. According to Peter Singer, perhaps the world's leading animal rights advocate, "From an ethical perspective, the most blatantly insupportable aspect of whaling is the slow and painful death inflicted upon the whales."[10] For the purpose of research into the humaneness of killing methods, slow generally equals painful, which means that the killing is inhumane. Thus, at least from the point of view of Western science, a quicker death is seen as a better death.

Anyone who studies whaling, though, is familiar with other ethical standards for what constitutes a humane—or at least proper—death for a whale. The geographer Chie Sakakibara writes about the rituals and traditions associated with whaling, as conducted by the Iñupiat in northern Alaska. Assuming the local worldview, Sakakibara described Iñupiat whaling not in the typical dichotomy of hunter and hunted—as does the Faroese ethnographer Jóan Pauli Joensen—but as a situation "in which the whale gives itself to the respectful hunters."[11]

Amid cultures such as the Iñupiat, a better death for the whale is often one that prioritizes proper behavior toward the whale, and especially its spirit—not necessarily a quick death for its body. In these contexts, a longer, more drawn-out killing method that properly cares for the whale's spirit during the time of its death is seen as better, more compassionate, than a quick death that disregards the spiritual aspect of whaling. The anthropologist Edith Turner, also writing about the Iñupiat, explains the requirement that a whale's head—"the home of its spirit"—be "returned to the water after the body has been cut up so the spirit can reincarnate and come back in a new body."[12] Similarly, the geographer and Asia scholar Michael Parnwell cites numerous examples of what he calls "whale veneration" found among whaling cultures throughout Southeast Asia and further across the Pacific.[13] These include funeral-like rituals held in honor of whales killed for food. Sakakibara's, Turner's, and Parnwell's many examples from diverse geographic and cultural settings show that respect for whales and consumption of whales are far from mutually exclusive.

Another ethical viewpoint takes into consideration the fact that a single whale can provide large quantities of food. While Buddhists are not required to practice vegetarianism, some, especially adherents to Tibetan Buddhism, teach that if one is going to eat meat, it makes more sense to eat the meat of large animals than of small ones.[14] A cow, for example, can feed many people by giving one life. Alternatively, it would take many shrimp—and therefore many lives—to make one person's meal. So when eating beef, one life sustains many. With shrimp, many lives feed only one. In this economy of mindfulness, whales—among the largest animals on earth—are the ultimate animal-based food. If methods of preservation can be worked out to keep the meat from spoiling, one large whale can feed an entire village for months. Even dolphins and smaller whales such as pilot whales provide far more meat than one meal requires.

This multitude of beneficiaries must have influenced the cooperative nature of the grindadráp. Not only would it be exceedingly difficult for a lone individual to hunt, kill, and bring back a pod of whales, but there would be more food than one person could hope to handle alone. In the Faroe Islands, there is little role for the solitary hunter, quietly stalking prey. The grindadráp—like other traditional Faroese forms of subsistence—demands collective action, presents collective risks, and provides collective reward. The Faroese may rely wholly upon Western science in determining their preferred killing methods and deciding what, exactly, a good death for whales is. But at a deeper level, the grindadráp represents one of history's many scenes of communal food procurement and, directly related to that, a case of cultural respect and valuation of the animals from which the food comes. The Faroese, in their modern, empirical way, attempt to continue providing whale meat and blubber for themselves while giving the whales the best death possible.

It Hurts to Die

Two methods of measuring time-to-death have been used to try to quantify the humaneness—or cruelty—of the grindadráp. The first measures the duration of the entire event from the killing of the first whale to the killing of the last. This method views the whale pod as a fundamental unit. The second method measures the time-to-death for each whale from the time its killing begins until it is dead. The fundamental unit in this case is the individual whale.

Dorete Bloch, along with a team of colleagues, followed the first method and timed forty-three grindadráp between July 1986 and July 1988.[15] They recorded the number of whales killed, the number of people involved, both on shore and in boats, and the total time from the death of the first whale to the last. Often anecdotal accounts of single grindadráp witnessed by ardent supporters of whaling will emphasize the quick and efficient nature of the event. By contrast, observers from environmental organizations with an anti-whaling focus tend to describe grindadráp as lengthy, drawn-out, and chaotic.[16] By looking back through the history of Faroese whaling, both groups can readily find examples of specific grindadráp that support their preexisting views. Bloch's team provided quantitative data collected from multiple events, averaging out the fastest and slowest examples.

An average of eighty-five whales were killed in each grindadráp recorded in Bloch's study and each event lasted, on average, just over twenty-eight minutes. This works out to a rate of about two whales killed per minute or one every thirty seconds. For comparison, this is a little less than half the rate at which cattle are killed in an industrial slaughterhouse, according to the political scientist Timothy Pachirat, whose book, *Every Twelve Seconds,* bluntly summarizes his firsthand participant observations starting right from the title.[17] Of course, "two whales every minute" is only a theoretical average rate; in reality, many whales are killed simultaneously by different teams of whalers.

Justines Olsen, a Faroese veterinarian and co-inventor of the mønustingari, used the second method—the individual whale approach—in his study, which measured time-to-death for 251 pilot whales killed in forty-seven grindadráp occurring between 1995 and 1998.[18] Controversially, Olsen split his timing for each whale's death into two phases. The first phase began the moment the whale was secured with the hook—crucially, both the sóknarongul, or sharp hook, and the blástrarongul, or blunt hook, were in use at the time—and ended with the first incision by the grindaknívur. (The mønustingari was not yet widely in use at the time of Olsen's study.) The second phase began with the grindaknívur incision and ended when the whale, having had its spinal cord severed and the blood supply to its brain interrupted, was dead, as evidenced by "immediate and violent muscle spasms, followed by total paralysis."[19]

The way in which these two stages were used to determine total time-to-death fostered some criticism of Olsen's methods. Distinguishing based upon which style of hook had been used, Olsen stated, in justification of his method, that "when the traditional whaling hook [or sóknarongul] is used to secure the whale, the total time-to-death is the sum of the first and second phases. When the blowhole hook [blástrarongul] is used, the total time-to-death is the second phase only . . . as the whales are not wounded with the blowhole hook."[20] This was not well received by advocates working against animal cruelty.

According to a booklet published jointly by the Whale and Dolphin Conservation Society and the Humane Society of the United States, "the [blástrarongul] causes no external bleeding and consequently, as it is presumed no wounding results from the insertion of this device into the blowhole, hunters may not count this as the starting point for measuring time-to-death. However, the [blástrarongul] may cause internal wounding, such as damaging the complex organs and tissue that lie below the blowhole (a particularly sensitive region in cetaceans) and burst blood vessels. It may also prevent the whale from breathing properly."[21] Expressing the same sentiment, though in his characteristically provocative style, Paul Watson—director of the Sea Shepherd Conservation Society—wrote to me, "I don't think that getting struck with [a] blunt hook is more humane than a sharp hook. That's like choosing between getting slugged over the head with a baseball bat or an ax."[22] Nevertheless, Olsen maintained that the time-to-death should not begin with the insertion of the blástrarongul. Inside the blowhole, according to Olsen, the "blubber is very tough and fibrous and will withstand considerable pressure."[23]

This timing decision makes possible one of the main arguments against the charge that the grindadráp is a cruel form of death for whales. Using Olsen's timing method, the death of each individual whale can indeed be said to happen very quickly: in as little as two seconds now that the mønustingari is the standard tool for the killing process itself. Critics have called for the "clock" measuring time-to-death to begin with the insertion of the blástrarongul into the blowhole or even with the beginning of the drive. These changes would of course result in a time-to-death minutes or even hours longer than is currently measured.

Do the whales suffer during a grindadráp? Inevitably yes. All forms of whaling involve some suffering. The head of the Icelandic Minke

Justines Olsen, Faroese veterinarian and inventor of the *mønustingari*,
holding an early prototype of the device, sheathed

Whaling Association, Gunnar Bergmann Jónsson, once gave me a
tour of his commercial whaling ship while it was docked in Haf-
narfjörður. I asked if the exploding harpoon head caused pain when
used to kill minke whales. Gunnar responded bluntly, "Yes. It hurts
to die." The Faroese, for their part, believe that the grindadráp
methods currently in place represent the quickest possible death for
the whales. When called upon to defend their practice in international dialogue, the Faroese consistently refer to the grindadráp's
efficiency and its interference in only a minuscule portion of the whales'
lives. Pilot whales are wild, free-ranging animals, whose lives inter-
sect the lives of humans only briefly at the end. The Faroese routinely
compare the grindadráp to domestic animal-based food production—
particularly in confined animal feeding operations (CAFOs)—to illustrate how, in the home countries of most grindadráp opponents,
humans interfere with animals throughout their entire lives. In

response to criticism, the Faroese also stress the connection between their culture and the natural environment, illustrated by the grindadráp and other aspects of Faroese life including sheep husbandry, haymaking, fowling, and artisanal fishing.

As more whales are killed, the rope teams haul them into orderly rows at the shoreline. Here they lie in the increasingly bloody water until the entire pod has been killed. The overall scene is one of constant motion: gradually reddening waves wash over the glossy black skin of whale carcasses that lie in repose at the water's edge, heads toward land.[24] As the work nears completion, some whalers become observers, taking in the sight of the grindadráp as it winds to a close. When the entire pod has been killed, most of the participants leave the scene and return home to dry off, warm up, and change clothes.

The Whaler Who Hates Killing Whales

A grindadráp produces a profound mix of emotions in the hearts of its participants. The anthropologist Jonathan Wylie describes the "eager, somewhat grim resolution" that pervades the scene.[25] There is, though, somewhat uncomfortably for a foreign observer, also joy. I have spoken with cocky teenagers who stab the air with imaginary whaling knives the way young American boys shoot imaginary cowboy pistols formed by their thumbs and forefingers. After a grindadráp, young children can often be seen playing around and atop the freshly killed whale carcasses. These expressions of enjoyment have brought strong criticism against the Faroese, claims that the entire operation is conducted merely for sport. Understanding that the ultimate reason for the grindadráp is indeed food production, we can still sympathize with these critics who take offense at the expression of joy amid the act of killing. The American food writer Michael Pollan zeroes in on this controversy in his bestselling book *The Omnivore's Dilemma:* "This, for many people, is what's most offensive about hunting—to some, disgusting: that it encourages, or allows, us not only to kill but to take a certain pleasure in killing."[26] If Pollan's understanding of the reason hunting provokes disgust is accurate, then how much more offensive is whaling when it's enjoyed?

I've been at the receiving end of some of this disgust myself—not as a whaler but merely as a whaling researcher. When I describe my work, it's often first assumed that I study whaling in order to stop it—that my research has the goal of shutting down the grindadráp and the Vincentian blackfish operation. As a scientist, not an activist, I have no such goal. When a friend, an acquaintance, or sometimes even an academic colleague realizes that I spend so much time among whalers without passing judgment or condemning their livelihoods, that I actually enjoy my work, both despite and even because of the proximity it gives me to whaling, and that I value the friendships, based on equality and mutual respect, that I've built with the many Faroese and Vincentian whalers I've come to know over the years, the offense and disgust described by Pollan can be unmitigated. I understand why I've had audience members walk out of my talks in tears. I've lost friendships and career opportunities.

But for every mob of stabby teenagers or happy hunters, I have also met a group of grave elders who invoke biblical imagery, describing whales as a "gift from God," and who regret their own need to personally kill in order to eat. You could hardly imagine these reserved men drumming up enough violent energy to participate in a grindadráp. The gentlest Faroese person I know is a schoolteacher named Ólavur Sjúrðarberg, a man so soft-spoken that his sentences, if transcribed, would end only in ellipses. This man is the president of the Grindamannafelagið, or Faroese Pilot Whalers Association. He has killed many whales.

"Ólavur hates killing whales," I was told by a Faroese biologist. A whaler who hates whaling? A man who advises the government on whaling policy—not on stopping it, but on making it more efficient, more humane and sustainable, and more in keeping with tradition—is personally saddened by the death of a whale? I needed to meet him. The biologist said she could arrange that.

Ólavur Sjúrðarberg

I was waiting on the quayside in Tórshavn when a silver Volkswagen sedan pulled up. Tinted windows. Immaculately clean leather interior. Ólavur, with aviator sunglasses perched between his mop of sandy blond hair and neat, sandy blond mustache, sitting in the driver's seat, suggested we talk while taking a drive around the southern tip of Streymoy, the largest of the Faroe Islands. He patiently stopped the car and waited for me each time I wanted to photograph one of the hundreds of postcard-worthy landscapes that the Faroese see every single day of their lives.

"They say you don't like killing whales," I asked. "Is this true?"

Ólavur thought for a long while before replying—a habit I truly admire and try to emulate daily. "I only think . . . can we do it right?" He told me how much the grindadráp has changed over the years. "In the old days . . ." He paused. "It could be best described as a war between people and whales." Now things are different. The mission of the Grindamannafelagið is to oversee the grindadráp, to ensure that it continues in a sustainable and humane way, to teach the skills necessary to conduct the grindadráp properly, and to advise those in the Faroese government who make policy on whaling.

When, exactly, did the "old days" of Faroese whaling begin? According to Kate Sanderson, it is "likely that some form of deliberate exploitation of whales has taken place in the Faroes from the earliest days of Norse settlement."[27] The Faroese ethnographer Jóan Pauli Joensen, would like to agree with Sanderson, but "cannot say for certain how old the pilot whale hunt is in the Faroe Islands."[28] He cites one Norwegian scholar who had "no doubts at all that 'the Faroese pilot whale hunt goes all the way back to' the time of the first settlements in the ninth and tenth centuries."[29] Joensen presents contrary evidence, though, in the writings of the Zeno brothers, Venetian noblemen who spent a total of nineteen years in the Faroe Islands during the late fourteenth and early fifteenth centuries. According to Joensen, the Zenos compiled a thorough account of their Faroese experiences "without relating one word about the pilot whale hunt."[30] He acknowledges, of course, that this doesn't automatically mean that the grindadráp did not exist at the time of the Zenos' residency. "Absence of evidence is not evidence of absence," goes the familiar scientific maxim. An interesting counterpoint to this truism, though, asserts that "in some circumstances it can be safely assumed that if a certain event had occurred, evidence of it could be discovered by qualified investigators," and that in these cases "it is perfectly reasonable to take the absence of proof of its occurrence as positive proof of its non-occurrence."[31] Whether the grindadráp represents one of these circumstances is at the heart of how we take the Zenos' failure to mention it. Joensen seems to think not. He mentions the distinct possibility that they simply didn't have an opportunity to witness a grindadráp during their time in the Faroes—a scenario with which I became quite familiar during the first two field seasons of my research.

The earliest reference to active whaling in the Faroe Islands—though not necessarily what we today would call a grindadráp—is from the 1298 Seyðabrævið, or "Sheep Letter." This letter, written by a duke in the colonial Norwegian government who would later go on to become king, detailed matters of sheep farming and other means of livelihood, including whaling. Three conditions by which people may obtain whales are mentioned: the finding of a dead whale at sea, a whale stranding onshore, and the active driving ashore of a whale. For all of these cases, the Seyðabrævið deals with how the meat and blubber should be divided. Clearly the first two situations cannot be called whaling, but the third undoubtedly can. Still, the driving ashore of "a whale"—singular in the original—does not equate to the current method of driving entire pods of pilot whales ashore.[32] While scholars draw connections between the rules delineated in the Seyðabrævið and the modern Faroese whaling operation, this document cannot be cited as the earliest reference to the grindadráp.

Joensen and Wylie seem confident in the hypothesis that the grindadráp is very ancient—perhaps dating to Sanderson's "earliest days of Norse settlement"—but that an economic decline during the fourteenth and fifteenth centuries, driven by climatic changes and political events on the Continent, along with their subsequent effects on Faroese-European relations, led to a time of austerity in the Faroe Islands that created an opportunity for the expansion and institutionalization of the grindadráp. According to Joensen, the grindadráp "could have assumed great importance in these times of crisis. It is conceivable that at about this time one began to create an organization around the hunting of pilot whales so that one could fully utilize an economic resource surely known of earlier but not to any real extent utilized."[33]

Wylie calls pilot whales "an import, as it were, for which nothing had to be traded."[34] It's reasonable to imagine the struggling Faroese of the fourteenth and fifteenth centuries searching their history for methods of survival that had proven successful to their forebears and that might yet again provide sustenance during times of scarcity. Let's consider these "earliest days of Norse settlement" to better understand the role of whales and whaling in the survival of these first Faroese people. For to visit a country without reading its history is to miss an opportunity to travel through time as well as space.

The Great Viking Exodus

Modern Faroese people trace their ancestry back to the Norse who arrived in the Faroes more than a thousand years ago during the major period of Viking expansion. In the late ninth century, Norway—which at that time included part of what is now Sweden—came to be ruled by Harald Fair Hair, the first king of what was considered a unified Norway. In fact, most northern parts of the Scandinavian peninsula were not brought under Harald's control. But then, just as now, the majority of the Norse / Norwegian population was concentrated in the south and along the coast. These are the regions that Harald unified and over which he became king.

Most of what we know as biographical information about Harald Fair Hair comes from the *Heimskringla,* one of many sagas written during the thirteenth century by the great Icelandic poet and historian Snorri Sturluson.[35] According to Snorri, the reason for King Harald's intense drive in conquering Norway was both simple and romantic: he did it for love. Before Norway was united, when Harald was a simple local ruler of a few small southern districts, he had sent messengers to propose marriage to a young woman named Gyda, daughter of a neighboring king. Gyda, not thrilled at the prospect of leaving her station as princess of one small kingdom to become queen of another small kingdom, sent word to Harald saying that she "would consent to be his lawful wife only if, before that, he would, for her sake, conquer all of Norway."[36] Apparently Gyda wasn't that into Harald and thought this to be a nicer way of letting him down. She clearly never thought the marriage would happen. "There is no king ambitious enough to claim Norway as his own and be sole king over it," she continued.[37] Gyda underestimated Harald's determination.

The messengers hurried back to Harald, no doubt assuming their king would react vengefully to Gyda's rejection of his proposal. Harald's reaction, though, was far from punitive. He responded that "the maiden had not spoken evil or done anything to merit revenge."[38] At this point, the king's revenge-happy messengers must have felt a bit let down. Harald continued, "She has reminded me of what it seems strange that I have never thought of before." Leave it to a king to be "reminded" of something that he "had never thought of before." Then Harald, puffing up his royal, lovesick chest, stated, "I make this vow, and call God to witness . . . that I shall neither cut nor comb my hair before I have conquered all of Norway."[39] It took him ten years to fulfill his vow.

This, of course, is not how Harald came to be known as Fair Hair. In the ensuing decade, Harald's hair grew long and matted. People called him—probably not to his face—Harald Lufa, meaning Harald of the Unkempt Locks. This was clearly not a title befitting a king who had just subdued the whole of Norway, so after winning the final battle and earning Gyda's love, Harald had his first haircut in ten years. What grew back in place of his previously unkempt locks was— at least by comparison—the most beautiful head of hair that his subjects had ever seen, or so they told him. Harald Fair Hair, his name would become.

Harald's hair may have been fair, but his rulings were not. As it turns out, all of Norway did not exactly want to be subdued. Vikings were the original "small government" bloc and didn't appreciate their disparate and autonomous estates being unified under one man's leadership, no matter how beautiful his hair might be. The twentieth-century geographer Carl Sauer wrote that Norway's unification initiated "a great Viking exodus to escape the rule of Harald" and to search for unsubdued lands.[40]

The Vikings sailed from Norway with all they had—families, possessions, livestock—clearly intending to settle where they landed, not merely to raid and return home. (They did not, however, bring horned helmets. That part is a myth.)[41] Some sailed south to the

British Isles, where they settled and ruled from Dublin for years. Others went east to the Baltic or into the Mediterranean. At least one group is said to have made it overland to Baghdad.[42] But the most famous route of Viking expansion was across the North Atlantic.

When first-time transatlantic passengers fly between the United States and Europe they are often surprised to see that the in-flight route map shows them passing over northeastern Canada and southern Greenland. "Why go north to get east?" they wonder. The shortest distance between two points is, of course, a straight line, but airplanes—and ships and trains and cars—have to follow the curvature of the earth. A truly straight line—one that ignores the shape of the planet's surface—between, say, Minneapolis and Oslo (the cities with the largest Norwegian populations in the United States and Norway) would dive into the Mississippi River, burrow through its left bank, and make the entire trip underground, only to emerge on the surface among the sculptures in Frogner Park like Bugs Bunny thinking he should have taken that left turn at Albuquerque. But try this: hold a piece of string taut against a globe, connecting Minneapolis and Oslo or any other two places. The shortest distance that one can actually travel—without digging—is a curve that follows what's called a "great circle route" across the earth's surface. This particular route leaves Minneapolis heading more north than east, crosses over northern Quebec and southern Greenland, starts bending to the south over Iceland, barely misses the Faroes, and enters Norwegian airspace just north of Bergen. Despite Minneapolis being a good fifteen degrees latitude south of Oslo, the final approach into Oslo Airport is from the west-northwest.

The Vikings, traveling west, also found the shortest distance for their voyages. Fortunately, this led them not across an open ocean but along a series of stepping-stone islands that connects Europe to mainland North America via the Faroes, Iceland, Greenland, and Newfoundland. They stopped in all of these places. Their residence in Newfoundland was probably short-term and seasonal. In Greenland their colony eventually disappeared, possibly, at least in part, because of a changing climate. But in Iceland and the Faroe Islands the Vikings established a presence that remains unbroken today. The Faroes, being the easternmost of these Atlantic islands, would have been the first reached by westward-sailing Norsemen. Today's Faroese like to joke that they are descended from the most seasick of the Vikings, those who got off the boat at the first opportunity.

Monks and Brigands

Most written histories of the Faroe Islands begin with the possibility that the islands' first inhabitants were Irish monks, arriving no later than the eighth century, well before the Vikings. Dicuil, a geographer and himself an Irish monk writing in 825 CE, mentioned these pre-Viking inhabitants in his *De Mensura Orbis Terrae,* which includes the oldest written account of the Faroes. Until recently, academic discussion of a pre-Norse settlement in the Faroes was self-consciously speculative since no hard evidence had yet been found. Then in late 2013 a multinational team of archaeologists led by Mike Church of Durham University published "The Vikings Were Not the First Colonizers of the Faroe Islands."[43] That's the title of the paper. It's also the conclusion. Church describes samples of burnt peat ash and carbonized barley grains unearthed in a deposit of windblown sand on the island of Sandoy. The barley was shown to have been cultivated, and has been dated to the fourth through the sixth centuries. So someone was there. While the archaeological evidence doesn't prove that that the pre-Norse inhabitants of the Faroe Islands were Irish, the findings and the legends taken together do point in that direction.

The most famous of the legends is that of Saint Brendan. This celebrated, possibly mythical, sixth-century Irish explorer is said to have visited a "sheep island" and a "paradise of birds." Brendan's descriptions of these islands sound remarkably like the Faroes. Of course, birds could have come to the islands on their own, but sheep would have to have been brought there. This necessitates the arrival of some sheep-bringing people even before Saint Brendan. Brendan's story allows for this situation by positing that his voyages were launched based upon information provided by an older monk—Saint Barinthus—who had already visited the islands in question.

If Brendan existed, which is not certain, and if he indeed traveled across the North Atlantic, which is even less certain, he most likely would have stopped at the Faroes—a natural waypoint between Ireland and Iceland. Tim Severin, a British historian, author, and explorer, spent two summers recreating Brendan's legendary voyage, complete with a built-to-specifications Irish curragh, or leather-hulled boat.[44] Severin and his multinational crew—which included Trondur Patursson, one of the Faroes' most famous artists and an accomplished sailor in his own right—successfully traversed the North Atlantic, from Ireland to Newfoundland. Along the way, Severin called at the Faroe Islands and solidified his conviction that Brendan had too.

Dicuil went on to explain that the Irish monks deserted the Faroes because the islands were increasingly being visited by "Norse brigands."[45] This is usually understood to mean that the monks remained until the Vikings arrived in the islands and then moved on in their quest for peace, quiet, and a place to meditate. The presence of Vikings understandably challenges this goal. Their destination is unknown but, based on past legends and some present place names, it's thought that the monks may have continued their way across the Atlantic, via Iceland and Greenland, only to end in North America. The Norse certainly took this route, and it's possible that the Irish were forced to move along ahead of an advancing wave of Viking settlers.

In 1035, the Faroes were formally politically united with Norway but remained relatively free to trade independently. Beginning in the thirteenth century, however, all trade was directed through Bergen in a government-run monopoly, initiating a period of isolation interrupted only by raids from pirates: first English, then Dutch and

French, and later Barbary. The last were called "Turks" by the Faroese, despite having come from North Africa, and were the most fearsome visitors that the Faroese have known. One raid took place on the island of Suðuroy in 1629, but as the pirates were sailing away with their newly captured Faroese slaves, two of the three ships struck rocks and broke up. The Faroese dutifully collected the dead "Turks" who washed ashore and gave these Muslim seamen a proper Christian burial. Today a low mound of earth is still visible on Suðuroy. A small sign marks it: Turkargravir, or Grave of the Turks.

In 1537, Norway entered a political union with Denmark, and brought the Faroes along. This union lasted nearly 300 years—an interim period, during which the Faroes were both Norwegian and Danish, politically. In 1814, when Norway was ceded to Sweden, the Faroes, Iceland, and Greenland remained with Denmark, still under a strict trade monopoly. The isolation would continue, under different colonial leadership, until Denmark lifted the monopoly in 1856. This six-hundred-year economic isolation led to cultural isolation as well, allowing Faroese folk traditions, language, and national identity to develop virtually uninfluenced from outside. It also helped the Faroes preserve their whaling traditions.

Even with the conveniences of today's travel and communication technologies, the Faroe Islands are remote. To go by ship from Denmark takes a day and a half. To fly to the Faroes from Copenhagen is to chance a free trip instead to Bergen, Norway—Atlantic Airways' designated alternative landing site. Pilots regularly find themselves circling the Faroe Islands' airport, waiting for the fog to clear or the wind to abate, until only enough fuel remains to get to Bergen. Without weather clear enough to land in the Faroes or sufficient fuel to make Bergen, there simply aren't any other options.

The isolation of the Faroe Islands, made even more acute during periods of bad weather, contributed to the Faroese dependence on local animals as sources of food. Many varieties of fish and seabirds occur in great numbers around the Faroes. Most have been integrated into the national cuisine, but none so much as the pilot whale. In an article explaining the risk of marine contamination found in the tissue of pilot whales, Dr. Pál Weihe, a Faroese physician and medical researcher, paid homage to the whale and its role in Faroese nutritional history. "There are many accounts of the importance of the pilot whale for us in this country," Weihe wrote. "If some years went by without any whales, it was reflected in the household, and the joy was great when this gift from God again appeared from the sea. There is no doubt that this food source in many ways has contributed to good health and has remedied imminent hunger in many homes. . . . The pilot whale has served the Faroese well for many hundreds of years and has likely kept many Faroese alive through the centuries."[46]

The ethnographer Jóan Pauli Joensen, perhaps the best living historian of the grindadráp, recounts the many uses for pilot whales that have arisen over the centuries.[47] In addition to eating the meat, blubber, and organs, the Faroese came up with myriad uses for other anatomical parts of the whales. Blubber was cooked down to make oil, which was used for lighting and later for lubrication of small mechanical parts. Strips of skin from the dorsal fin and tail were used to tie oars to the gunwales of rowboats. Long ropes made of whale skin allowed the Faroese to rappel down their islands' sheer cliffs, retrieving eggs from the nests of squawking and defensive seabirds. Shoulder blades became shovels; skulls were stacked into fences. Children played with smaller bones as toys. Sinews became thread. Shoes were made from whale esophagi. (Let me repeat: people would wear pieces of a whale's esophagus on their feet.) Stomachs were tied off, inflated, and dried to become oil containers and buoys called kíkar (sing. kíkur). Sámal Johansen, a Faroese author translated by Joensen, described what it was like to make these inflated stomachs.[48] In typical Scandinavian understatement, he referred to the task as "not a particularly pleasant job" before detailing the process of inflating the stomach by mouth, in which the person inflating the kíkur "placed his tongue into the hole every time he inhaled." Imagine the taste that would leave. Indeed, Johansen wrote, "the person who inflated the kíkur should not have a weak heart." While kíkar have long been replaced by plastic floats for fishing lines and glass or plastic containers for liquid products such as oil, they live on linguistically as part of Faroese slang. Someone who drinks too much coffee (*kaffi*) is called a *kaffikíkur*. An alcoholic—one who drinks too much *øl*—is an *ølkíkur:* literally an inflated whale stomach full of beer.

Isolation and Obsession

Today, isolation and obscurity are two of the Faroes' most intriguing characteristics. They remain relatively unknown. The word *Faroe* sounds similar to *pharaoh,* which leads some to think that the islands must be in Egypt. Travel websites sometimes autocorrect to Faro, Portugal; be careful when booking your flight! I've seen academic literature reference the Falkland Islands when the author really meant the Faroes. In fact, it was just such a mistake that once sent me searching for more details after finding an obscure document referencing a hunt for pilot whales that supposedly happened in the Falklands. Another geographer, Kent Mathewson, my mentor at Louisiana State University, let me down gently when my literature review turned up nothing: "I think they meant the Faroes." Of course they did.

When I talk about the Faroe Islands—usually before even really describing them in detail—a common reaction is, "I have never heard of this place but now I want to go there." A photograph of a sheep atop a turf-roofed house or a waterfall dropping into the sea usually seals the deal. One of the most extreme cases of "Faroe-philia" is the story of Matthew Workman of Medford, Oregon. In 2007, like many new parents, Matthew kept a blog, mostly featuring pictures of his twin boys, humorous stories about his family at home, and the everyday miscellany that makes up so much of the internet's content. As online communication goes, this was one of the better examples, owing to Matthew's training as a professional journalist. (In other words, he kept his *there* from his *their* and *your* from *you're*—and never ventured into *ur.*)

Matthew checked his visitor statistics from time to time, just to see how much traffic his blog was generating and where the viewers were from. Through software provided by Google, his blog hosting service's parent company, he was able to view a world map with small markers representing the locations of his visitors. This pleased Matthew, a self-professed "map geek," who described in a blog post the interesting geographical discovery that kicked off his relationship with the Faroes: "Two months ago, I was looking at my Google Analytics map and saw a tiny orange dot in the middle of the North Atlantic. I clicked on it and found that I had gotten a hit from the Faroe Islands. I was fascinated because, despite the fact that I'm a huge map geek, I had never heard of the Faroe Islands. A few hours of research later, I learned the Faroes are a semi-independent set of islands about halfway between Iceland and Norway. They have their own language, their own flag, and a stunning green windswept landscape. I actually signed up to get their tourist brochure. One week later, it arrived in the mail. I'd actually like to go there one day. They've got a summer music festival that looks quite cool. (Note to Faroe Islands Tourism Board: fly me out there and I'd be happy to write a lovely piece about the event.)"[49]

Matthew's interest in the Faroe Islands only grew from there. It became, in his words, "a full-on obsession."[50] At the time there was not much information available online in English about the Faroe Islands. Even so, Matthew was interested in mundane details of everyday life that would hardly be website material: villages, shopping malls (or mall, as there is only one in the Faroe Islands), banks, football stadiums, and the airport. He began to dedicate one day per week on his blog to the Faroe Islands. These "Faroe Friday" blog posts contained Matthew's latest discoveries as well as increasingly persistent pleas, such as the one above, to the Faroese tourist board to fund a visit in exchange for a glowing piece of journalism.

One day he received a response from an online visitor going by the handle "Faroe Man" who expressed his appreciation for the positive attention and encouragement to keep going. This mysterious visitor turned out to be Tollakur Hansen, a—yes—Faroese man, who later would be instrumental in Matthew's continued involvement with the Faroe Islands. In 2009, with Tollakur's help on the ground, Matthew launched *The Faroe Islands Podcast,* basically an audio version of his Faroe Friday posts. Later that year, his work, pleas, and publicity paid off, as Matthew received an invitation from the Faroese Ministry of Foreign Affairs to come to the Faroes, fully hosted, and report on two important summer events: Ólavsøka (St. Olav's Wake), the Faroese national holiday, and the G! Festival, a music event founded in 2002. Matthew announced the exciting news via his blog: "Needless to say, I am thrilled beyond words. It's really a stunning turn of events. Two years ago, I stumble upon a country I'd not previously heard of and become deeply obsessed. As the months pass, I begin blogging about the place and eventually start a podcast about it. And now I'm going there."[51]

After his first visit—many more would follow—Matthew's reporting on the Faroe Islands began to grow in seriousness and insight. He discussed cultural, political, economic, and environmental issues. He interviewed government officials and their opposition. Sports, music, and human-interest stories continued to provide entertainment for his blog readers, and increasingly for his podcast audience, but these stories began to carry the gravitas of having come from a veteran—no longer an obsessed but distant blogger, researching online from halfway around the world, but an experienced traveler, someone who sought firsthand information to the questions he puzzled over.

It is a testimony to his holistic interest in the Faroe Islands that Matthew has addressed whaling only about a dozen times on his podcast. This is out of more than three hundred episodes to date. The first, in 2009, included interviews with me (conducted via Skype while Matthew was in Oregon and I was in Tórshavn) and Dr. Pál Weihe, the physician and medical researcher. It covered the basic process of the grindadráp and focused on the twin controversies of international protest and environmental contaminants. Despite his broad interest in all things Faroese and his—perhaps intentional—tendency to pay less attention to the grindadráp than to other aspects of Faroese life, Matthew finds himself serving as something of a whipping boy for those with anti-whaling sentiments to express. He regularly receives messages through the podcast or social media, attacking whaling, attacking the Faroese, and attacking him personally.

Or perhaps he receives those negative comments precisely *because* he doesn't focus on the grindadráp: whaling opponents might consider that, by discussing the more mundane and pedestrian aspects of Faroese life, Matthew's work normalizes the Faroe Islands, showing that a whaling society can also include mothers, fathers, musicians, football enthusiasts, social activists, chefs, scholars, and bus drivers—all former guests and interviewees of the podcast. More than once Matthew has received a photo of a bloody grindadráp scene along with the demand "Why don't you cover this on your podcast?" Matthew can respond with links to the handful of episodes he has produced on the subject, but he can also steer the conversation to any number of topics related to the larger context of Faroese life.

These anti-whaling messages are sometimes vulgar, often threatening, and regularly misinformed. Matthew describes it as "an endless torrent of bile thrown at me from strangers all over the world," and confesses, "That sort of thing can wear a person down."[52] He has received death threats. Occasionally, though, the communication borders on the sublime. Consider this darkly lyrical message Matthew received in 2014 from a Facebook user going by the name Oltalmazó Oposszum, reproduced here verbatim: "fear from me, im a whale, in the hell i will eat out your eyes what a red ladscape! do you like to erase this post? do you like to erase a heart?" I know Matthew and I am certain that he does not "like to erase a heart." Soon after Matthew made this threat—or is it a poem?—public, another American Faroe Islands enthusiast, Miranda Metheny, translated it into Faroese, complete with the "ladscape" misspelling, for Matthew to share with the podcast's Faroese listeners.

After the 2009 podcast about the grindadráp, more than six years elapsed before Matthew dedicated a second episode wholly to the issue. This time the bulk of the recording was made live at the scene of a grindadráp that Matthew witnessed during the summer of 2015 in the village of Bøur.[53] To anyone who wants to experience—not only read about, but actually experience—what being present during a grindadráp is like, I suggest listening to this fantastic piece of journalism. Matthew's reflections at the end are especially poignant. Listening to the confluence of human effort, joy, and conflict overlaying cetacean death and the unconcerned cycling of the ocean's waves conjures a powerful juxtaposition of emotions. The long sections of ambient sound together with Matthew's unrehearsed narration capture this uneasy mix of reactive feelings about as well as any medium I know.

Today, information about the Faroe Islands is much more readily available online than it was in 2007, when Matthew first became interested in the subject. With the increased attention comes an increase in information—and misinformation—about the grindadráp. *The Faroe Islands Podcast,* for the most part, leaves that topic for others to discuss. Under Matthew's direction, the podcast is a testimony to the complex, culturally rich, and interesting archipelago hiding out under a small orange dot on a world map.

4

—

Barrouallie, St. Vincent's Blackfish Town

The small museum inside Fort Charlotte, perched on a hill above Kingstown, St. Vincent, contains a series of paintings by American artist William Linzee Prescott, depicting a shipwreck that occurred in 1675 on the shores of Bequia, the northernmost of the Grenadine islands.[1] This shipwreck is one of the more significant events in the history of the archipelago because it brought together two cultures that would be foundational to the development of today's Vincentian nation. Aboard the ship was a cargo of enslaved Africans, destined for various island plantations in the Lesser Antilles and Bahamas. The caption below one of the paintings describes the survivors of the shipwreck as having "made their way to St. Vincent, where they were welcomed and accepted by Carib Indians living there." These African castaways assimilated into the indigenous Carib culture, adopting such traits as dress, diet, burial traditions, and the flattening of their infants' foreheads. The descendants of the Africans and Caribs came to be known as the "Black Caribs." They gained a reputation for the tenacity with which they defended their land from the incoming colonizers, in this case the English and the French.[2]

The history of an island being fought over by two or more European colonial powers is common throughout the Caribbean. Julianne Maher, an American linguist and historian, coined the term "history's shuttle-cock" to describe the back-and-forth transfer of colonial rule experienced by tiny St. Barthélemy, but the term could apply equally well to any number of other colonized places.[3] On St. Vincent, however—arguably more than anywhere else in the insular Caribbean—the main threat to European settlement was seen as coming from the island's indigenous inhabitants rather than pirates or competing colonizing nations. The Black Caribs were no doubt aided in their struggle to protect their land by the land itself. St. Vincent's interior landscape—rugged, mountainous, forested, and lushly provisioned with both food and water resources—provided ample opportunity to establish hidden settlements and to execute surprise offensives. To this day, the cannons at Fort Charlotte point inland rather than out to sea, a reminder of how the British prioritized threats to their colonial possession.

In 1796, the British defeated the Black Caribs and deported the remnant survivors to Roatán, an island off the Caribbean coast of

Cannons at Fort Charlotte, pointing inland

Honduras. From Roatán, these deportees—the Garifuna, as they came to be known—crossed to the Honduran mainland and spread along the Caribbean coast of Central America, where their descendants live today.[4] St. Vincent, the Garifuna's place of origin, maintains a strong connection to its Carib heritage despite only a small percentage of the population claiming direct Carib ancestry.

After their violent and forcible removal of the native population, the British were able to bring St. Vincent fully under colonization and cultivation. As was the case on most of their Caribbean colonies, sugar was the primary crop, though on St. Vincent it thrived only in the coastal areas, not on the wetter upland slopes. Experimentation with other crops—especially cotton and arrowroot—ensued, with varying degrees of success, until finally bananas emerged as the largest export for the island, booming in the 1980s as a result of preferential pricing arrangements in Europe, and then declining as prices dropped amid foreign market shifts to Latin American bananas.[5] Today, bananas still account for the majority of St. Vincent's official agricultural production, with illicit marijuana cultivation supplementing legal agriculture to a large degree. The United Nations Environment Programme (UNEP) estimates that some 1,500 Vincentian farmers are involved in marijuana cultivation.[6]

In his public address at the Fisherman's Day festivities in 2009, Vincentian prime minister Ralph Gonsalves issued a plea to the marijuana growers to "come down from the mountain." The term "the mountain" is used colloquially as a euphemism for the marijuana fields located in the island's rugged and roadless northwest. By contrast, the island's most prominent mountain, La Soufrière, is more often referred to as "the volcano." The prime minister urged the marijuana growers to seek honest employment, specifically mentioning possibilities in the whaling operation at Barrouallie. He offered government assistance in training and provision of capital for the establishing new trades—including funds for boats and whaling equipment. Thus, whaling has become a national issue in the context of its potential to provide legitimate, legal work to impoverished

Vincentians who might otherwise turn to illicit occupations. This may strike the non-Vincentian reader as odd, considering that whaling itself is often thought of as a marginalized activity—not something that would replace marijuana cultivation, but something that would, itself, need to be replaced. A look at the history of whaling in the Caribbean helps to explain the context of the prime minister's remarks.

Yankee Whalers

The existence of Vincentian whaling today traces its origin to the high historical status of fishermen in the Caribbean. The geographer Bonham Richardson, in his exploration of the transition from slavery to free societies throughout the region, acknowledged this status when he called fishing "an occupation to which many aspire, possibly because of its relative prestige as much as the financial rewards."[7] During the plantation era, when a select group of the enslaved were developed as fishermen, Richardson notes that "fishing . . . would have been attractive to the slaves, since it meant periodic physical removal from the islands and even chances for escape."[8] Anthropologist Richard Price called the enslaved fishermen "a privileged slave subgroup within the plantation system" and noted that "their special socioeconomic role permitted a particularly smooth transformation to a life as free fishermen."[9] Both Price and Richardson also mention the unique and valued skill set that these enslaved fishermen would have obtained through their trade, skills that stayed with these individuals after emancipation and allowed for a level of prosperity that other freed slaves may not have been able to access.

Beginning in the early eighteenth century, ships based mainly in New England began visiting the islands of the Lesser Antilles in search of whales.[10] The primary target species of these so-called Yankee whalers were the humpback and the sperm whale, but they often took short-finned pilot whales and other small cetaceans for meat to feed the crews and to give novice harpooners a chance to practice their skills.[11] As was the case throughout the whaling grounds of the world, the history of whaling in the Caribbean evolved gradually from abundance during the eighteenth century to declining takes in the late nineteenth century, due primarily to the unsustainable rates at which whales were removed from the oceans.[12]

St. Vincent was among the later-visited islands in the region. The multidisciplinary scholar Aldemaro Romero found archival records of twenty-five whaling voyages from New England to St. Vincent & the Grenadines, beginning in 1864 and ending in 1886.[13] Forty whales were killed in Vincentian waters during this twenty-two-year period. Despite the relative paucity of Yankee whaling in St. Vincent—by contrast, Romero counts ten times as many whaling voyages to Barbados—both the practical legacy and cultural influence of whaling have remained stronger in St. Vincent and Bequia than any of the other Caribbean islands.

A hundred years after American whalers began exploiting Caribbean cetacean populations, the decline was seen not only biologically, but economically as well. Whaling, like fishing, usually pays its workers a share of the total catch rather than a set hourly or daily wage. After 1870, with catches declining, American seamen increasingly began to turn down crew positions aboard Caribbean-bound whaling ships, owing to the reduced profitability of the voyages. Captains filled these vacancies by hiring local men, "half castes from all parts of the West Indies," in the words of one early twentieth-century economist.[14] The Caribbean whalers accepted lower pay than their New England counterparts, which helped to offset the losses of the increasingly unproductive voyages. Of course, those locals with skills in fishing and experience as seamen were the first to be selected by the Yankee whaler captains.

These familial and occupational descendants of the original enslaved fishermen augmented their fishing skills with the specialized knowledge required for whaling. When their employment with the Yankee whalers ended, some sought ways to continue putting their newfound skills to work. The rise in locally run whaling operations coincided with the continued decline and eventual collapse of American whaling in the Caribbean. Over time, Caribbean whaling came to be dominated by local labor and management.

One of the Caribbean seamen who joined a Yankee whaling crew was William Thomas Wallace Jr., of Bequia. After participating in whaling voyages within the Caribbean and abroad, Wallace returned to Bequia having learned the skills necessary to start his own whaling operation.[15]

Wallace began whaling out of Friendship Bay, Bequia, to fill the niche left by the decreasing presence of the Yankee whalers. While humpback takes had not been sufficiently profitable to justify the long, costly voyages that the Americans had been undertaking, enough whales did remain to support a local operation. The geographer John Adams mentions the coincidence of the rise of locally managed whaling opportunities with the decline of cash-crop agriculture, indicating increased incentive for local subsistence populations to turn to the sea for their livelihoods.[16] In the mid-1880s, Wallace joined with another Bequian, Joseph Ollivierre, to expand their island's whaling operation. These two families—the Wallaces and the Ollivierres—would come to dominate the entire history of Bequia whaling, first as partners and later as rivals.[17] Athneal Ollivierre, the famous Bequia harpooner, was a descendent of the latter whaling family.

Locally directed whaling began to spread from Bequia throughout the Eastern Caribbean as the occupation proved profitable. During the late nineteenth and early twentieth centuries, local Caribbean whalers established many more stations throughout the Lesser Antilles. Bequia was the entrepôt through which local whaling entered the region, and thus the source of knowledge, technique, design, and culture for most of the subsequent Caribbean whaling operations, including the blackfish operation at Barrouallie. During the peak period of Caribbean whaling, between 1870 and 1925, tiny Bequia boasted at least five whaling stations. Within the southeastern Caribbean, Bequia-influenced whaling stations were established on at least eleven other islands.[18]

The Caribbean tradition of hunting large baleen whales, introduced by the Yankee whalers, survives today only on Bequia. Because of the humpback whaling operation based at Bequia, St. Vincent & the Grenadines was given an International Whaling Commission (IWC)–sanctioned quota of two humpback whales per year, since increased to four—the only aboriginal subsistence whaling quota given to a tropical country by the IWC. Two whales is of course a maximum allotment and not a guarantee. As Raymond Ryan, St. Vincent & the Grenadines' chief fisheries officer at the time, explained to me in 2009, "Sometimes we don't get two. Sometimes we get none."

The Last Whalers

The journalist Sebastian Junger began his article on Bequia whaling by introducing Athneal Ollivierre with this provocative sentence: "The last living harpooner wakes to the sound of the wind."[19] Junger's poetic license notwithstanding, the motif of the current generation of Caribbean whalers—and to a greater extent, artisanal whalers globally, including the Faroese—as "the last" in the world has been circulating for so long as to become self-contradictory. For example, in 1994 John Adams described the pilot whalers of Barrouallie as the "last of the Caribbean whalemen."[20] Another, more recent use of the phrase can be found in the subtitle of the 2014 documentary about whaling in Bequia, *The Wind That Blows,* by director Tom Weston, which identifies the film as "a portrait of the last Yankee whalers."[21]

As the continued practice of whaling in both St. Vincent and in Bequia would indicate, though, Junger's, Adams's, and Weston's subjects by no means constituted the last practitioners of their trade. These premature eulogizations can even happen from within. During

the late 1980s and into the 1990s, the Vincentian government made
the case to the IWC that whaling for humpbacks on Bequia was a
soon-to-be extinct phenomenon. According to one legal scholar of
whaling, "St. Vincent and the Grenadines argued that no proactive
measures to end whaling were necessary as 'the phasing-out of whaling
would take place naturally as the single harpooner was 67 years of age.'
Moreover it claimed that 'no young people [were] interested in continuing the tradition.'"[22]

Other whaling cultures also have been held up as the last of their
kind. An operation targeting sperm whales off the Azores until the
late 1980s was memorialized in a 1973 documentary, *The Last Whalers*.[23]
Another operation, also pursuing sperm whales, based in Indonesia,
was described in a 2000 article titled "The Last Whale Hunters."[24]
Despite the nearly antipodal settings of the subjects of these works,
the titles are almost identical and the sentiment is exactly the same.

Similarly, the end of the Faroese grindadráp has been predicted
for some time now. A representative of Greenpeace Denmark was
quoted in the *Los Angeles Times* in 1991 saying, "I think it's a matter of
a couple of generations before they drop the pilot whale hunt. . . .
The younger generations are losing interest."[25] While "a couple of
generations" have not quite passed since that statement was made,
the evidence that young people are not interested in the grindadráp
is yet to be shown, except perhaps to some degree within Tórshavn.

Although these "end of an era" discourses remain dominant, the
data indicate that whaling does, in fact, comprise a widespread set
of contemporary practices, diverse in both method and spatiality, as
marine mammalogists Martin Robards and Randall Reeves showed
in their wide-ranging and amply sourced 2011 paper that tallied all
known marine mammal takes since 1970.[26] Robards and Reeves's findings, coupled with the active participation by young people in both
the blackfish operation in St. Vincent and the grindadráp in the Faroe
Islands (along with myriad other marine-mammal-focused operations around the world), suggest that whaling isn't going away anytime
soon. It would seem, then, that like the premature reports of Mark

Twain's death in 1897, current predictions that the end of whaling is imminent are probably "exaggerated."[27]

Today's whalers in St. Vincent and the Faroe Islands are most likely not the last whalers in the world. They may not even be the last Vincentian or Faroese whalers. Athneal Ollivierre woke to the sound of the wind for the last time on July 4, 2000—he died that afternoon—but another living harpooner took his place. When I first visited Bequia in 2008, I paid five Eastern Caribbean dollars (about US$1.85) to a young girl named Nyoka, one of Athneal's granddaughters, for a tour of the small "museum," really just a shrine, dedicated to her grandfather's legendary whaling. Among the artifacts, I saw a painting of Athneal, standing erect in the bow of his whaleboat, the *Why Ask,* thrusting a harpoon into a surfacing humpback. Instead of a canvas, the artist had used a humpback's scapula.

A painting on a whale scapula, depicting Athneal Ollivierre harpooning a humpback from the *Why Ask* (signed, "Obby 2005")

I asked Nyoka where the *Why Ask* was docked or beached now. She looked down sadly and told me in her Bequian brogue that "him mash up"—meaning that the whaleboat had been smashed on the rocks. But despite the loss of both their famous harpooner and his boat, Bequians still hunt humpbacks. Vincentians and Faroese still hunt pilot whales and dolphins. When I returned to Bequia in 2015, the *Why Ask* lay prominently on the beach at Port Elizabeth—lovingly restored and repainted from its unfortunate "mash-up." Whaling traditions, especially when conducted for food, have the resilience to endure such setbacks.

From Humpbacks to Blackfish

By the early twentieth century, at the same time that humpback takes were declining throughout the local whaling operations of the southern Caribbean region, fishermen from the leeward villages of Barrouallie, on St. Vincent, and Castries, on nearby St. Lucia, had begun to hunt pilot whales and a variety of dolphin species, which were still abundant.[28] The connection between the whaling communities on St. Vincent and St. Lucia goes beyond mere coincidence of timing. Whalers from Barrouallie often take whales from within St. Lucia's territorial waters. This fact first appears in the scientific literature in the early 1970s and I confirmed that it was still true as recently as 2009 with GPS tracking.[29] Additionally, pilot whale meat and blubber from St. Vincent is exported to be sold in St. Lucia, though any international sales of cetacean products that take place without a permit are in violation of the Convention on International Trade in Endangered Species of Wild Fauna and Flora (CITES).[30]

Until the early 1930s, Barrouallie whaling was primarily opportunistic, meaning that cetaceans were not the main target but fishermen would take them if the opportunity arose. It was then that Griffin Arrindell, a local fisherman, purchased two Bequia-built whaling boats, themselves modeled after the Yankee whaleboats from the nineteenth century (recall Junger's words: "Take the guys from Melville's *Moby-Dick* and put them in Athneal's boat, and they'd know exactly what to do"), and began regularly and directly hunting small cetaceans. Adams cites Arrindell's mentors as "some old-timers at Barrouallie and Saint Lucia who had periodically hunted dolphins."[31] Over time, the village of Barrouallie became known for its unique food products. Since pilot whales—"blackfish"—were the most commonly sought species, if not always the most commonly caught, Barrouallie earned the nickname "Blackfish Town."

Guns and Boats

From the 1930s until today there have been two major technological innovations in Vincentian whaling: the harpoon gun and the motorboat. From the beginning of the operation, whaling crews set out each morning in oar- and sail-powered vessels. When a whale or dolphin was sighted, a hand harpoon virtually identical to the ones used by Yankee whalers was thrown—or in some cases, skipped across the water surface—at the targeted cetacean as it rose to breathe.[32] The introduction of motorboats and harpoon guns greatly extended the range at which whalers could hunt. Hand harpoons can, in theory, be thrown several meters or more, but in practice I only ever observed them being thrust nearly straight down into a whale or dolphin that had risen just next to the boat. Sailboats, even when their propulsion is supplemented with rowing, are limited in the speed at which they can approach cetaceans, and if a chosen spot proves to be unproductive, they are slow to reach another potential whaling area.

In addition to simply extending the whalers' range, the introduction of the harpoon gun allowed whalers to target what they termed "wild" whales and dolphins. Among Barrouallie whalers, pilot whales and dolphins are considered either "wild" or "tame" depending upon their behavior. The local usage of these terms is slightly different from their standard definitions and requires some explanation. Tame ce-

A harpooned spinner dolphin, brought alongside the whaling boat.
Photo © Andy Fielding

taceans are ones from pods that have not been hunted before and do not yet avoid boats and humans. They will often approach the boats quite closely and can sometimes be seen swimming in the bow wake. These are the easiest targets. They can be struck easily with the hand harpoon. Wild whales and dolphins have been hunted before, avoid humans, and flee boats. They are difficult to hunt and must usually be taken with a gun harpoon. When whalers are recounting the day's events to friends on shore in the evening and they mention sighting a pod of whales or dolphins, the first question asked is often, "Were they wild or tame?" The answer to this question often foretells the rest of the story.

During the mid-twentieth century, the whaling operation at Barrouallie witnessed a gradual shift from hand harpoons to gun harpoons. One reason that the gun was introduced gradually, rather than as an overnight innovation, is the permit. St. Vincent, having no equivalent to the United States' Second Amendment, regulates gun ownership tightly. A license to keep a firearm is difficult to acquire in St. Vincent and must be held by any whaler wishing to use a harpoon gun. The license itself costs 250 Eastern Caribbean dollars (US$93) per gun per year and is given only to whalers who have completed the appropriate paperwork, have clean criminal records, and, according to a Vincentian police officer with whom I spoke, are deemed to be "of good character."

During the same time period that Barrouallie whalers were adopting the harpoon gun, they were also shifting from sail power to engine power in their boats.[33] At the time of John Adams's 1964 fieldwork, "dramatic and costly plans were being made to install inboard and outboard engines" but the boats were still powered solely by sails.[34] Then in the early 1980s, another researcher, William Price, found the boats to be "sail powered with auxiliary [inboard] diesel or outboard [gasoline] engines."[35] By the early 1990s, all of the boats were equipped with outboard gasoline engines, as they still are today.[36] It is interesting to note that the humpback whalers from Bequia continue to use sailboats to approach and harpoon whales.[37] This was explained to me as essential to maintain the quota given by the IWC for aboriginal and subsistence whaling. The IWC does not actually require aboriginal subsistence whalers to refrain from using engine-powered vessels, but the whalers of Bequia perceive this lack of technological advancement as working to their advantage in keeping their quota year after year.

Shanties and Societies

In addition to the technological changes, two main areas of cultural change have taken place with regard to whaling in Barrouallie over the last half century as well. The first of these is the decline of shanty singing, and the second is the establishment and tumultuous history of a cooperative fisherman's society in Barrouallie. Both the shanties and the cooperative were formerly very important to the whaling operation. Today the shanties have vanished in their original form but have seen renewed interest as a piece of folk cultural heritage. The current iteration of the cooperative society struggles against debt and negative perceptions among the whaling and fishing communities.

Shanties are working songs sung by seamen and serve two primary purposes aboard ships: they provide a rhythm by which men could synchronize their physical labor—actions such as rowing, raising sails, or hauling anchors that require timed collaboration—and they offer a pleasant diversion from the tedium of shipboard life.[38] The American folklorist Roger Abrahams described songs that were associated with specific events aboard a whaling boat: the harpoon strike, hauling in a whale, rowing home.[39] Abrahams also cited certain prescribed periods of silence, such as when a whale had been harpooned and was hauled close to the boat, enforced in order to keep from frightening the whale and causing it to dive. On shore the whalers would sing shanties extolling their own strength in dealing with the perils of whaling, or parodying or calling out the boat owners, vendors, and public for their stinginess in haggling over the price of their wares.[40]

Many shanties followed a call-and-response structure by which the leader, called the shantyman, would sing a line, followed by the sailors who sang a line in response or a repetitive chorus. In the context of Barrouallie whaling, shanties served one additional purpose besides those mentioned above: by singing as they approached shore at the end of the day, whalers could alert community members onshore of a successful catch and request their help in the hauling and processing work that would soon follow.[41] Many of the shanties used in Barrouallie follow the same geographical line of transmission as whaling practices themselves: from New England to Bequia to Barrouallie.[42] Of course, some of the songs were adapted along the way. As such, the shanties often contain lyrics about places that were known to Yankee whalers but would have seemed exotic to the whalers from Barrouallie—Alabama, Baltimore, Bermuda, Calais, and Dover—as well as some that would have been more familiar, such as the neighboring villages of Rose Bank and Wallilabou, and the

Grenadine islands of Bequia, where they learned the whaling skills, and Mayreau, where they bought their salt.

During the 1960s and 1970s, changes both cultural and techno-logical led to the decline and eventual abandonment of the shantying tradition in Barrouallie. As boat owners began to replace their oars and sails with inboard and outboard engines, crews grew smaller and the need for the crewmembers to work in rhythm with each other disappeared. Along with the need for keeping time, so went the time-keeping shanties. The other practical use for shanties—to alert com-munity members on shore that a catch had been made and help would soon be needed—declined as the shanties proved perhaps too effec-tive. Specifically, crowds larger than necessary began to arrive at the shore where whaling crews unloaded their catch, offering to help and demanding to be compensated. At first, whalers incorporated new shanties into their repertoire that spoke directly to the excessive and demanding crowds that had been turning up at the beach for a free share. This social commentary is reminiscent of that other great Ca-ribbean musical tradition, calypso.[43] Consider, for example, the fol-lowing lines from the shanty "Bear Away Yankee": "Who na been off, / Na come a bay. / If you want de liver you have to buy. / If you want de guts you have to buy." Vincent Reid and folklorist Daniel Lanier cite these lyrics along with their translation to standard English ("whoever hasn't gone out [whaling], don't come to the bay") and note "that the whalers expected payment for even the most undesirable parts of the catch."[44] These new, critical shanties were not sufficiently effective against the demanding crowds, and the whalers soon aban-doned the notion of broadcasting news of their catch. Coupled with the transition from sails to motors, this led to the practical abandon-ment of shanties altogether.

In 2001, St. Vincent witnessed a small renaissance of interest in the Barrouallie whaling shanties. That year, under the leadership of Vincent Reid, a group of eight former whalers formed a singing group called the Barrouallie Whalers. This group began performing locally in 2002 and later internationally. Through this group, the tradition of shantying remains alive on St. Vincent despite no longer being used in the whaling operation.

The future of the tradition is uncertain, however, owing to the fact that few, if any, of Barrouallie's youth have taken an interest in the shanties. I stood on the pier in Barrouallie one afternoon in 2016, enjoying a private, spontaneous concert performed by Vincent Reid and George "Tall Twelve" Frederick, a former whaler and member of the Barrouallie Whalers singing group. Standing with me were two of my students, a colleague from St. Kitts, and a young man from Barrouallie named Diallo Boyea. While Vincent and Tall Twelve harmonized, I looked over at Diallo, who was smiling and shaking his head. When the singers finished, Diallo told me—confessed, really—"I've lived in Barrouallie my whole life and I've never heard these songs before."

If only the youth of St. Vincent could be motivated to embrace this aspect of their heritage. In Atlantic Canada, for example, I've sat in living rooms with Newfoundlanders, Nova Scotians, and Prince Edward Islanders, all of us under the age of thirty, singing authentic old sea shanties and modern ones, written and arranged by regional artists such as Stan Rogers, Ron Hynes, and Great Big Sea in a style that honors their roots. Perhaps Vincent Reid will someday be to Kingstown what Stan Rogers was to Halifax. Tall Twelve could bring the pride to Barrouallie that Ron Hynes brought to St. John's, Newfoundland. Great Big Sea will most likely never tour the Lesser Antilles, but the Barrouallie Whalers might—if audiences want to hear these history-imbued songs of yesteryear's adventures.

The presence of a cooperative society for the fishermen and whalers of Barrouallie has a history not unlike that of the shanties: a period of utility, a decline, and a final—perhaps symbolic—renaissance. The first iteration of a fisherman's cooperative in Barrouallie began in 1952 as the Barrouallie Fisherman's Cooperative Society with the main focus being the support of the pilot whaling operation. The Cooperative Society had a period of functionality, utility, and profit from its beginning in 1952 until the early 1970s when its decline began.

George "Tall Twelve" Frederick

Between 1972 and 1973 the society's profits decreased by an order of magnitude.[45] The timing of this decrease is directly related to the passage of the United States' Marine Mammal Protection Act of 1972, which forbade the import of whale oil into the United States, previously an important source of income for the Barrouallie whalers who exported the product, primarily for use in lubrication of small mechanical instruments.[46] In the early 1980s, both the productivity of the whaling operation and the morale at the Cooperative Society were low. Attempting to increase both, the society began several projects that were intended to stimulate the industry but which, in hindsight, led to the closure of the Cooperative Society itself.

One of the major projects that the Cooperative Society took on was the construction of more modern, more hygienic facilities for the processing and storage of whale meat, blubber, and oil. Unfortunately, this project was not completed satisfactorily, despite the contractual oversight and funding from international agencies including the United States Agency for International Development (USAID). It is interesting that USAID contributed funds directly toward the development of the whaling operation at Barrouallie in 1984—six years after the establishment of the Marine Mammal Protection Act. Apparently not all U.S. agencies were against the promotion of whaling in Barrouallie.

A Norwegian consultant oversaw the construction of the processing facility and the USAID funds covered the construction of a whaling boat.[47] Neither project went smoothly. The facility was built at Wallilabou, the next village north along the leeward coast from Barrouallie and a place without a whaling history. Traditionally, Barrouallie has always been the center of St. Vincent pilot whaling.[48] To construct a whale and dolphin processing center at another village was a misguided and culturally uninformed venture. The structure was never used for its intended purpose. It was used as a place to do laundry rather than as a whale and dolphin processing facility. Similarly, the whaling boat was built amid controversy as to both its cost and its seaworthiness. The boat was launched in 1989 and did well but only lasted until 1993, when it, along with the Barrouallie Fisherman's Cooperative Society as a whole, was put out of commission.[49]

The next attempt at a cooperative society in Barrouallie began humbly: according to an archived 2000 memorandum, one of the early meetings of the steering committee was to be held "under the almond tree next to the fishery center." In 2003, the steering committee for the new society registered the Barrouallie Fisheries Development Cooperative (note the slight name change from the previous incarnation) with the Vincentian national government. The cooperative—which exists still today—was not officially launched, though, until January 2005. The reliance upon international funding for the whaling operation continues. The building that the cooperative currently occupies, called the Barrouallie Fisheries Centre, was built with Japanese funds in 1999. This, to some conservationists, is problematic, owing to the well-supported link between Japanese foreign aid to small-island developing states and the voting records of those aid recipients in decisions related to the international whaling regulation.[50]

So pervasive is the connection between Japan and the pro-whaling stance at the IWC that the mere mention of the country can be enough to call into question one's conservation credentials. Personally, I am by no means pro-whaling. As an academic researcher, I do my best to withhold value judgments and instead emphasize the importance of three data-centric questions when assessing a particular whaling operation. The questions I use are: Are the cetacean populations being hunted able to withstand the current hunting pressure? Are the whales and dolphins that are taken being used efficiently? And finally, do the hunting methods employed strive for a quick and respectful death for the animals? These are my criteria. You're entitled to your own.

Once, however, I applied for a fellowship at the Harvard Center for the Environment with the intention of studying the relationship between Japanese foreign aid and small island states' voting records on whaling policy. I planned to work under the supervision of Ted Bestor, a renowned anthropologist and East Asia scholar. This would have been the first time my research touched on Japan directly. In the end, I was not awarded the fellowship, but just the proposal was enough to raise questions about my motives among the research community in the Caribbean. I received a cryptic message from a colleague on Bequia, mentioning that she had been "hearing some crazy rumors about your Japanese connections." The lesson learned is this: to maintain the impression of scientific objectivity when conducting whaling research, steer clear of Japan.

In addition to the questions raised by Japanese involvement, today's Fisheries Cooperative experiences its share of local controversy within St. Vincent as well. Of the four pilot whaling boat owners in Barrouallie, only one is a member of the cooperative. While the benefits of membership would seem appealing to local fishermen and whalers—credit for fuel and gear purchases, access to cold storage facilities, and a guaranteed wholesale market—many fishermen and most whalers see the board of directors as not prioritizing their interests.

How well the cooperative is now functioning is a matter of debate. The cooperative's president, Vibert Pierre, "boast[s] of success," and its members agree that its establishment was "a good move."[51] Patterson Homer, chief inspector at the ministry that oversees cooperatives, is more ambivalent. In a 2009 interview he told me that "there are two functioning [fisheries] co-ops: Kingstown and Calliaqua. There are several that are non-functioning, including Chateaubelair and Bequia." When I asked him to evaluate the cooperative at Barrouallie, the one about which I had originally asked him directly and which he had strategically avoided mentioning, he said, "Barrouallie is doing okay. They have a Fish Fest from time to time."

By most accounts, the Hairoun Bagga Fish Fest was the major accomplishment of the Cooperative. Hairoun is the local beer, named after the Carib name for the island of St. Vincent, and the festival's major sponsor. Bagga is a nickname for Barrouallie. For about three years, beginning in February 2007, the cooperative held a seafood-themed festival in the center of Barrouallie on the first Friday of every month. The Fish Fest attracted people from all over the island, who came for the live music, the festivities, and the fish and whale dishes that were sold. The Fish Fest was advertised on St. Vincent radio with the slogan "Remember, nobody can cook blackfish like Bagga people!"

As indicated by the success of the Fish Fest, the major accomplishment of the cooperative may be different from its primary stated purpose—service to the whalers and fishermen of Barrouallie. Like the shanties sung by the Barrouallie Whalers, the cooperative has the potential to be a positive representation of Barrouallie fishing and especially whaling to the Vincentian community at large. If the cooperative is to survive, it must find new and innovative ways to resume and continue this representation. Perhaps community outreach efforts to better understand the needs of the local fishers and whalers, increased sponsorship and promotion of cultural institutions such as the shanty singers, a minimization of the role of Japanese aid, and better and more transparent financial accountability could help this iteration of the cooperative, and with it, the Caribbean's foremost "Blackfish Town."

The village of Barrouallie in St. Vincent & the Grenadines

Two Vincentian whaling boats pursuing a pod of dolphins

A Risso's dolphin, harpooned and drawn alongside the whaling boat

Whale meat, hung to dry in the sun in Barrouallie

(Photo © Andy Fielding)

Chopping blubber at a processing station on the beach

Turning whale meat as it dries in the sun

Stirring whale blubber over a fire to make crisps

The whaling beach at Leynar in the Faroe Islands

Boats driving pilot whales toward shore
(Photo © Terji S. Johansen)

Shore-based whalers entering the water with ropes and hooks
(Photo © J. Remmer and K. Remmer)

Driving a *sóknarongul* (the old-style sharp hook) into a pilot whale
(Photo © Tracy H. Ostrofsky)

Hauling a hooked pilot whale toward shore
(Photo © J. Remmer and K. Remmer)

Preparing to kill a hooked pilot whale with a *mønustingari,* or spinal lance
(Photo © Tracy H. Ostrofsky)

Breaking the spinal cord of a pilot whale with a *grindaknívur,* or pilot whale knife
(Photo © Tracy H. Ostrofsky)

The scene of a *grindadráp* nearing its conclusion
(Photo © J. Remmer and K. Remmer)

the ventral grooves running along their throats—to take in large amounts of seawater for filter-feeding. As this blue whale decomposed, lying on its back, its throat expanded like a hot air balloon. Town residents thought an explosion was imminent. One enterprising marine biologist and blogger even started a watch site, the now-defunct hasthewhaleexplodedyet.com. The whale did not explode. After swelling to a maximum, it began to naturally deflate and was eventually towed away by a team from the Royal Ontario Museum to be studied, its skeleton preserved as a museum display.[5]

A year earlier, in 2013, a sperm whale had stranded on the coast in the Faroe Islands and died. It began to swell, and local experts—the same team of scientists who collect data at every grindadráp—decided to open its body cavity using a large flensing knife to relieve the pressure. Bjarni Mikkelsen, a soft-spoken marine biologist, was tasked with the job. Bjarni smartly donned fisherman's attire before he began cutting. After only a few small incisions, the knife apparently pierced the cavity where the gases had accumulated and a great horizontal explosion of organs, putrefied liquid, and tissue erupted. Bjarni quickly dropped the flensing knife and ran to safety. The whole incident was filmed and is available online after a brief search combining the terms *Faroe Islands, whale,* and *explosion.* The video, predictably, went viral. Bjarni had his Warholian fifteen minutes of fame.

Origins

In the Caribbean, although terrestrial landscapes were generally more productive than those of the North Atlantic, stranded cetaceans were still likely an appreciated and unexpected food source for ancient peoples. Many of the same cetacean species hunted today by Vincentian whalers are known to occasionally strand on Caribbean beaches.[6] Archaeological evidence indicates the use of marine mammals—probably restricted to stranded and scavenged whales and dolphins—by prehistoric Caribbean peoples.[7] The use of cetaceans in both the Caribbean and the North Atlantic was likely greater than extant archaeological evidence would indicate, though. Medievalist Vicki Szabo explains that because the butchering of whales—whether stranded or actively hunted—almost always takes place on the beach rather than in a settlement, the bones and teeth that otherwise would serve as evidence to future archaeologists are often lost to the tides.[8] In this sense, the ancient use of whales becomes "invisible" to future researchers who are accustomed to identifying animal-based food sources through the bones and other preserved items excavated from a settlement site.[9]

Active whaling operations, as opposed to the harvesting of stranded cetaceans, originated independently in several locations worldwide and cannot be said to have a single point of origin. The earliest whaling appears to have been conducted at several locations in the Arctic, although the degree to which these distinct operations were connected by cultural and technological exchange is unknown.[10] It's very likely that the first whalers had become familiar with their eventual quarry first through the use of stranded whales. Each whale that was then successfully harpooned and towed back to shore was itself a godsend—albeit in the manner of God helping those who help themselves.

Try to imagine what it must have been like for that first-ever whaler.[11] The setting may have been what is now northern Alaska, during a particularly bleak time about two thousand years ago, when food from other sources was especially scarce. As the memory of the last time a whale stranded on his village's coastline had begun to fade, some desperate and enterprising man, a father of hungry children, stood on the beach and noticed a whale spout not far offshore.

Acknowledging no other options besides starvation, he took to a small boat with an assemblage of gear normally used for fishing, sealing, and hunting—a bundle of fishing harpoons attached to lines made from braided sealskin, a spear used to hunt caribou, and a few inflated seal-stomach buoys—with the vague hope that he might avoid the long wait for a whale to strand on its own. As he approached the spot in the bay where he had last seen a vapor spray from the blowhole, he stopped paddling, stood in his shaky birch-framed and sealskin-hulled boat, and stared into the frigid water. Misshapen circles of pancake ice drifted by. He half hoped that the whale had dived, disappearing under the waves, and that he wouldn't have to actually face the beast. The unsteadiness of the boat amplified his legs' shaking, driven by nerves, cold, and low blood sugar.

Suddenly, directly behind him, he heard a massive blast from the whale's blowhole. He spun on his heels, lost his balance, and fell onto the rail of his boat, nearly dropping the harpoon. For a moment he paused there, hands gripping the boat's gunwale, head hanging over the side, staring directly into the sea. The whale surfaced again in nearly the same spot and the man took its next exhalation directly in his face, grimacing at the fishy, fermented smell of the whale's breath.

As this whale—like all whales—had never before been hunted, it had no fear of this tiny man in a tiny craft. After drawing a breath, the whale lolled on the surface, rotated its body slightly so its massive eye was above water, and stared directly at this would-be first whaler. Did the man sense the "emotional connection" that today's whale-watching tourists feel upon encountering whales up close for the first time?[12] Probably not. He was too hungry and too afraid. As the man and whale regarded one another, the hunter tightened his grip on the harpoon. He knelt first then stood slowly, bracing himself, and raised the harpoon above his head. Cupping the base of its shaft in his right hand, smoothing the rawhide line that coiled at his feet, the man took a deep breath. Pushing his fear to the back of his mind, he forced his muscles to explode, driving the harpoon deep into the flesh of the whale at his feet. The reaction was instant. Blood shot from the wound, first splashing the man's face and clothing and later freezing in place. The whale's fluke rose from the water and instantly slapped back down at a distance from the boat that revealed the sheer size of the animal. The whale dove but rose again nearby. Ready, the man lobbed another harpoon, which held fast and initiated another blood eruption. Each harpoon trailed its line a dozen meters or so to its buoy, an inflated and tied-off seal stomach that floated on the surface behind the whale as it swam.

The activities of the next half hour were a blur. The whale meandered frantically around the bay, growing tired from blood loss and trying to swim against the drag of the seal-stomach floats. When it dove, the floats submerged and provided even more drag underwater. The whale lost an enormous amount of blood. The man followed its erratic course, paddling as fast as he could to keep up. Exhausted, the whale's breathing became more rapid, which exposed it to more attacks with the harpoons and the spear. It convulsed, then slumped on the surface. The whale took one last, shallow breath and died, blood mingled with spray in the final, weak blast from its blowhole. Our whaler, the world's first, collapsed backward into his boat, utterly spent.

The process of towing the whale's carcass to shore required many boats and most of the men in the village. The effort was greatly aided by the fact that this particular whale species—which would later be named *Balaena mysticetus* by scientists and called the bowhead or Greenland right whale by whalers—has the unusual characteristic of floating when dead. As the whale came to rest on the village's rocky shore and was quickly and efficiently butchered—its meat, blubber, skin, and organs divided among the village's hungry population—this prototypical whaler faded into obscurity, content to provide food, first for his family and then for the rest of the village.

This adventure had been a proof of concept that others from his village and other Arctic settlements would follow. Future whalers would refine his rough and experimental techniques, applying technologies he couldn't even imagine. Spiritual beliefs would grow to incorporate whaling, and his culture would embrace the bowhead as part of its own ancient story. In time, whaling and the aboriginal peoples of the Arctic would become inseparable to the point that the Iñupiat—today's living descendants of the villagers whose lives were preserved through this first act of whaling—would come to call themselves "the People of the Whales."[13]

The arrogant and foolhardy notion that a person could kill a whale would arise several times independently elsewhere and would be tested using vastly different techniques. We don't know the name of the first whaler, but because of his actions the biblical questions posed by God to the patriarch Job can no longer be considered merely rhetorical: "Canst thou draw out Leviathan with a hook, or his tongue with a cord which thou lettest down? / Canst thou put a hook into his nose, or bore his jaw through with a thorn? . . . / Shall thy companions make a banquet of him, shall they part him among the merchants? / Canst thou fill his skin with barbed irons, or his head with fish spears?"[14]

Once whaling had proven possible, it was opened to the refinement, expansion, and modification by thousands of enterprising individuals. Today's diverse seascape of whaling, meticulously organized into a multivariate "taxonomy" by scholars Randall Reeves and Tim Smith, has evolved and adapted from those first brave and desperate people who considered whether they could "draw out Leviathan" and answered, perhaps while attempting to hide their own self-doubt, "Yes."[15]

Whaling Methods

Humans have captured cetaceans, and continue to do so, using a surprisingly diverse array of methods. Whales and dolphins have been poisoned, trapped in nets, trapped in weirs, trapped by the receding tide, hooked, lanced, shot with firearms, killed with explosives, electrocuted, harpooned, and driven ashore. The latter two methods of whaling are the most relevant to this book as they represent the methods used in St. Vincent and the Faroe Islands, respectively.

Oceanographers divide the Atlantic Ocean into two major basins: the North Atlantic and the South Atlantic. Picture for a moment the North Atlantic, not just the realm of icebergs and Vikings but the ocean basin in its entirety. Let's consider the border of this North

Atlantic as beginning at the southern tip of Greenland. From here, moving counterclockwise, it follows the coast of North America southward, and skips along the chain of Caribbean islands to the northeast coastline of South America. The North Atlantic's southern limit is defined, conveniently, by the equator, which crosses from northern Brazil to Gabon. From there the border of the ocean basin tracks northward along the coastline of West Africa, leaps the Strait of Gibraltar, and continues along the west coast of Europe, taking in the British Isles and southern Scandinavia, before completing its circuit along the path the Vikings took to the Faroes, Iceland, and Greenland.

This oceanographic North Atlantic, bounded by continents and islands, contains a circular ocean current rotating in a great gyre around its edges. In the center, found in a region known as the horse latitudes, is the Sargasso Sea—a high-pressure zone with frustratingly (to sailors) calm winds stretching roughly from Bermuda to the Azores. This North Atlantic basin counts the islands of the Lesser Antilles, including St. Vincent, as part of its southwestern boundary and reaches its northeasternmost extent at the Faroes.

Harpooning and whale-driving, the two whaling methods of relevance here, are generally split geographically in their occurrence between the south and north halves of this gyre, respectively. In the north, whales have mainly been driven; in the south, they've been harpooned. This geographical division of whaling methods likely reflects the informal diffusion of techniques from one place to another as well as the serial introduction of techniques from outside sources to several new and nearby locations. We cannot rule out the possibility of the convergent evolution of technologies and methods, though, especially in the case of drive-style whaling, based on close observations of cetaceans' natural behaviors and the ability of human societies to adapt their hunting techniques to observed cetacean behavior.

Of course, neither whale-driving in the northern North Atlantic nor harpooning in the south is an unbroken rule. Exceptions exist in both areas. Large-scale commercial whalers make use of the harpoon

Atlantic whaling regions, separated by whaling method. Cartography
by Alison DeGraff Ollivierre, Tombolo Maps & Design.

nearly everywhere they go. Today, commercial whaling operations
in Iceland and Norway both use large, cannon-fired—not hand-
thrown—harpoons. On a subsistence level, the Inuit of Greenland
and northern Canada are known for their expert use of the hand harpoon. In the Faroes, until the government forbade it, harpoons were
sometimes used in the grindadráp too. Drive-style whaling rarely
occurs in the southern North Atlantic, but a few examples do exist.
A colleague recently sent me photographs of a few small, black
cetaceans—possibly short-finned pilot whales, melon-headed whales,
or false killer whales—driven ashore by fishermen from the Grenadine island of Mayreau.[16]

Another exception, across the ocean from the Grenadines and
more than a century ago, is found in an 1890 American consular report, which described a "porpoise fishery" in France that seems to
have used a drive-style method.[17] There are three important caveats

to note about this "porpoise" drive, which most likely involved a species of dolphin, rather than true porpoises. First, the plan was to drive the animals "into shoal water, where they are killed with harpoons," indicating that this would have been a hybrid driving / harpooning form of whaling.[18] Second, the operation was judged to be unsuccessful, owing to the ability of many of the porpoises to escape before being killed. Third and finally, for what it's worth, the authority of the report's writer to comment credibly on any aspect of marine mammals whatsoever is called into serious question by his use without correction of a quotation from a colleague who referred to the porpoise as "a reptile."[19]

A final outlier, the Azores, located in the middle of the North Atlantic, would seem to have its pick of whaling techniques, due to the geographical ambiguity of its location. Probably owing to their contact with early American whalers, as well as to the steepness of their volcanic shorelines, which makes whale-driving difficult, the Azoreans chose the harpoon.[20]

In the development of these distinct North Atlantic whaling regions, the physical environment indeed may have played a role. Whale-driving generally requires a sandy beach, not a muddy, rocky, or cliff-bound shoreline, and the presence of appropriate coastal morphologies may have aided the development of whale-driving in the places where it occurred. While I'm careful not to overplay the role of the physical environment in determining the type of whaling that would arise in a certain place, I acknowledge its tendency to prevent—or at least make very difficult—the importation of specific techniques from one setting to another. A memorable example of this came for me during a midday break from whaling off St. Vincent. Samuel, the Barrouallie harpooner, regularly asked me questions about the grindadráp in the Faroe Islands and on this day hinted that he would like to learn how to drive whales ashore en masse in St. Vincent, rather than harpooning them one by one. We weren't far offshore but the water below us was already hundreds of meters deep, rising steeply toward the island along a slope that would make driving difficult, if not impossible. To make a whale drive even less likely, St. Vincent's leeward coastline is broad, not deeply embayed, and certainly not fjorded like the Faroes. If whales were to be driven toward shore, they would find ample opportunity to escape, either to the unbounded left or right or by diving deep, directly under the boats. St. Vincent, with its history of association with American whalers and its challenging physical geography, is a perfect example of why harpooning and not whale-driving became the dominant form of whaling in the southern North Atlantic.

Harpooning

The Basques, the mysterious people of the Pyrenees whose linguistic and cultural origins are lost to history, developed the methods of whaling that would be most influential in St. Vincent and much of the rest of the southern North Atlantic. Basque-style whaling involves pursuing whales in "small open boats, attacking them with hand harpoons and lances."[21] In their whaling taxonomy, Reeves and Smith describe the American style of whaling, which directly influenced the development of Vincentian whaling, as having "employed the basic Basque techniques of killing and processing whales."[22] So Vincentian whaling traces its legacy to the Basques, via the Americans. While the Basques were not the first whalers, nor even the first whalers to use the harpoon, they arguably perfected the technique of harpoon-based whaling, a technique that spread around the Atlantic Ocean and beyond. Basque-influenced whaling is a theme that has inspired countless variations.

Whaling by harpoon ranges from the use of the simple, hand-thrown harpoon of the Vincentians (or of our hypothetical ancient whaler) to the massive, cannon-launched harpoons with exploding heads, based on a nineteenth-century design attributed to the Norwegian whaler Svend Foyn.[23] While nearly all commercial whalers use harpoons with exploding heads, most subsistence whaling operations still make use of the simple harpoon with a barbed or toggling head today. This ancient design has probably been used for fishing for tens of millennia.[24] The modern, high-tech harpoons are intended to be immediately lethal, exploding on impact, whereas simple harpoons are intended only to secure the whale, either to a float or to the boat from which the harpoon was thrown or fired, via a rope or cable. A whale struck with a simple harpoon is drawn alongside the boat, where it can be dispatched with a lance or by gunshot if it has not died of blood loss or organ rupture following the initial strike and ensuing struggle.

Based primarily upon techniques learned from American or European whalers, but sometimes developed indigenously, artisanal whalers of the southern North Atlantic have tended toward the harpoon as their whaling implement of choice. Along the southern arc of the North Atlantic Ocean, the harpooning of cetaceans at a subsistence or artisanal level by local peoples from the Americas, Africa, and southern Europe has been recorded in Florida, Dominica, Martinique, St. Lucia, St. Vincent & the Grenadines, Trinidad & Tobago, Venezuela, French Guiana, Brazil, St. Helena, Gabon, Equatorial Guinea, Cameroon, Ghana, Côte d'Ivoire, Guinea, Senegal, Gambia, Mauritania, Cape Verde, Madeira, Portugal, Spain, and France.[25]

With the decline of whaling in St. Lucia and other Caribbean islands where it was once practiced, it would appear that St. Vincent & the Grenadines may soon stand as the only remaining whaling nation in the Caribbean region. It is possible, however—though infrequent—for whaling to begin in a country where it was not previously practiced or had not been practiced for a long time. For example, after a hiatus of more than seventy years, the Makah Nation of Washington State obtained permission from the IWC and legally killed its first gray whale in 1999.[26] Their practice—to some an efficient blend of old and new, to others a mockery of what it means for whaling to be "aboriginal"—was to harpoon the whale first to secure it to the boat, then kill it with a shot from a big-game rifle. The revival and reinterpretation of this traditional practice after the passage of more than two generations sparked passionate debate about the meaning of tradition and the place of whaling in the modern world.[27]

While it's highly unlikely that a new whaling operation would start in the Caribbean anytime soon, an interesting event at least gives me cause to consider the possibility. In 2012 I met with fisheries officials in St. Vincent to discuss my research and the government's own efforts to compile records of cetacean takes by Barrouallie whalers. I sat in a small, aggressively air-conditioned office with fisheries officer Lucine Edwards, who casually rotated her computer monitor to show me an image.[28] It was a photograph of three men standing in the bow of a motorboat—the blur indicated that they were moving fast—and the bulge of a humpback whale rising from the water just a few meters ahead of the boat. One of the men held a harpoon. "They're from Grenada," Lucine told me, "chasing a whale by PSV." Petit Saint Vincent, which is normally referred to by its initials, is the southernmost Grenadine island belonging to St. Vincent & the Grenadines. The islands to the south and west—Petite Martinique and Carriacou—are part of Grenada. Yankee whalers visited Grenada during the nineteenth century and locals established commercial whaling stations there in the years that followed, lasting until the 1920s and probably influenced by the success of the Bequia whaling operation, but no small-scale whaling operation for food ever developed in Grenada.[29] It could be, as the fisheries officers suspected, that the people in the photograph I saw in Lucine Edwards's office were just local fishermen causing trouble and not an early attempt at Grenadian artisanal whaling. But if so, why had they thought to bring along that harpoon?

Another interesting case of whaling by harpoon in the southern North Atlantic comes from Annobon, a small island off the west coast of Africa, a part of Equatorial Guinea but separated from the mainland portion and other islands of that country by an intervening archipelagic nation: São Tomé and Príncipe. Equatorial Guinea is remote. Within Equatorial Guinea, Annobon is remote. This double remoteness led to Annobon's inclusion alongside such insular obscurities as Diego Garcia, Tristan da Cunha, and St. Kilda in the acclaimed *Atlas of Remote Islands,* an intriguing and aesthetically beautiful reference for any islophile or would-be explorer.[30]

In 1957, a Catholic priest named Aurelio Basilio published an obscure ethnographic text in Spanish titled *Caza y pesca en Annobon* (Hunting and fishing in Annobon).[31] This book was based on Basilio's nearly thirty years' residence on Fernando Pó, now called Bioko, the island containing Equatorial Guinea's capital at the time, Malabo, and his travels among the other islands in the region. Nearly half the book is dedicated to traditional whaling, "la pesca de la ballena," on Annobon.[32] Based on his own eyewitness account, Basilio goes into great detail describing the ecology, methods, and cultural significance of the hunt for humpback whales off Annobon—a major food production strategy for islanders at that time. The history of whaling in Annobon, like that of St. Vincent, is directly related to the practice of locals laboring aboard foreign whaling vessels. Like the Vincentians, the Annobonese retained the skills and knowledge they had gained from contact with foreign whalers and continued their own locally driven whaling operation after foreign whaling in the area ceased. Perhaps the best analogy would be Bequia, the Grenadine island where the IWC-sanctioned aboriginal subsistence whaling operation takes a maximum of four humpbacks per year. Bequia and Annobon are found on opposite sides of the Atlantic but both apply skills learned from foreign whalers more than a century and a half ago in the pursuit of humpback whales today.

Or do they? In 1970, Equatorial Guinea fell into a dictatorship from which nearly all foreigners were expelled. Basilio himself was sent away in 1972.[33] Since that time, little has been known about Annobonese whaling—whether it still occurs, and if so, to what degree. The most recent investigation, itself now more than thirty years old, was unable to confirm any activities occurring later than 1975, though the researchers could not confirm the cessation of Annobonese whaling either, owing to the inaccessibility of the location.[34] In Annobon we have a case of what may be the least understood whaling

operation in the world. Even the most basic question—do the Annobonese still hunt humpbacks?—remains unanswered. The fact that
the last confirmed whaling there occurred at least a generation ago
means that if the knowledge was not passed down, it could remain
only in the minds and muscle memories of men too old to whale. In
the case of Annobon, though, an absence of confirmation of whaling
is certainly not a confirmation of whaling's absence. Outside researchers simply haven't been able to investigate.

Our final notable case of whaling by harpoon is found not in the
North Atlantic but in the western Pacific. It warrants inclusion in
this discussion because of its reliance upon culturally embedded conservation strategies, as well as the sheer uniqueness of its method.
In the Solor archipelago of Indonesia, between the better-known
islands of Flores and Timor, lie two islands called Solor—the namesake of the entire island group—and Lembata. These small neighboring islands host whaling operations that can only be described as
symbiotic. Whalers from the village of Lamalera, on the island of
Lembata, hunt only the sperm whale and smaller, toothed cetaceans.[35]
Whalers from Lamakera on the island of Solor—note the single letter
difference in the villages' names—hunt only baleen whales and a few
species of dolphins.[36] Each village claims traditional justification for
its own taxonomic niche in whaling; the whalers do not claim to be
focused on sustainability. Consider, however, the ecological impact
of this specialization: if both villages pursued both kinds—or exclusively the same kind—of whale, they would be more likely to overexploit the resource. Of course, whalers from either island could still
overexploit the whales they target. The traditional whaling taboos
in the Solor archipelago, though, like the culturally embedded conservation strategies of the Faroe Islands and St. Vincent, have served
to divide the resource and to make sustainable rates of whaling a more
likely outcome.

Just as impressive as the culturally embedded conservation strategies at work in these Indonesian whaling villages is the spectacle of
the whaling method used. Rather than throwing or shooting har-

poons at their target animals, the whalers of Lamalera and Lamakera use their own body weight to drive the implements into the flesh of the whales, thus ensuring a secure catch and minimizing struck-and-lost whales. To achieve this, as the boat approaches the whale the harpooner stands at the end of a long "harpooning platform" built like a diving board protruding from the bow.[37] When the whale surfaces to breathe and the harpooner is close enough, he leaps from the platform onto the back of the whale, driving his harpoon into its flesh. Author Tim Severin, who witnessed this form of whaling in the late 1990s describes the scene in which "harpoon head, shaft, and human were all one single projectile, hurtling through the air."[38] The harpooner is usually dragged for a short distance by the whale before letting go of the harpoon and being picked up by his quickly passing boat.

Based on the uniqueness of this method—it is found only among the traditional whaling communities of Indonesia and the Philippines—whaling taxonomists Randall Reeves and Tim Smith conclude that the Lamalera and Lamakera operations are truly aboriginal, with "no obvious link to the activities of visiting foreign whalers," concurring with what anthropologist Robert Barnes stated, setting straight the record that "these villages were hunting whales long before the English and American whalers entered the Indian Ocean."[39]

The Lamakera operation has shifted in recent years from whaling to manta ray hunting. According to marine biologist Heidi Dewar, this shift was not the result of a decline in whale numbers caused by overhunting, as has been the case with most other ceased whaling operations, but was due to increased demand for the skin, gill plates, and meat of rays.[40] Lamalera still hunts sperm whales. Despite their shift in target species, the whalers-turned-ray-hunters of Lamakera continue to use the spectacular method of hunting that they and their neighbors, the sperm whalers of Lamalera, developed. Whether hunting whales or rays, these intrepid harpooners perch on the bows of their chase boats, harpoons in hand, waiting for the right moment to leap onto the back of their quarry.

Whale-Driving

Drive-style whaling is similarly diverse and exists on a spectrum from the highly organized and methodical grindadráp to the chaotic dolphin drive of the Solomon Islands, in which spinner dolphins and pantropical spotted dolphins are made to strand in the shallow, muddy water where swimming or wading participants capture them by hand.[41] The most famous, or infamous, dolphin drive is probably the one that occurs in Taiji, Japan, and was brought to public attention mainly through the 2009 documentary film *The Cove*.[42] There, dolphins and small whales are driven into a bay, penned in with nets, and either slaughtered for their meat or captured alive to be sold to aquaria and zoos.

Whale-driving has been practiced for centuries in diverse geographical settings and is called by several terms including "porpoise drives," "dolphin drives," "drive-style whaling," and "drive fisheries." This method almost certainly arose from the observation of natural whale or dolphin strandings and the desire to induce such an event to occur. The Canadian author Farley Mowat states this theory succinctly: "In prehistoric times, such accidents must have been spectacularly rewarding to shoreside scavengers, including man. Eventually our ancestors realized that they had no need to wait passively for such gifts from the gods but could arrange for them to happen on a regular basis. So the whale drive was born."[43]

In general, drive-style whaling involves the use of one or more boats to force a pod of whales into a shallow bay or onto the shore where they can be killed. Occasionally whales or dolphins have been driven into nets rather than onto the shore. Drive-style whaling often employs sound—produced through such diverse methods as clapping rocks together underwater, blowing trumpets, shouting, firing rifles, throwing stones, and slapping the hulls or rails of the boats—to keep the whales swimming in the desired direction.[44] Just as with whaling in general, there is no clear single point of origin for the rise and diffusion of drive-style whaling. Rather, it appears to have begun independently in several locations and among various peoples. Whale-driving is recorded as having been developed independently by the Basques, various North Atlantic societies, aboriginal inhabitants of the Arctic, multiple Japanese villages, and various peoples of the tropical Pacific.[45]

From these points of origin, drive-style whaling spread to many locations, and was most prevalent among the Norse-influenced cultures of the North Atlantic. The Faroese researcher Arne Thorsteinsson, in a paper exploring the origins of the grindadráp, states that whale-driving "is part of the common Norse culture which the first settlers brought with them to the Faroes."[46] Within the northern North Atlantic, records exist of whale and dolphin drives occurring in Ireland, England, the Scottish mainland, the Hebrides, the Orkney Islands, the Shetland Islands, Denmark, Norway, Sweden, the Faroe Islands, Iceland, and Greenland, as well as in the Canadian provinces of Newfoundland and Labrador, Quebec, and Manitoba, and in the United States in Maine, Massachusetts, Connecticut, New Jersey, and North Carolina.[47] Among the countries and subnational jurisdictions along the northern arc of the North Atlantic, from Ireland to the United States, more have driven whales than have not. Remember this when tempted to think of the grindadráp, in all its Faroese uniqueness, as unprecedented. The Faroese may be the last North Atlantic people to drive whales today, but that status is the result of attrition, not exceptionalism.

North Atlantic whale drives have ceased in all locations except the Faroe Islands. The last holdout was Newfoundland in Canada. For a long time, prior to the twentieth century, in several small, coastal villages—known locally as "outports"—on the Atlantic-facing coasts of Newfoundland, local fishermen and opportunistic whalers took stranded cetaceans and occasionally drove ashore pods of long-finned pilot whales. This is the same species as is taken in the Faroe Islands, called "potheads" in Newfoundland, but from a distinct population with little to no interbreeding.[48] In 1947, immediately following the Second World War and just two years prior to Newfoundland's confederation with Canada, whalers from several outports along Trinity Bay began to drive pilot whales commercially. The main product was oil, rendered on the beaches and sold to local consolidators. The lean muscle and other tissue such as organs and bones were often left on the shore to decompose. Older residents recall the stench of rotting whales on the beaches of Trinity Bay.[49] In the 1950s, the newly established provincial government of Newfoundland and Labrador began to promote the pilot whale drive as a source of animal food for the captive fur industry, which raised mink and foxes. Whale drives became more common in response to the increasing demand.

The take of pilot whales in Newfoundland peaked in 1956 with 9,794 whales and began a steady decline from that year forward.[50] By 1970, pothead drives had become rare events and the number of whales taken per drive had decreased from hundreds to dozens. When the government of Canada banned the pothead drive in 1972, along with all commercial whaling, the practice had already all but exhausted the resource. During the twenty-six-year run of the commercial pilot whaling operation in Newfoundland, opportunistic whalers took about 54,000 pilot whales.[51] The annual average of 2,077 whales taken in Newfoundland was about two and a half times the long-term annual average in the Faroe Islands—833 whales—and has proven, in hindsight, to have been unsustainable.[52]

Another historically recent pilot whale drive occurred in the Shetland Islands of Scotland. According to archivist Brian Smith, whose comparative study is unique because of the distinctly Shetlandic perspective with which the author writes, Shetland Islanders never ate whales.[53] Instead, like the Newfoundlanders, they would drive—or *caa,* to use the local Scots term—pilot whales and other small cetaceans ashore, kill them, and render their blubber into oil. Later, Shetlanders ground whale bones and other tissues to make fertilizer. But to eat a whale in the Shetland Islands seems to have always been only an act of desperation. The Scottish ethnologist Alexander Fenton mentions one such desperate time in 1740 when Shetlanders were "forced to eat [whale meat] in time of famine."[54] While thorough records of the number of whales taken in the Shetlands do not exist, the profit-driven motivation for whaling seems to have led to overhunting as in the Newfoundland case. By the late nineteenth century, the cetaceans they hunted had become rare in Shetland waters. The last whale caa took place in 1920. When Parliament finally banned whale-driving officially in 1981, the activity had already ceased, owing to both the scarcity of whales and the changes in Shetlandic culture. Modern Shetlanders, according to Smith, "would never dream of hurting a whale."[55]

Our final example of whale-driving in the North Atlantic comes from Cape Cod, in Massachusetts. While the whale drive there never grew into the industry that arose in Newfoundland or Shetland, occasional and opportunistic drives were common enough to have served as a supplemental source of income for fishers and other local residents. Because Cape Cod has long been a destination for tourists, the occasional outsider's description exists in the published record to offer a perspective on the activity. One such outsider was Henry David Thoreau, who witnessed the immediate aftermath of a pilot whale drive on Cape Cod in 1885. Thoreau's narrative is included in his travelogue *Cape Cod.* His account speaks to the priority of oil production over food production and gives some indication of the subaltern status of the consumption of whale meat, as in the Shetland Islands, by describing it as a food of last resort, eaten, for example, by boys who would "sometimes come round with a piece of bread in one hand" onto which they would lay a slice of blubber or smear a knifeful of oil. In their desperation, these boys reminded Thoreau of "the poor of Bretagne."[56]

Food and Oil

Whales have been used to make many useful and necessary products for people. Meat, blubber, skin, and some organs can be consumed either cooked or uncooked. Generally, food products derived from whales are high in vitamins, fatty acids, marine oils, and protein.[57] But as marine pollution increases throughout the world's oceans and concentrations of various toxins in whale tissue increase accordingly, the health benefits of a diet that includes whale products begin to be outweighed by the risks.[58]

Historically, the most economically valuable non-food whale product has been oil. The blubber—and to a lesser extent the muscle and bone—produces oil when heated. Whale oil has been used in a variety of industries and in the production of various household products including soap and especially margarine.[59]

Time and again we have seen the same history of artisanal whaling unfold: people who take whales for food are loath to give up the practice; those who whale for oil do not cling to it so tightly. Artisanal whaling cultures more interested in oil than food fell into a pattern similar to that of large-scale commercial whaling, described by one whaling historian as a situation in which whalers "killed without any regard to the consequences for the animal or the future of the whaling industry."[60] We know that food production likely motivated the first whalers. It would appear, as well, that food production is the reason for the continuation of whaling in nearly all the places where it still occurs today. We can think of the commercial production of whale oil, then, as a short-term exception to the long history of whaling—an exception, however, that had disastrous consequences on both whale populations and outside perceptions of whaling.

The divergent motives of profit and subsistence lead to vastly different outcomes through the different management regimes that follow. In this way, it is no surprise that the Vincentians alone continue harpooning whales at any significant scale in the Caribbean and that the Faroese constitute the only remaining whale-driving society of the North Atlantic. Others hunted whales for oil or whaled for food only as a last resort. These operations ceased either when whales became rare, their meat was no longer needed or desired, or whale oil became obsolete. In both St. Vincent and the Faroe Islands, whaling is done for food and that food is a mainstay of the local diets. Food, unlike whale oil, is never obsolete, and so the Vincentians and Faroese continue whaling.

6

Laws and Traditions

Since the beginning of my research into artisanal whaling, when discussing this work with friends or colleagues, I have been asked one question more often than any other: "Isn't whaling illegal?" This is a difficult question, not because there is no answer but because there are so many different answers depending on what, exactly, is meant by "whaling" and "illegal." Whaling is a diverse subject. It is and has been practiced by many different peoples for different economic, subsistence, cultural, and political purposes, taking place in all the world's oceans and many seas, gulfs, bays, fjords, inlets, coastlines, and even some rivers. Whaling occurs in waters territorial and international, coastal and pelagic, and employs a wide range of hunting and killing methods. Whaling involves a variety of cetacean species, from small porpoises and dolphins to the largest animal that has ever lived, the blue whale. The International Union for the Conservation of Nature (IUCN), "the world's largest and most diverse environmental network," assigns a conservation status to every species on earth, ranging from "critically endangered" to "of least concern."[1] Whaling operations target cetaceans from every conservation status within this range, including "data deficient," the IUCN's default status for species that we don't yet know enough about to even define the size of their populations.

The various activities that fall under the broad category of "whaling" have developed within a wide variety of legal regimes. Regulations range from total bans on nearly all forms of marine mammal interactions to a complete absence of whaling policy. And then there are some policies that even encourage whaling as a form of food production and economic development. For example, during the Allied occupation following the Japanese surrender at the end of the Second World War, General Douglas MacArthur actively promoted commercial whaling as a solution to the food shortages facing Japan.[2] It is far too simple to ask whether whaling is legal or illegal. We must even go beyond the categories of "permitted," "proscribed," and "promoted." To understand the diversity of laws and traditions that regulate whaling, we need to know first what we mean by "whaling" in terms of the identity of the whalers, the species of the whale, and the purpose and location of the activity.

When people assert that whaling is illegal, they are most likely referring to the 1986 zero-quota (more familiarly known as the "moratorium") for commercial whaling established by the International Whaling Commission. This international body, formed in 1946 through the International Convention for the Regulation of Whaling, was established to manage whales as a shared resource. Its original goal was decidedly pro-whaling. The convention text calls whales "great natural resources" and states that "increases in the size of whale stocks will permit increases in the number of whales which may be captured."[3] Over time, that changed.

For the first several decades of the IWC's existence, its membership comprised only whaling nations. The fourteen original member states—Argentina, Australia, Brazil, Canada, Chile, Denmark, France, the Netherlands, New Zealand, Norway, Peru, the Soviet Union, the United Kingdom, and the United States—all had significant interests in whaling. IWC membership, though, is open to any nation. Beginning in the 1970s, countries with no history of—or interest in—whaling began to join the IWC, according to one whaling historian, "apparently for the specific purpose of changing the balance of votes and thus to institute a moratorium policy."[4] This apparent goal was met in 1982, when the IWC passed a resolution that, beginning in 1986, reduced the annual quota for commercial operations targeting all whale species to zero, so that scientists could conduct a "comprehensive assessment of whale stocks."[5] At the end of this assessment period, the IWC would consider establishing new take limits. What was originally intended to be a temporary pause in whaling, though, has continued to be upheld by annual vote; the zero-quota remains in place today.

Part of the reason that the 1986 moratorium is still in effect is that the IWC has become more precautionary, more environmentally conscious, and less tolerant of whaling. Per IWC regulations, each member state has an equal vote, regardless of its population, seniority, or history of whaling. The IWC has shifted in its philosophical framework from conservation, which is the sustainable use of a resource, to preservation, which requires completely abstaining from the use of a resource. Under the precautionary philosophy of the IWC, "the burden of proof has been moved to those who wish to utilize the resource to demonstrate that any resumption of whaling will not be harmful."[6] Today commercial whaling remains forbidden by the IWC. Of course, whaling still occurs and in most cases is not in violation of the moratorium.

Citizens of some countries may whale and others may not. The first set of countries not bound by the IWC moratorium, nor any of its other policies, is made up of those who are not member states of the IWC. Some whaling nations, such as Indonesia, have never joined the IWC. Others, like Canada, were early signatories but have since left the commission. In either case, as a voluntary international organization of sovereign states, the IWC has no authority to compel membership. As such, some whaling nations have simply opted out.

Environmental historian Kurkpatrick Dorsey's history of the IWC, *Whales and Nations,* recounts the comings and goings of several of the commission's founding member states during the years before the moratorium, as the IWC struggled to establish quotas that were both acceptable to its members and supported by scientists as actually being capable of effecting conservation.[7] For many years, the cohesion of the IWC itself was threatened by the real risk of member states simply leaving the commission when they felt they could not accept its rules.

This risk led to the second category of nations where whaling can be legal: those that have objected to the IWC moratorium. As an organizational compromise, designed to keep the IWC from disbanding altogether, the so-called objection clause was included in the commission's framework. In essence, this allows any member state to file an objection to any resolution adopted by the IWC. After filing an objection, the objecting state is not bound by the resolution. So when someone asks whether whaling is "illegal" and makes clear reference to the IWC moratorium, I cannot help but think, *Yes, but only in the most unenforceable way possible.* Imagine if other illegal acts suddenly became legal for those who had lodged objections to the relevant laws:

> "Sir, I pulled you over because you were driving eighty-five miles per hour in a thirty-mile-an-hour school zone."
>
> "But officer, I can drive as fast as I want—I filed an objection against the speed limit."
>
> "I see. Sorry for the trouble. Have a nice day."

As an organization built by voluntary membership, the IWC saw the objection clause as a necessary guarantor of its own cohesion.[8] Even policies as broad as the moratorium are subject to objection, as in the cases of Norway and Iceland, both of which currently support commercial whaling operations while maintaining IWC membership, in objection to the IWC moratorium. Thus, the two categories of countries that may host legal commercial whaling operations despite the moratorium are those that are not member states of the IWC and those that are but have filed objections to the moratorium.

The purpose of a whaling operation also affects its permissibility under the rules of the IWC. Two types of whaling are allowed under the moratorium: aboriginal subsistence whaling and scientific whaling. According to the IWC, from the beginning of its existence, the commission "recognised that indigenous or 'aboriginal subsistence' whaling is not the same as commercial whaling."[9] The IWC makes provisions "to enable native people to hunt whales at levels that are appropriate to cultural and nutritional requirements" by allowing an aboriginal subsistence exemption to the moratorium for qualified cultural groups.[10] Currently, four countries have permission to hunt whales under the aboriginal subsistence exception to the IWC moratorium: Denmark, Russia, St. Vincent & the Grenadines, and the United States. The specific cultural groups permitted to whale for aboriginal subsistence purposes are the Inuit peoples within Russia, Alaska, and Greenland (the last, like the Faroe Islands, is a dependency of Denmark); the Makah of Washington State; and the humpback whalers of Bequia.[11] All of these communities, except one, host active whaling operations today: the United States government is currently reviewing Makah whaling to decide whether to allow the operation to resume.

The second reason whaling may be permissible, based upon its intent, is if killing the whales is a necessary part of a scientific research program. The IWC recognizes that some research questions can be addressed only through the analysis of a whale carcass, not a living whale, and that scientists may occasionally have to employ what are referred to as "lethal research methods" to collect the data they need. The commission's scientific committee reviews proposals from member nations regarding upcoming and ongoing research, especially when such methods are included. Despite this review, the IWC does not regulate scientific whaling through allowing or forbidding specific proposed programs; rather, the commission, through its scientific committee, just makes comments on proposed research.

As such, some scientific whaling programs—most notably those of Japan—have provoked controversy and accusations that the scientific objectives were actually secondary to the killing of whales for commercial purposes. The fact that meat from whales killed for allegedly scientific purposes makes its way into the Japanese food system is used as evidence for the claim that scientific whaling is really just thinly veiled commercial whaling. The Japanese say they're just being efficient and that the avoidance of waste is exactly in line with the rules regarding scientific whaling.[12] Opponents maintain that the food was the whole point all along.

The final way that whaling may be practiced legally depends upon the species targeted. When it began, the IWC was intended to regulate commercial whaling in international waters. While the commission never explicitly defined the species of whales over which it claims jurisdiction, the names of fifteen whale species were included in an annex to the original convention establishing the IWC. These were the blue whale (*Balaenoptera musculus*), bowhead or Greenland right whale (*Balaena mysticetus*), Bryde's whale (*Balaenoptera brydei*), common minke whale (*Balaenoptera acutorostrata*), fin whale (*Balaenoptera physalus*), gray whale (*Rhachianectes glaucus*, since renamed *Eschrichtius robustus*), humpback whale (*Megaptera nodosa*, since renamed *Megaptera novaeangliae*), North Atlantic right whale (*Eubalaena glacialis*), North Pacific right whale (*Eubalaena japonica*), northern bottlenose whale (*Hyperoodon ampullatus*), pygmy right whale (*Neobalaena marginata*), sei whale (*Balaenoptera borealis*), sperm whale (*Physeter catadon*, since renamed *Physeter macrocephalus*), southern bottlenose whale (*Hyperoodon planifrons*), and southern right whale (*Eubalaena australis*).[13]

Because of their inclusion on this list, the sperm whale and baleen whales—but, curiously, not the bottlenose whales—came to be known as the "IWC whales" in the context of international conservation. It is generally agreed that IWC policies relate only to IWC whales. The convention made no explicit claim, though, as to the exclusivity of their protection. Since the establishment of the IWC, several changes to the list of IWC whales have occurred. In addition to the altered scientific names of the species mentioned above, several newly defined species have been added to the list of IWC whales. After the commission was founded, the Antarctic minke whale (*Balaenoptera bonaerensis*) was recognized as a species separate from the common minke whale, and Bryde's whale was redefined as a "species complex" that also includes Eden's whale (*Balaenoptera edeni*) and possibly Omura's whale (*Balaenoptera omurai*).[14] These latter whales are assumed to fall under IWC jurisdiction because they were known at the time of the convention and their current designations are merely the result of taxonomic restructuring.

As a result of the de facto extension of IWC regulation to only the IWC whales, the protection of other cetacean species falls unilaterally to each of the individual countries in whose territorial waters they are found. Collectively, these species are called "small cetaceans," although as one legal analyst points out, this designation is not necessarily based upon a smaller physical size than that of the IWC whales.[15] Some conservationists have called for the establishment of an international regulatory body for small cetaceans, either as part of the IWC or as a separate entity altogether.[16] Others favor the expansion and empowerment of existing regional conservation treaty organizations to oversee the protection of small cetaceans.[17] The lack of a global international management body for small cetaceans has led one environmental organization to call these species "the forgotten whales."[18] Whether or not small cetaceans are indeed "forgotten" by conservation and management policy depends upon the national or subnational level of protection they are afforded.

So, to answer a common question: yes, whaling is "illegal" and has been since the implementation of the IWC's moratorium in 1986. Still, some major exceptions exist to that general rule. Because pilot whales and the other species taken by both Vincentian and Faroese whalers are small cetaceans and not among the species protected by the IWC, we must narrow our political scale to examine the legality of these whaling operations. In the case of the grindadráp we will look at the possibility of international protection via the European Union, national protection under Danish law, and finally subnational protection under Faroese law and traditional custom. In St. Vincent & the Grenadines—an independent country not part of any international organization on par with the EU—we will consider only national law, including international treaties to which St. Vincent & the Grenadines is a signatory state, and local laws and customs as the relevant regulatory powers.

Faroese Laws: The Essence of Home Rule

The Faroe Islands, population roughly 50,000, are a dependency of Denmark. American readers are sometimes told to think of Puerto Rico as an imperfect analogue for the Faroese-Danish political relationship, although the U.S. Virgin Islands—which were the Danish West Indies until 1916—might be a more fitting stand-in. British readers can think of Bermuda or any of the other "outposts" remaining from the old colonial empire.[19] Denmark is a member state of the European Union. The Faroes, though, are not. The Treaty on the Functioning of the European Union states rather plainly that it "shall not apply to the Faeroe Islands."[20] The same is true for Denmark's other dependent territory, Greenland, although the separation of Greenland from the EU may seem more natural given the geographical distance of Greenland from mainland Europe and the non-European ethnicity of the native Greenlandic people. Some territories of EU member states, however, lie much farther from the European mainland than Greenland does and yet still maintain full EU status. The Caribbean islands of Guadeloupe and Martinique, along with the French side of St. Martin; and the Indian Ocean islands of Mayotte and Réunion—all French territories—are fully part of the EU. EU law applies in all of these islands, albeit with the possibility of some modification owing to "the structural social and economic situation" as well as the territories' "remoteness, insularity, small size, difficult topography and climate, [and] economic dependence on a few products."[21] The Canary Islands, the Azores, and Madeira are treated the same as these French territories under EU law; however, these Spanish and Portuguese territories lie much closer to mainland Europe than Greenland does. It should be noted, however, that geographically the Faroes are even closer than these Iberian archipelagos and are populated by people of European ancestry, yet remain politically and jurisdictionally outside of the EU.

During the Second World War, Iceland—then also a part of the Danish kingdom—declared independence while Denmark was Nazi-occupied.[22] The British occupied the Faroes during the war, an experience that showed some Faroese that they too could function independently from involvement with Denmark. Beginning in 1946, with the possibility of independence on the minds of many Faroese, negotiations were carried out between representatives from the Faroes and Denmark, finally resulting in the establishment of home rule in 1948.[23] The home rule arrangement transferred most domestic authority to the locally elected Faroese government but left all international representation to Copenhagen. The balance of power has been slowly tilting toward Tórshavn, the Faroese capital, ever since.

Today the Faroe Islands remain an autonomous province of Denmark under the home rule arrangement, with the official status of "a self-governing community within the Kingdom of Denmark."[24] Since 1948, the topic of full independence has been discussed within Faroese public and political discourse.[25] Denmark supplies the Faroes with an annual subsidy, staffs police and military forces, and handles some international representation. The Faroese home rule government handles most domestic affairs, including the regulation of whaling, and an increasing amount of foreign relations. Denmark forbids whaling; the Faroe Islands embrace it. In Copenhagen, I asked Danes for their opinions of Faroese people. A common response was, simply, "whale-eaters." In the Faroe Islands, however, whaling is problematic only to a small minority. According to former prime minister Kaj Leo Johannesen, with whom my students and I met in 2012, the biggest environmental debate in the Faroe Islands at the time was

about fishing limits. The grindadráp did not register as a major domestic environmental issue.

The distinction between Denmark and the Faroe Islands, with regard to EU laws and treaties, is especially relevant to the grindadráp
because of the Convention on the Conservation of European Wildlife and Natural Habitats, commonly known as the Bern Convention.
The Sea Shepherd Conservation Society rightly points out that
Denmark is a signatory to the Bern Convention and that this convention prohibits "all forms of deliberate capture and keeping and
deliberate killing" of species listed in its Appendix II, which includes the long-finned pilot whale along with twenty-nine other cetaceans.[26] If the Faroe Islands were subject to the Bern Convention,
the grindadráp certainly would be in violation of the treaty. It is the
interpretation of the Danish government, however, that decisions
regarding the grindadráp are not within Copenhagen's jurisdiction.
According to a former adviser on Faroese matters at the Danish
Ministry of Foreign Affairs, Denmark defers all decisions on whaling
policy to the Faroese home rule government. This adviser stated em-
phatically that "if the pilot whaling is going to be drastically reduced
or stopped, it will be a result of a Faroese policy decision. Danish authorities have no legal means to stop it."[27] That is to say that the
Danish government views neither its own legislation nor its participation in the Bern Convention—or any other treaty—as capable of
impacting the grindadráp in the Faroe Islands. Perhaps the best illustration of how Copenhagen views Faroese autonomy on matters
such as whaling is the fact that the Danish government addresses
Faroese concerns through its Ministry of *Foreign* Affairs.

At the international level, there is no treaty to which the Faroese
home rule government is a signatory that would forbid the grindadráp. The IWC moratorium does not apply to small cetaceans. The
Bern Convention does not apply because Denmark defers to the home
rule government on all whaling matters. Therefore, the laws governing
the grindadráp exist only at the domestic level and are enacted and enforced by the Faroese government itself. This location of authority is

made explicit by the Executive Order on Pilot Whaling, part of the Faroese legal code, which states plainly that "the Faroese Government is the highest authority in all matters pertaining to pilot whaling."[28]

Throughout much of the grindadráp's early history, the activity was regulated locally by those who participated, with the greatest authority resting with the landowners upon whose shores the whales were driven. An early departure from the rule of the landowner was initiated in 1779, when the Faroese scholar Jens Christian Svabo called for the establishment of a kind of hierarchy by which "one or two of the most responsible men from each whaling bay" would each become the absolute authority regarding all aspects of the grindadráp, including the division of the meat and blubber within his district.[29] Svabo's idea proved to be popular, and gradually the authority to regulate whaling began to move from the landowners to the government, which oversaw the identification and installation of these "most responsible men," whose role eventually grew into—and was formally established as—that of the grindaformenn today.

The Løgting, or Faroese Parliament, first codified pilot whaling regulations in 1832. Today, Faroese laws regarding the grindadráp maintain the empowerment of the grindaformenn, but share that power with the sýslumaður. The charge is repeated several times throughout the English translation of the whaling regulations, using the standard translation of "sheriff" for *sýslumaður,* that "all boats and people on land must follow the instructions of the Sheriff and/or the whaling foreman."[30] Together, these authority figures direct Faroese whaling. Several grindaformenn might participate in any given grindadráp, but it is the first grindaformann on the scene who hoists *Merkið*—the white, red, and blue Faroese flag—on his mast and thus assumes the leadership role at sea in the drive. The sýslumaður normally stays on shore to share power with the grindaformenn in this land-and-sea dichotomy.

Grindaformenn are expert whalers and representatives of a Faroese tradition that predates Danish rule. Faroese law prescribes nine whaling districts containing twenty-five approved whaling beaches, chosen for their historical connection to whaling and, ostensibly, their physical appropriateness, and states that each whaling district must have four grindaformenn and two deputies.[31] With their whaling experience and nautical knowledge, grindaformenn are the most qualified to decide how to best handle a particular pod of whales within particular oceanic, meteorologic, and economic conditions. As the boats arrive on the scene to assist with the drive, the grindaformann instructs the other boat captains on how to best steer the pod into the chosen bay. When the whales begin to strand in the shallow water, the grindaformann signals the men on shore to enter the water and begin the kill.

After the whales are killed, a distinct shift in authority occurs. The most pressing practical need is that the whales must be counted, measured, evaluated, and divided. The sýslumaður, not the grindaformann, is solely responsible for these organizational processes. The work has shifted from whaling to resource allocation. Faroese law prescribes a complex yet adaptable system of division by which the meat and blubber are distributed among those who participated in the grindadráp and / or the residents of the village where the event took place. Fairness and equality are the ideals of the system, but often not all are satisfied with their lot. Sometimes the sýslumaður makes decisions regarding the distribution of food that leave out certain people—even sometimes those who have participated most directly in the grindadráp. The sýslumaður's decision is final and, according to the Faroese whaling regulations, he receives twice the amount of food in compensation for his duties as the grindaformenn each receive for theirs.

Vincentian Laws: Maintaining a Tradition

St. Vincent & the Grenadines is a sovereign, independent state—population about 100,000—made up of the main island, St. Vincent, and seven other inhabited islands. Since independence from

Britain, which came in 1979, intellectuals from St. Vincent & the Grenadines have emphasized the need for nation-building and recognition of the African and Carib influences present in modern Vincentian culture. Anthropologist Virginia Young cites the recognition of St. Vincent Creole as a legitimate language as one of many ways the Vincentians "search for their culture."[32]

Whaling is another. In 1995, an international group, reported to have originated in the United States, threatened to organize a boycott of tourism to St. Vincent & the Grenadines in protest of both pilot whaling on St. Vincent and humpback whaling on Bequia. As is often the case with Caribbean politics, the people's reaction was voiced by the region's endemic troubadours, the calypsonians. One of the popular songs at that year's carnival included the line "No, Uncle Sam, we will not give up blackfish."[33] Even the United States' passage of the Marine Mammal Protection Act in 1972 did not bring about the termination of pilot whaling in St. Vincent. Prior to passage of the act, the majority of the blubber from pilot whales had been rendered into oil for export to the United States. After 1972, when marine mammal products were no longer imported into the United States, whalers from St. Vincent discovered a higher-than-expected demand in local and regional markets for blubber and whale oil—the former fried and sold as "crisps" (the first s is silent, so the word is pronounced "crips"), a popular snack food, and the latter used for cooking, fuel, and medicinal or cosmetic purposes. The idea of whaling as both a unique signifier of Vincentian identity and a form of resistance to international hegemony has likely buoyed its continued public support throughout St. Vincent.

Once, in 2009, aboard an inter-island ferry that was about to depart St. Vincent for the southern Grenadines, I stood on the deck among a group of Vincentian teenagers. After having mentioned my interest in whaling, I noticed a framed portrait of Barack Obama hanging on the wall of the boat's luggage cabin. President Obama was—and remains—very popular throughout the Eastern Caribbean. A teenager saw that I had noticed the picture and asked me, "Do you work for Obama?" Recalling in quick succession the history of anti-whaling attitudes originating in the United States and the basic tenets of American government—"of the people, for the people, and by the people"—I responded, "Do I work for Obama? Obama works for me!" This, it turns out, was the right answer. The teens laughed and we were able to have a pleasant conversation about pilot whaling, the United States, and, of course, President Obama.

A few days later I discovered that this would not be the last time these topics were discussed together in this part of the Caribbean. A full-page advertisement in *Searchlight,* one of St. Vincent & the Grenadines' major newspapers, juxtaposed an official portrait of the American president alongside an image of a breaching humpback whale. The headline read, "President Obama Needs Our Help to Save the Whales." The ad's message was an effort to mobilize the Vincentian public in support of the U.S. position at the IWC against commercial whaling. It urged them to contact their prime minister, Ralph Gonsalves, and ask him to appoint a different national representative to the IWC, one that "will protect whales in the Caribbean and worldwide."[34] While this advertisement was paid for by a foreign organization, its presence in a Vincentian newspaper may hint at a nascent change in attitudes regarding whaling there.

Official whaling regulations that would apply to Barrouallie do not exist in St. Vincent & the Grenadines. In fact, marine mammals are not mentioned at all in the country's fisheries regulations.[35] Therefore, any discussion of policies applicable to the blackfish operation must begin at the international level. Two international treaties to which St. Vincent & the Grenadines is a party are occasionally cited in discussions of whaling legality, but neither is actually relevant to the Barrouallie operation. The first, the International Whaling Commission's moratorium, we know, applies only to the so-called IWC whales, not to the small cetaceans targeted by Barrouallie whalers. Another treaty, the Convention on International Trade in Endangered Species of Wild Fauna and Flora (commonly referred to by the acronym

CITES, pronounced "SIGHT-ees"), regulates—among other things—the international export of cetacean products. CITES does not address the local sales and consumption that define the market for the whale-based food products from Barrouallie.

A third treaty is more relevant—and also more problematic for the legality of St. Vincent's pilot whaling operation. In 1990, St. Vincent & the Grenadines ratified the Convention for the Protection and Development of the Marine Environment of the Wider Caribbean Area, commonly known as the Cartagena Convention. This broad treaty is supported by three specific agreements: one related to oil spills, one focusing on land-based sources of marine pollution, and—most relevant to the discussion of Vincentian whaling—the Protocol Concerning Specially Protected Areas and Wildlife in the Wider Caribbean Region (colloquially called the SPAW Protocol, or simply SPAW). SPAW's objective is "to protect, preserve and manage in a sustainable way" both species and their habitats that are threatened with depletion within the Caribbean.[36] To achieve this goal, the protocol includes three annexes that list species to be afforded varying levels of protection.

The first, Annex I, deals only with plants. Annex II and Annex III, however, include lists of animal species and differ dramatically in the way these species are protected. According to the text of the SPAW Protocol, countries that ratify the agreement "shall ensure total protection and recovery to the species of fauna listed in Annex II by prohibiting . . . the taking, possession or killing . . . or commercial trade in such species, their eggs, parts or products [and] . . . to the extent possible, the disturbance of such species."[37] According to SPAW, then, all species listed in Annex II are to be given complete protection from hunting. The approach to Annex III species is of a different character entirely. According to the text, participating countries "shall adopt appropriate measures to ensure the protection and recovery of the species of flora and fauna listed in Annex III and may regulate the use of such species in order to ensure and maintain their populations at the highest possible levels."[38] The difference between Annex II and Annex III, then, is stark: complete protection versus managed use, preservation versus conservation. If the species targeted by the Barrouallie whalers were listed in Annex III, a regulated hunt would be within the scope of the SPAW Protocol. They are not, so it is not. Annex II, the list of species to be given complete protection, contains the following simple entry with profound ramifications: "Order: CETACEA, All spp."[39]

This means that SPAW protects all cetacean species from "taking, possession or killing."[40] Any whaling in St. Vincent & the Grenadines— including both the blackfish operation in Barrouallie and humpback whaling from Bequia—is therefore at odds with this agreement. As yet, however, St. Vincent & the Grenadines has passed no laws to enforce this aspect of SPAW. In fact, when sea turtle hunting became illegal in early 2017, Vincentian prime minister Ralph Gonsalves assured his audience at a speech in the village of Calliaqua that he had no intention of also banning what he called "traditional whaling."[41]

The prime minister likely chose his words carefully. Speaking at the opening of a newly upgraded fisheries facility, Gonsalves would have known that ideas of subsistence and future food security were on the minds of his audience. The purpose of his speech, at least in part, was to introduce new legislation that would ban a traditional method of food production—turtle hunting. This new policy was likely inspired by St. Vincent & the Grenadines' commitments under SPAW, since all species of sea turtles that occur in the region are also listed in Annex II—the list that forbids any "taking, possession or killing."[42]

The prime minister's pivot from turtle hunting to whaling probably anticipated the concerns of his audience: *If he's banning turtling because of SPAW, and SPAW also forbids whaling, is he going to ban whaling next?* By referring to both the humpback operation in Bequia and the blackfish operation in Barrouallie as "traditional whaling," Gonsalves laid the foundation for a legal exception to compliance with the SPAW Protocol. Article 14 of the treaty enumerates "exceptions for traditional activities."[43] A signatory country is allowed to make exceptions to the enforcement of its treaty obligations in order "to meet traditional subsistence and cultural needs of its local populations."[44] The Vincentian government has not fulfilled its obligation to "inform the Organization accordingly" about its intention to allow a traditional exception for whaling. Still, the government's conceptualization of whaling as "traditional" likely explains the seeming contradiction between its ratification of SPAW and continued permission of whaling.

Herein lies the weakness of international treaties. Many, such as the Cartagena Convention, include very little in terms of enforcement authority. If a signatory country opts out of enforcing its own agreement to a treaty, there is often no mechanism for other participating countries to enforce compliance. The ideal of "international law," rather than resembling federal or state laws—which can be enforced—is often reduced to something along the lines of an "international handshake agreement," based on stated good-faith intentions to implement policies that enforce international treaties on a national scale. When, for reasons of competency, misstated intentions, changing political climates, or simply changing national priorities, a country signs a treaty but fails to implement national policy in harmony with its goals, the treaty's other signatory countries have little recourse to force the first country's hand. Coercion may be possible, especially in the form of international trade sanctions or public statements of disapproval, but actual enforcement is often elusive.

The blackfish operation based at Barrouallie remains both internationally and domestically unregulated in terms of formal, enforceable laws. This is not to say that that artisanal whaling at Barrouallie is anarchistic. Rather, it is bound by its own cultural traditions in the absence of formal law. These traditional regulations can sometimes be stricter, more effective, and more consistently enforced than official laws, owing to the deep and unquestioned adherence that their cultural rootedness can demand.

Traditional Ecological Knowledge

In 1949, the forester and author Aldo Leopold introduced a concept known as the "land ethic." Leopold's simple but profound proposition was that, when considering the community to which a person's ethical obligations apply, the nonhuman inhabitants of the planet should be included alongside the human ones. Specifically, the land ethic recognizes "that the individual is a member of a community of interdependent parts. His instincts prompt him to compete for his place in the community, but his ethics prompt him also to co-operate. . . . The land ethic simply enlarges the boundaries of the community to include soils, waters, plants, and animals, or collectively: the land."[45]

Since the late 1990s, the study and practice of environmental conservation has witnessed the development of something of a land ethic in reverse. Scientists and policymakers interested in conservation have expanded their purview to include, within their broader ecological strategies, not only "the soils, waters, plants, and animals," but the needs of indigenous human societies as well.[46] This inclusive focus is based upon a foundational concept in American cultural geography, dating back at least to the 1920s: the idea of a "cultural landscape" that includes not only the geology, watersheds, flora, and fauna that are normally considered constituents of the natural environment, but also the presence, history, culture, and agency of a place's human inhabitants.[47]

Local communities, of course, are not merely passive elements of the ecosystem, surviving or perishing as a result of the effective, or ineffective, conservation measures implemented on their land. Conservation efforts can be aided by allowing the knowledge compiled within these cultures to inform and instruct the actual conservation plans that are implemented. For example, conservation geographer Mark Bonta suggests "that we analyze and appreciate local conservation knowledge and practice before attempting to impose new beliefs and new techniques."[48] By following this advice, conservationists can recognize local people as colleagues, not merely as constituent parts of the landscape or, worse, as their adversaries in the struggle to protect a place, species, or resource. Cultures with long histories of natural resource use and subsistence have often had to adapt to a variety of changing environmental conditions throughout their histories. By recognizing the hard-won lessons that these cultural adaptations have produced, conservationists can gain access to a wealth of traditional knowledge about the local and regional ecologies—knowledge that can support and inform the empirical findings gained through more scientific methods.

Ecologists and anthropologists often describe this "traditional ecological knowledge" (TEK) as more holistic, systems-based, and multidimensional than the linear, empirical, reductionist sciences typically categorized as "Western." Historically, scholars have upheld this dichotomy between Western science and TEK, the latter of which is almost exclusively framed as residing within "tradition-based, non-industrial societies."[49] These "two parallel modes of acquiring knowledge" are generally represented as just that: parallel, like railroad tracks, and therefore not intersecting.[50]

In recent decades, though, the stated goal of much of the literature reflecting upon the importance of TEK has been to integrate these "two parallel modes" by recognizing the holders of TEK as valuable conservation partners and bringing them into the processes of planning, conducting research, and analyzing data. While the Western / TEK dichotomy may often be accurate, and its associated conservation prescriptions prudent in many cases, it is not true that TEK is always absent from the collective knowledge of societies that are more apt to be characterized as modern, Western, and industrial. Indeed, both TEK and Western science can exist within the same society, even within the same individual. A memorable illustration of this fact is a short, charmingly titled paper by physiologist-turned-geographer Jared Diamond, "This-Fellow Frog, Name Belong-Him Dakwo."[51] In his own words, Diamond learned "to be a better bird watcher" by integrating TEK with his scientific knowledge.

The Faroese and Vincentian whalers do the same thing, but in the reverse order as Diamond: both groups integrate scientific knowledge and technological development with the TEK that has long existed within their cultures.[52] For example, Samuel Hazelwood directs his sternman where to steer the boat based on a variety of environmental observations that his predecessors would have used going back to the origins of the Barrouallie operation and beyond. He watches the behavior of seabirds—whales will frequently pursue the same schools of fish for which the birds dive. He pays attention to ocean currents and winds, noting when access to certain reliable yet notoriously turbulent whaling areas might be possible. Yet when he finds a large piece of flotsam—a discarded net or a raft of Styrofoam—he marks its location on his GPS so he can return to it again and see whether it has attracted fish and maybe whales. Samuel's repertoire includes useful tools, both traditional and modern. Likewise, in the Faroe Islands, the skills of the grindaformenn are based upon generations of nautical experience, while decisions about sustainability and knowledge of pilot whale movement, behavior, and abundance are informed by scientific data gained through the use of satellite tracking and genetic analysis. These artisanal whaling operations show that TEK and science can—and should—work together toward common goals, especially toward the goal of conservation.

Often this traditional knowledge is not overtly recognizable as conservationist. Rather, profound principles can lie hidden within traditional practices—the ecological implications of which may remain obscured even to those who adhere to them most strictly. Geographer Stan Stevens writes of "patterns of resource use and resource management that reflect intimate knowledge of local geography and ecosystems."[53] He notes examples of ways that this knowledge aids the "conservation of biodiversity through such practices as protecting particular areas and species as sacred, developing land use regulations and customs that limit and disperse the impacts of subsistence resource use, and partitioning the use of particular territories between communities, groups, and households."[54]

Notice, from Stevens's examples, that the practices ingrained into the cultural traditions of an indigenous group may be represented as religious, customary, or organizational, but often are not seen as overtly ecological. Carl Sauer recognized the intrinsic and practical value of understanding these "wise and durable native systems of dealing with the land."[55] Sauer's observations, in the words of another geographer, Clark Monson, "helped spawn an intellectual renaissance among geographers and anthropologists in re-examining and revitalizing indigenous environmental knowledge."[56]

This "renaissance" has continued to produce studies that examine the value of ritual, cultural traditions, and TEK to policies of resource conservation. To discover these culturally embedded conservation strategies, an outside researcher must employ the methods of the ethnographer and the anthropologist in addition to becoming well versed in the science of the ecologist, the forester, the oceanographer, or the biologist.

In both the Faroe Islands and St. Vincent, TEK is a major factor in the conservation of cetaceans through the establishment of culturally embedded conservation strategies. The fact that many of the customs and traditions based on this knowledge, and related to the grindadráp, have been codified into written law in the Faroes should not be seen as detracting from the importance of older, less overt, unwritten traditions. In the absence of written laws related to whaling in St. Vincent, the regulation of the blackfish operation there remains wholly governed by TEK through the adherence to culturally embedded conservation strategies.

Let us now turn to the activities that occur in each location after the whalers have completed their work and the task of making and distributing food products commences. These actions resemble a kind of wake for the whales—a vigil kept to ensure that post-death behaviors are conducted correctly. It is at this time that many of the culturally embedded conservation strategies guiding whale and dolphin conservation become most apparent.

7

The Fragile Link

In 1967, the Canadian environmentalist and author Farley Mowat witnessed a spectacle in the small Newfoundland town where he had been living. After a particularly high tide, a large fin whale had become trapped in a nearby saltwater lagoon and attracted the attention of the town's residents. A few, like Mowat, saw the event as an opportunity to closely observe an animal that, though huge, remained mostly hidden from their daily, terrestrial experience. Others though, driven by curiosity, aggression, or perhaps just bored apathy, began to torment the whale. They shot it with rifles when it would surface to breathe, frightened it by approaching closely and quickly in a motorboat, and, at least once, lacerated its back with the boat's propeller. The whale eventually died from its injuries, which had become infected, and from starvation. Mowat had tried to rally attention both in Newfoundland and nationally across Canada, in the hopes of aiding the whale, but had only succeeded in alienating himself from the local people.

Mowat's account of these events, published five years later in his book *A Whale for the Killing,* framed the narrative within the broader context of humanity's estrangement from the natural world. He saw the senseless killing of the whale as evidence that humans viewed themselves as—and in some ways had become—above the rest of nature. More than a century earlier, in 1864, the scholar and statesman George Perkins Marsh concluded his broad survey of human-environmental interactions by calling for more data, more study, and more observations. Marsh stated at the end of *Man and Nature* that "every new fact, illustrative of the action and reaction between humanity and the material world around it, is another step toward the determination of the great question, whether man is of nature or above her."[1]

For Mowat, the answer was clear. The senseless death of the fin whale in Newfoundland at the hands of cavalier and ignorant humans served as further confirmation of the answer to this "great question," or at least of humanity's perception of the answer. Regardless of whether "man" actually is of nature, Mowat witnessed evidence that humans—at least as represented by those among whom he lived—certainly viewed themselves as being "above her." After the tragedy, Mowat sat on the beach and wept, "not just for the whale that died but because the fragile link between her race and mine was severed."[2]

The link between modern humans and the natural environment, including all its living and nonliving components, may indeed be strained—if not severed completely in some cultural contexts. This disconnect can be seen in the wantonness, wastefulness, and cruelty that drove people to torment Mowat's trapped whale in 1967 or to carry out commercial hunts for some whale populations well past the point of sustainability, but it does not necessarily follow that all takes of wild animals—or indeed, even all takes of whales—come from this polluted wellspring in humanity. To compare these examples of commercial whaling or senseless killings to what happens in St. Vincent and the Faroe Islands, especially considering the order, regulation, and purpose of these whaling operations, seems out of place. This is not intended to justify the Faroese and Vincentian whaling operations; rather, it is meant to distinguish them from other forms that might superficially appear similar. The purposefulness and lack of malice in Vincentian and Faroese whaling is all the more evident in light of the processes that occur in both places after the killing is complete.

Whale Tickets

At the end of the grindadráp, we are left with dozens or hundreds of whales lying dead in the shallow water or on the beach, and a comparable number of proud, exhausted whalers. Residents of the district villages who did not participate in or observe the killing have begun to arrive at the whaling bay with knives and large plastic tubs, eager to take home their share of meat and blubber. Faroese law prescribes a complex yet adaptable system of division by which the food produced through the grindadráp is distributed among those who participated in the killing and the residents of the village where the event took place.

As the Faroese population grows and communication networks and infrastructure improve, it becomes possible for large crowds of nonparticipants to assemble at the site of the grindadráp after receiving the grindaboð. They come for the food and the camaraderie. Regulations for the division of the whales vary by district, and in some districts there is much room for subjectivity in how the meat and blubber will be divided. Final authority in all post-grindadráp decisions rests with the sýslumaður, whose first step in making a fair division is to have all of the whales lined up and measured in the place where they will be processed. Adjacent to some whaling bays, such as Tórshavn, a large paved area serves as an ad hoc processing facility. In others, such as Øravík, whales are processed directly on the beach where they were driven. In either case, the first task is to haul all the whales, either by hand or by machine, into orderly rows in the designated assessment area.

Since at least 1584, stranded and hunted whales in the Faroe Islands have been assessed using a unit of measurement known as the *skinn*. According to the ethnographer Jóan Pauli Joensen, a skinn is made up of approximately thirty-eight kilograms of meat and thirty-four kilograms of blubber. Since the early nineteenth century, a measuring rod has been used to determine the skinn value of a whale. Prior to this time whales were entirely assessed visually. Today, visual inspection can shift the measured skinn value slightly, but the value is based first upon the measuring rod. Forty such rods exist in the Faroe Islands. Two are in the historical museum in Tórshavn and the rest are distributed throughout the whaling districts, still in contemporary use as tools in the grindadráp. The fact that these rods simultaneously fulfill their utilitarian purpose of measuring whales while also being enshrined as material relics of Faroese culture points to the common North Atlantic habit of drawing no fine line between past and present, legacy and utility, art and science. Why, in a place where the gray sea and foggy sky are often indistinguishable, where horizon lines are never guaranteed, would a culture develop sharp divisions anywhere at all?

In 1989, Faroese biologists Dorete Bloch and Martin Zachariassen examined all forty measuring rods and described them in an article.[3] Skinn values on the rods are marked logarithmically in Roman numerals, usually from I to XX, though there are examples of both shorter and longer rods. Six rods are marked at the half skinn as well. The nonlinear spacing takes into account the fact that there is more body mass toward a pilot whale's head than toward its tail. Although the rods are said to have all been made using the original rod as a standard, there does exist significant variation in the marked units from rod to rod. The effect of these variations is modulated, though, by the fact that the final designation of skinn value for each whale is based not solely on the measurements taken by the rod but also on such qualitative factors as size of the pod from which the whale was taken; physical condition of the whale, including factors such as stoutness, gravidity, lactation, and wounds; and time of year—winter whales have thicker layers of blubber than those taken in summer.

When the whales are lined up in the processing area, certain people appointed by the sýslumaður set to the task of measuring them. These *metingarfólk,* or measurement people, chosen for their trustworthiness and impartiality, fill an ancient role in Faroese society. Jóan Pauli Joensen cites the earliest reference to these folk and their job from a 1710 report, which stated that after the whales are killed, "then they are all assessed, small and large, by men who have been appointed by the sheriff, and each fish [is marked with] its number and value."[4] Don't be misled by the use of the term *fish.* In older literature, whales are often referred to as fish. Their taxonomic description as mammals seems not to have been widely accepted until

Two *metingarfólk,* or measurement people, recording the lengths of a pod of Atlantic white-sided dolphins driven ashore at Øravík

the mid-nineteenth century.[5] Today whales' "fishy" legacy lives on in terms like *finder's fish* and *blackfish*.

Whales driven ashore in the Faroe Islands are literally "marked" by the use of a *grindajarn* (pilot whale iron), a handheld tool specifically designed to peel away a small strip of the whale's black skin, exposing the white blubber beneath. Metingarfólk mark whales with both their "number," by making consecutive Arabic numerals on each whale's head, and their "value," by carving each whale's determined skinn value, using Roman numerals, into its pectoral fin.

As each whale is measured, the metingarfólk, or other helpers of the sýslumaður's choosing, open the body cavities and remove the entrails to allow the carcasses to cool, thus preventing the meat from spoiling. This is common practice in the butchery of any animal, whether raised domestically or taken from the wild, but, like all aspects of the grindadráp, the "dressing" of pilot whales takes place in the public sphere rather than behind the walls of an abattoir or at a remote hunting site. Faroese towns, with only one exception, are built around sea harbors. The exception is Vatnsoyrar, a village situated not on the sea but on the shore of the Faroes' largest lake. Harbors are often the most convenient site for processing pilot whales, but their centrality contributes to the vulnerability of the grindadráp to outside criticism.

When the metingarfólk have finished their work, they present the tally to the sýslumaður. He then retreats to his temporary office—normally a simple workspace with a desk in a nearby house or other building—to calculate the divisions. The purpose of the calculations is to ensure that the meat and blubber are divided fairly and that any special shares are properly assigned. Special shares include the finningarfiskur or "finder's fish," which goes to the person who first sighted the whale pod, as well as extra portions for the grindaformenn, the metingarfólk, local schools and nursing homes, and others whom the sýslumaður deems deserving. Aside from assigning the special shares, the sýslumaður's main task is to portion out the bulk of the whales among the grindadráp participants and the resi-

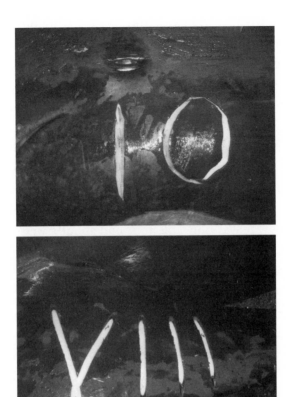

A pilot whale, showing markings on the head for identification *(above)*,
and on the fin for its value in *skinn (below)*

dents of the local village. If the take is large enough, some of the meat
and blubber will be shared with residents outside the village—usually
beginning with other villages in the district and reaching even further in the case of an exceptionally large grindadráp.

The most traditional and most egalitarian method of distribution
is called the *heimapartur,* or "home share." With this method, every
home in the village—or district, depending on the size of the take—
receives an equal share of whale meat and blubber. Strict adherence
to the heimapartur gives no preference to the actual participants in
the grindadráp and assumes they are from the village or district where

the killing took place; otherwise, those whose work directly resulted in the catch might actually be left out of the distribution. The exclusion of nonlocal grindadráp participants from the distribution is rare but does sometimes occur, leading predictably to feelings of disappointment and questions regarding the value of intervillage participation and aid.

One memorable event in Øravík, on Suðuroy, the southernmost of the Faroe Islands, taught me directly about how out-of-town participants can feel left out when the division follows a strict heimapartur. In 2009 a fellow geographer, Bill Rowe, came to visit me in the Faroes. He was only able to spend about a week there and I had told him not to get his hopes up about witnessing a grindadráp during his trip. But Bill was lucky. We happened to be on Suðuroy just in time for a *springardráp,* or dolphin slaughter. Atlantic white-sided dolphins are driven ashore and killed in the Faroe Islands in the same manner as pilot whales. As the killing came to an end we met two men who had come to participate in the springardráp from Fámjin, a village on the other side of the island from Øravík, only about fifteen minutes' drive over the intervening hills. They were soaked, their traditional Faroese sweaters hanging from the weight of the seawater. Both men had deeply receding hairlines and their bald heads were spattered with dolphin blood. They had worked hard driving, hauling, and killing dolphins. When Bill and I returned to the beach a few hours later for the sýslumaður's announcement, detailing how the meat and blubber would be divided, we found these men sitting in a pickup truck, smoking cigarettes and staring out the windshield at the sea. "It's going to be a heimapartur," one man told us. "We're from Fámjin, so we get nothing." Their disappointment, though, would be short-lived. Five days later another pod of dolphins was driven ashore in Suðuroy—this time onto the beach at Fámjin.

There is another form of distribution that stands as an exact opposite to the heimapartur. Occasionally a small pod of whales will be divided only among those who participated in the grindadráp. This type of distribution—called a *drápspartur*, or killers' share—is generally unpopular because it strays from the traditional, intended purpose of grindadráp: to provide food for the general population. In populous areas—especially Tórshavn but increasingly, Klaksvík and other growing towns—the entire village cannot adequately be served by the heimapartur. The shares would simply be too small to be of any real value to everyone. In Tórshavn, the sýslumaður maintains a roster of local residents and divides the proceeds from each grindadráp among those of a portion of the list, beginning where the last distribution ended. For example, if the distribution of the last grindadráp went to residents with surnames beginning with the letters A through J, the next distribution will begin with those whose names start with K.

At its most basic level, the division of the whales after a grindadráp is a process of human geography. The Faroe Islands are divided into a series of *grindadistrikter*, or pilot whaling districts. Ideally, if a grindadráp is large enough, its proceeds will be shared among everyone in the district. To facilitate the heimapartur, the inhabitants of each district are organized into groups of no more than fifty individuals each. In most districts, these groups are called *bátar*, "boats" (sing. *bátur*). This system of organization was based on the assumption that the crew of an eight-man rowing boat together with their families comprised twenty-five people.[6] A bátur then represented two boat crews and their families. Today, actual boats can be crewed by any number of people but the bátur as a unit of human organization remains set at fifty people. When the whales are divided, they are assigned to individual bátar; further division among individuals is left up to informal group leadership to decide.

While the sýslumaður is working on the division, nearly everyone else who was involved in the grindadráp leaves the scene. Most who were in the water go to bathe and change clothes. The sýslumaður usually needs several hours to prepare the division before he can announce the shares. This mass departure has led to accusations of abandonment by anti-whaling groups who portray the grindadráp as sport, with no practical purpose for the whales after the killing is complete.[7] One would give up the notion of abandonment quickly upon returning at the appointed time to see the crowds eagerly listening to the sýslumaður's traditional oral recitation of the shares. During this speech, the sýslumaður gives a representative of each bátur a slip of paper called a *grindaseðil* (pl. *grindaseðilin*), literally "pilot whale ticket," which lists the numbered whale or whales that one particular group of people will receive.

Grindaseðilin in hand, recipients descend to the beach or the otherwise designated processing area to claim their shares. Representatives from each bátur who will share the meat and blubber from an individual whale first must locate that whale by the number marked on its head. Once the whale has been located, the bátur members quickly and methodically cut the blubber and meat from the carcass. While the processing is usually left to those with more experience, children can often be seen helping, observing, and in some cases, practicing the skills needed to get meat and blubber from a whale.

The entire scene is one of communal cooperation and parallel labor. Small groups of people work independently to efficiently cut meat and blubber from their assigned whales. Blubber is stripped away in broad sheets the size of chessboards and the thickness of rooks. Meat is taken in large cuts at first—the long flank muscles removed whole—then smaller pieces as the carcass is stripped further.

To a foreign observer the activity on the beach can seem surreal, anachronistic: large groups of people appearing to scavenge food from beached whales. The open, public nature of the butchering process contributes to its character. Nothing is hidden. Everyone can see what everyone else takes. To achieve fairness, some interesting methods of sub-bátur division have arisen. Some groups divide themselves in two and each takes the meat and blubber from one side of

A man cutting blubber from a pilot whale in Klaksvík

their whale. Other groups pile meat and blubber on the ground—always blubber on the bottom, skin side down, to keep the edible parts clean—in distinct stacks, then ask one member to look away. "Whose is this?" someone asks the one who is looking away, and they respond with a group member's name. Whichever stack had been pointed to goes to the person who was named.

After the division, people carry home meat and blubber in plastic buckets, wheelbarrows, or pickup trucks to be processed at home. Nearly all of the blubber is salted and left to dry for three months or more. Some of the meat is frozen or cooked fresh and the rest is cut into long, thick strips to be dried in the wind. The Faroese dry whale meat at home, or at the home of a neighbor, in a structure called a *hjallur* (CHUT-ler). These little rooms, sometimes separate from the house and sometimes attached, are built with centimeter-wide openings between the slats of the walls so that wind can blow through and dry the meat. I visited one family in Toftir that had an ingenious

A man placing a cut of whale meat into a bucket to carry home

method of accessing their hjallur. A painting, mounted in their living room on hinges, opened to reveal a small, hidden drying room on the other side of the wall. If James Bond had been Faroese, this would have been his hjallur of choice.

When the whale meat is sufficiently dried, usually after three to five weeks, it is ready to be eaten, cured but uncooked. The most common, and most traditional, way to prepare a meal of whale meat in the Faroes is to slice the dried meat and salted blubber thin and to serve both together with boiled potatoes. This dish is called *grind og spik*—literally, and straightforwardly, "pilot whale meat and blubber." It is widely considered to be the national dish of the Faroe Islands.

A *hjallur,* or drying shed, in Vestmanna

The Liminal Coastline

Off the coast of St. Vincent, when the harpooner feels that the day's whaling is complete, he signals the sternman to return to port. The harpooner usually remains at his post—standing upright in the bow of the boat, a harpoon and cartridge loaded in the gun—until the boat is very near the dock. The purpose of this continued vigilance—common to many cultures that whale by harpoon—is to be ready if any whales or dolphins are sighted on the journey home. Melville, in *Moby-Dick,* noted that the lookout positions on the *Pequod* were "manned almost simultaneously with the vessel's leaving her port . . . and kept manned to the last . . . [in] the hope of capturing one whale more."[8] If it's been a productive day at sea, several pilot whale or orca carcasses may be seen be flanking the boat, their flukes tied to the gunwales with nylon rope. Or, instead, a half dozen or more smaller

Dolphins, dead and dying, piled at the author's feet inside the *Sea Hunter*

dolphins—spinners, spotteds, or Rissos—may lie in the boat, piled between the center and front seats. While the pilot whales or orca would be lanced before they were tied alongside, the smaller dolphins are rarely killed intentionally. Rather, they are left to die, either of blood loss or crushed under each other's weight.

Critics of the Faroese grindadráp have often claimed that the whales cry—or even scream—as they are being killed. Aside from the clicks and whistles used for echolocation, I've never noticed any sound coming from the whales during the multiple grindadráp I've witnessed in the Faroe Islands. But I have heard the awful calls of dying dolphins in the hold of Samuel's boat. It resembles something between a dog's bark and a child's croupy cough. It's troubling to hear.

On most whaling days, I carried a small hunting knife that I used to take tissue samples after we arrived back in Barrouallie. At sea, when the dolphins began bark-coughing, their lungs struggling against the sudden loss of buoyancy, I often wanted to do what I had seen done many times in the Faroe Islands but had never put into practice myself: place my hand behind the blowhole to measure the distance, cut once through blubber, once through muscle, and plunge the knife through the spinal cord, ending the dolphin's drawn-out suffering. I never did it. Instead, I would look at the horizon, watching the island approach, and try to think less empathetically and more economically. In St. Vincent, whales and dolphins delivered alive bring a higher wholesale price to the whalers. The common belief among the vendors is that the meat will be fresher, a misguided notion that actually results in a gamier taste and a longer period of suffering. Still, perceptions being firmly held, I knew that quickening the dolphins' deaths would have been seen as stealing from Samuel and his crew. I kept my knife, sheathed, in the waterproof bag.

As the boat approaches Barrouallie, the sternman cuts the engine, the harpooner unloads the gun, and the crowd gathered on the dock peers anxiously to see what was caught. A small group of women can usually be found among this crowd, standing at the base of the pier, sharpening knives on its concrete pylons, waiting to do business. These are the blackfish vendors. After we arrived, secured the boat, and hauled the day's catch up onto the pier or the beach, I always stood back to watch the negotiations that took place between the whalers and the vendors.

The whales and dolphins were carcasses now, having either died at my feet in transit or been killed on the dock upon arrival. I noticed that the vendors referred to the animals with names that were much more generic than those the whalers had used. This was only the first of many indications that a profound transformation was taking place on the pier. At sea, myriad local names are used for the various cetacean species that whaleboat crews may encounter. Vincentian whalers are experts at identifying a cetacean at great distances by the shape and color of the dorsal fin or the pattern of spray from the blowhole. The names they use, descriptors of living animals and of whole carcasses, constitute a "folk taxonomy" found only at sea.[9] For example, a Risso's dolphin is known by whalers as an Americano while it is alive, and it retains this distinction until its carcass is delivered to the shore and sold wholesale to the vendors. Every other species of cetacean taken by Vincentian whalers has an equally specific local name, used at sea.

On shore, by contrast, cetaceans from a dozen or more species are reduced to a simple list of three possible names: blackfish, papas, or whale. Upon transfer from the whalers to the vendors, the meat from the Risso's dolphin—formerly the Americano—is known in Creole simply as papas, the same name given to meat from a number of small cetacean species, each of which has its own name while alive. Likewise, pilot whales, orcas, and melon-headed whales are distinguished from one another while at sea—called *blackfish, whitefish,* and *black hard-knocks,* respectively—but the processed meat of all three is sold as blackfish. Coming to understand these name changes opened a window for me into the multifaceted transformation that occurs as cetaceans are brought ashore in St. Vincent to be turned into food.

Any animal that is captured, killed, and processed for human consumption necessarily undergoes multiple important transitions: from life to death, from animal to food product, from whole to divided, raw to cooked, unsanitary to clean, specific to general. To explain profound changes such as these and the spaces in which they occur, ethnographers and anthropologists have long used the concept of "liminality."[10] Liminality is the state of transition from one form or status to another. The term not only describes the state of being in between but also provides a temporary definition when neither the pre-transition state nor the post-transition state is tenable. Like Schrödinger's cat—being neither alive nor dead, and therefore equally alive and dead—people, animals, and objects in a state of liminality are no longer what they were before but not yet what they are becoming. Liminality itself has come to define them. Liminal spaces are where these transitions happen. They are places of change, of uncertainty and hybridity.[11]

The liminal space relevant to the transformation of whales and dolphins into food products in St. Vincent is the pier, solid and fixed to the earth yet suspended over water, or the beach, alternating between land and sea as each wave ebbs and flows. In these liminal spaces identities are broken down and reformed. Neither fully land nor fully sea, the beach is equally land and sea. At the same time, it is something wholly different. It is fitting to view the beach, then, as a space where liminality can occur. Even more, one might even come to expect liminality to be the dominant state in a space so rife with transition. Culturally, island populations have sometimes come to view their beaches as thresholds, spaces that must be crossed in order to transition from the outer to the inner.[12] This concept is enshrined in

Children assisting in and watching the butchering
of dolphins on the pier in Barrouallie

Vincentian law, which defines all beaches as public spaces—even those immediately adjacent to privately held resorts or other property. These liminal spaces, being both land and sea, belong both to everyone and to no one.

At sea, on the water, the harpooner is in control. His is the role of captain of the ship, and the sternman and centerman must obey his directions. On shore, on land, the vendor is in control. She gives orders to her helpers and decides what will become of the meat she processes. Indeed, she owns the catch, having purchased it in its entirety from the harpooner. In St. Vincent, whaling adheres to strict gender norms. These are largely traditional, very straightforward, and rarely questioned. Whalers are always men; vendors are almost always women. This is just the way it's always been. I've only met one male vendor. He reluctantly took over his mother's business when she died.

In the Faroe Islands, the grindadráp is similarly divided along gender lines, but with some interesting complexity. First, there was the traditional prohibition—no longer in force—against women viewing the killing process. Pregnant women were especially forbidden. As the flotilla drove the whales into the fjord, most women and certainly all expectant mothers would be ushered inside, doors shut behind them and shades drawn. Why should women be kept away from a grindadráp? Opinions differ as to the reason for this superstition. One Faroese research team said that women were seen as "marginal persons."[13] An American botanist, Elizabeth Taylor, who lived in the Faroes for a decade at the turn of the twentieth century, told how women were considered "unlucky creatures" when it came to the success of the grindadráp.[14] Kenneth Williamson, an English soldier stationed in the Faroes during the 1940s, preferred to think that this taboo "was originally designed for the woman's sake rather than any advantage which might accrue to the hunt."[15] The Faroese poet V. U. Hammershaimb—who, you'll recall, described Faroese whaling as "a dreadful sight for whomever stands on the shore peacefully watching"—also considered the prohibition on female observers.

He wondered if the rule might have arisen "because the men were embarrassed by those people seeing their behaviour in the whale kill."[16]

Today, no one is forbidden to watch the grindadráp. Men, women, and children stand by as the whales are driven ashore, hooked, hauled, and killed—actions conducted almost exclusively by men. The second factor complicating the strictness of gender roles in Faroese whaling, however, is the determined, persistent participation of a small minority of Faroese women. In a 2017 academic paper about the grindadráp, two female Faroese social scientists explained that "neither of us has ever taken active part in the slaughter itself, one reason for this being related to the gendered dimension of the practices involved, since few women are involved in the slaughter."[17] Of course, "few women" is not the same as "no women." One of the few *grindakvinnur*—pilot whale women—is named Liljan.[18]

Liljan recently moved back to the Faroe Islands from Denmark and now lives in Klaksvík. She told me that her father is the driving force behind her grindadráp participation—he answers the grindaboð, arriving at the beach with both Liljan and her younger brother. There he sends both of his children into the surf to hook whales and haul them ashore. Liljan told me that she doesn't have a license to participate in the actual killing process, so she leaves the mønustingari, or spinal lance, to others—for now. Liljan's father has encouraged her to complete the training process and to obtain, in her words, "a license to kill," something Liljan says she wants to do. If she follows through on her father's suggestion, she will become one of very few women in the Faroe Islands licensed to kill pilot whales; women make up a little more than 48 percent of the Faroese population but account for only about 2 percent of all licensed "killers."

The licensure requirement was instituted in 2015. Certainly women occasionally killed pilot whales in the Faroe Islands before then. The anthropologist Jonathan Wylie recounts an 1896 grindadráp in Tórshavn that was recorded in a local newspaper. The story ended with the observation that "the women of Nólsoy also took part in the *dráp*—because too few of the menfolk were at home—and it seemed to most people that they were just as strong and zealous as other *grindamenn*."[19] Another grindadráp, this one in 1938 at Hvalba, on Suðuroy, relied even more on women for its success. The men of the village, answering the grindaboð, had gone to help with a grindadráp over the mountain, in another fjord, at Trongis-vágur. While they were away, a second pod of whales was sighted near Hvalba itself. Not willing to let this pod escape, the women of Hvalba—along with the village priest and a visiting grindaformann from Vágur—took to the remaining boats and conducted the drive and slaughter themselves.[20] Imagine the surprise, perhaps mingled with embarrassment, the men of Hvalba would have felt. At Trongis-vágur they had helped drive in a pod consisting of fewer than 200 whales. Afterward, the men returned home, each bearing a small portion of meat and blubber, to find their wives and daughters proudly exhausted, soaked with seawater and blood. The women had taken nearly 900 whales—to this day, the fifth-largest grindadráp in Faroese history.

At Liljan's first grindadráp after she gets her license, a team of men—maybe including her own father and brother—will hold taut the stout rope at the end of the blástrarongul while Liljan wades through bloodied water toward a beached but living pilot whale. She'll place her hand behind the blowhole to measure the distance, press the point of the mønustingari's double-edged blade against the whale's jet-black skin, take a breath, and thrust the lance downward into the whale. She'll be ready for the spasm and the eruption of blood—the training required for her license will have prepared her for it. After the whale's first violent thrashing, Liljan will reaffirm her grip on the lance, rock the tool back and forth to sever the spinal cord, and withdraw it from the now-dead whale. The event will be momentous—a contribution to the changing history of the grindadráp—but there will be more work to do. It's typical at a grindadráp that every licensed killer on hand is needed, their quick actions necessary to make the whales' suffering as short as possible. After quietly making her contribution to the new history of whaling in the Faroe Islands, Liljan will simply move on to the next whale on the beach, place her hand behind the blowhole, and move the needle slightly further in the direction of equality.

St. Vincent's whaling operation hasn't yet had its Liljan. Until she arrives, men will provide and women will prepare. This preparation—the butchering of the whale and dolphin carcasses—takes place at temporary processing facilities set up on the beach. They consist of three stations: the dividing station, where large pieces of meat and blubber are cut, roughly, from the carcasses; the meat station, where large pieces of meat are cut into thin sheets for drying; and the blubber station, where sheets of blubber and skin are cut into small cubes to be cooked. All of the work is done with cutlasses and smaller, handheld knives.

After the workers have cut the meat and blubber down to manageable sizes, they process these materials for sale and consumption. The meat is sometimes sold "fresh," meaning raw, or *scalled* (a Creole word derived from the English *scalded*), meaning steamed. But by far the most common method of preparation in St. Vincent, just as in

Vendors and their assistants processing
dolphins on the beach in Barrouallie

the Faroe Islands, is drying. Vendors and their assistants dry cetacean meat on racks made of bamboo and wood that are set up near the beach. They hang the meat directly on the horizontal bamboo poles at a height of about a meter and a half above the ground, out of reach to Barrouallie's many stray dogs. After drying for several days, during which it is turned at least once each day, the meat is ready to be divided into portions and packaged for sale. The vendor cuts the large sheets of dried meat into small strips and bundles these strips together, either tying the bundles with strings made from banana leaf fiber or simply placing the bundles, untied, in plastic bags. I examined several of these bundles and found that the weights ranged widely. Despite the variation in weight, at the Kingstown market the bundles all cost the same price—EC$2.50 (about US$1.00) each. Prices vary in the villages.

Prislet Francis, an employee of the Barrouallie Fisheries Cooperative, bundling dried blackfish meat with banana fibers

While the meat is being dried, the vendor and her assistants will usually prepare the blubber for sale and consumption. During the processing stage, the blubber was cut into small cubes with the skin left on. These cubes of blubber are then placed into a metal pot or an old oil drum and heated over a fire. A small amount of salt is added to the pot. As the blubber heats, it releases oil, which boils. The blubber is fried in its own oil. Sometimes the cook will use a halved calabash—the gourdlike fruit of the *Crescentia cujete* tree—to scoop bowlfuls of the oil out of the pot, with the oil used to further stoke the fire.[21] The blubber provides both the fuel and the fat for its own cooking. After several minutes, the blubber cubes take on a brownish color and begin to float in the oil. This indicates that the crisps are done. Consumers buy crisps in plastic bags, sometimes drained and sometimes still soaking in oil.

If you don't live in Barrouallie, there are two ways to buy cetacean meat and blubber in St. Vincent: you can visit one of the permanent market stalls in Kingstown or you can buy from a mobile vendor. Mobile vendors are like the Vincentian equivalent of the American ice cream truck. They travel from village to village, usually on a regular weekly schedule, and sell meat and blubber either directly from their vehicles or from temporary roadside booths. When a vendor arrives in a small Vincentian town, instead of playing "Turkey in the Straw" through tinny, truck-mounted speakers like our ice cream vendor, she blows a conch shell to announce her presence. The ancient, amphoric sound of the conch summons potential buyers to her makeshift stand. I met one vendor who carried along two conch shells; each played a distinct note. One was for when she had fish to sell; the other called her blackfish customers. Blackfish vendors know that their best customers are to be found in "the country," as the windward, east coast of St. Vincent is called. Despite its distance from the whaling center at Barrouallie, the country has some of the island's most dedicated connoisseurs of blackfish.

There is no true "blackfish season" in St. Vincent, though the whalers do take a holiday in late December and early January to celebrate Christmas and the New Year. The boat owners often use this time to upgrade and repair the equipment and the vessel. This holiday season is the only time, according to my analysis of the records going back to 2007, when total takes tend to decrease. In an interview with a local radio station, Samuel Hazelwood stated that the season runs "from January to December," echoing the words of Alston Becket Cyrus, a local calypsonian, who sang not only of his love for—and cultural identification with—traditional Vincentian foods including "blackfish crisps" but also that "whaling time is anytime and anytime is whaling time."[22]

The Ordeal of the Blubber

I have often been asked to describe what whale blubber tastes like: a difficult task because it is so unlike any other food. Of course, bacon comes to mind—the fattiness and the oil. Bacon has often been used as an analogue by travelers to describe blubber to their readers. The geographer John Adams referred to Vincentian blackfish crisps as "island bacon," citing what may have been a local term at the time.[23] But the flavor of pork has nothing to do with the sea, an essential component of the complex taste of blubber. Also, bacon is marbleized to an extent rarely found in blubber, which is almost completely white, the fat totally separated from muscle tissue.

The best way that I have found to describe the flavor and texture of whale blubber is this. Imagine you put on a pair of knee-high rubber boots and stomp on a pile of fish that had been pulled from the sea and left in the sun for three days or so. You step on the fish; you twist to grind your feet into them; you dance. The pile is deep. Think of making wine the old-fashioned way, except instead of stomping grapes you stomp fish. You would never want to drink a glass of the juice that is pressed out from this exercise. To get an idea of what it's like to eat blubber, both the flavor and the texture, after the fish have been thoroughly pulverized, stop stomping . . . and eat your boots.

The taste of lean whale meat, on the other hand, is more influenced by its method of preparation than is blubber. A dark, smooth-grained red meat, it resembles a lean beef filet. The most basic flavor of whale is like beef if it had been cooked with fish sauce. Toothed whales are mammals, but they feed almost exclusively on fish and squid. The flavor of their food becomes incorporated into the flavor of their own meat. You are indeed what you eat. The Vincentian method of drying whale meat produces a food that looks like American beef jerky or South African biltong—thin, irregular strips of meat cut along the grain. When the Faroese dry whale meat they use much thicker cuts, nearly the length and diameter of your arm, yielding a finished product that more resembles a thick, hardened column of pâté, or perhaps the largest and darkest blood pudding you've ever seen.

When whale meat is cooked, rather than dried, it takes on the flavors of the other ingredients. In the Faroes, whale meat is often roasted with onions and served with whale gravy and boiled potatoes. It can replace beef in almost any recipe but has a tendency to get dry. The Vincentians slice whale meat thin and add it to a mixture of cabbage, carrots, onions, spices, and tropical fruits for a kind of "whale slaw," served over roasted breadfruit, that seems appropriate to eat with chopsticks. The Japanese eat whale sashimi—raw and cold—or fried in tempura batter. At the Hairoun Bagga Fish Fest—the Friday night community celebrations that used to be held in Barrouallie—tempura-style blackfish, prepared by a Japanese development volunteer, was a crowd favorite. During one field season in the Faroe Islands, I brought along a jar of Tony Chachere's Original Creole Seasoning that I had picked up in Louisiana. Printed boldly on the jar was the phrase, "Great on Everything." While I'm sure that Mr. Chachere never intended it, I can confirm that his slogan holds true, even with regard to whale meat.

Blubber is sometimes used as a test of loyalty, attitude, outlook, or convictions. In multiple field sites, I've been offered a bite or two of whale blubber as a way of gauging my biases and of determining my reason for approaching a person with questions about whaling. In Newfoundland, where whales are no longer hunted, I was given seal. Usually when I would approach someone involved in the whaling operation—a whaler, a processor, or sometimes just a consumer—to ask a few questions, the potential interviewee would be somewhat standoffish until offering me a piece of blubber: "Here, eat this first." The assumption was that undercover anti-whaling activists, which whaling researchers are occasionally suspected of being, would not consume whale blubber, but that a neutral academic researcher might. After I passed the test, the tenor of the conversation would change, for I was now "one of them," having shared a symbolic, communal meal. Blubber, by its status as a unique and—to those not raised on it—unappetizing food product, takes on a new meaning, transcending that of ordinary food, to become a symbol of solidarity with those of the whaling community.

I have empirical evidence from the Faroe Islands to support this observation of solidarity. Faroese citizens are given the choice of whether to carry a red Danish or green Faroese passport. The Danish passport makes international travel easier owing to its higher level of recognizability, especially outside of the Nordic countries. Which would you rather slide under the window at some far-flung customs desk: a red European Union passport or a green one with the odd-looking word *Føroyar* emblazoned on the cover? Imagine the skeptical look an immigration official at St. Vincent's new Argyle International Airport would give you: *Faroe? Is that in Egypt?*

Arguably, only someone who prioritizes the expression of Faroese nationality over the convenience of traveling on a familiar passport would opt to carry a green passport. Green Faroese passports can thus be seen as a statement of national identity and, based on a sample that I surveyed, are carried by about a quarter of the population. The grindadráp has also been held up as a symbol of Faroese national identity and to a large degree remains in this role today.[24] It's interesting to examine how these two symbols coexist. Comparing the consumption habits of people who hold green passports with those of their red-passport-holding counterparts, we see that the two groups eat whale meat at rates that are statistically similar. Blubber, however, is a different story. Significantly more of the green passport holders reported eating whale blubber, compared with the red passport holders. It appears that those who identify more strongly with their Faroese nationality, as their choice of passport attests, also express their nationalism through their consumption of the grindadráp's most iconic food product.[25]

The first time I was confronted with blubber as a statement of solidarity was aboard a family's boat tied up in the harbor of Nólsoy in the Faroe Islands in 2005. I wanted to talk with several of the family members about whaling. Soon after I came aboard and explained my intentions, the son—about my age—disappeared into boat's cabin briefly, only to return with a slab of blubber about the size of a loaf of bread. He pulled a grindaknívur from his belt and cut me a bigger-than-bite-sized portion. I stood on the deck of the boat, watching oil trickle down the knife blade as he extended the point toward my face and said, using the Faroese term for whale blubber, "Here, try some *spik*." Conversation halted and all eyes were on me. What else could I do? I plucked the morsel from his knife tip and ripped a piece away with my teeth. I had never tried blubber before and was unprepared for its consistency. I chewed, but the portion in my mouth remained whole. The family members resumed talking as I ground the blubber between my molars, trying to break it into smaller pieces. No luck. Oil was extruded, coating the inside of my mouth, but I couldn't break the blubber down. I started to panic: *I can't swallow this and I can't chew it up!* Fortunately, we were on a boat, floating on the water. I waited until I thought no one was looking, turned, and spat the blubber into the harbor. "He spit it out!" I heard the mother cry in English. "Give him another piece!" Which is exactly what the son did, this time bigger than the first. Slightly more prepared the second time, I gave up on chewing, ripped a smaller bite, and swallowed it whole. Satisfied that I was not fundamentally opposed to blubber-eating, the family opened up to me about whaling. The son told me how he had been participating in the grindadráp since his teens and how he felt that the practice rooted him to his heritage, his ethnicity, his "Vikingness." During our conversation, I glanced inside the boat's cabin to notice that the family's young daughter, a girl of about seven, had slipped her brother's knife from his belt and was cutting her own piece of blubber to snack on. Hers was at least twice the size of the first one I had been given. She looked very happy.

A nearly identical scenario played out four years later in the village of Soufrière, St. Lucia.[26] I was walking around the village with Methodius Paul, a marine ranger for the Soufrière Marine Management Area. Methodius and I were talking about Caribbean whaling when we happened to pass a woman standing on the sidewalk and tending to two large pots atop charcoal fires. In one, large green leaves—the Caribbean delicacy, callaloo—were being cooked down. In the other I could see the sheen of oil swirling in the yellowed water and large chunks of meat stewing. "That's blackfish," the woman told us. Methodius emptied the cup from which he'd been drinking water and took a large serving of whale meat, blubber, and the broth in which it was cooking. Next, the woman plunged a two-pronged fork into the oily water, withdrew an irregularly shaped piece of blubber, the whale's glossy black skin still attached, and extended it to me. I held the scalding piece of fat gingerly between my fingers. Both the ranger and the woman stared at me. By now I knew the routine. I popped the blubber into my mouth, chewed it a few times—it was more pliable than its Faroese counterpart, since it had been cooked, but it was still quite tough—and swallowed it whole. The woman smiled. Methodius resumed telling me about St. Lucian whaling traditions.

I had come to St. Lucia to investigate the possibility of incorporating the few ports on that island from which fishermen occasionally hunt pilot whales into my broader Caribbean whaling study. This was not to be, it turned out, for in response to my research proposal to the St. Lucia Department of Fisheries, I received a letter from Rufus George, the chief fisheries officer, kindly informing me on beautifully embellished letterhead that my project was not welcome there. In his words, the proposed work would "not provide added benefits to the cetacean fishery in Saint Lucia."[27] I've always wondered whether he thought I might have had some kind of anti-whaling agenda and that it was safer to simply deny my request to conduct research than to allow it and take the risk. I wish Mr. George had been there to see me eat the blubber.

While eating whale blubber must sound foreign—or even repulsive—to many readers, this revulsion is, of course, not universal. In the 2000 comedy film *Me, Myself & Irene,* Jim Carrey's character tests the devotion of his wife by asking her whether she would stay with him if they had to move to the Arctic and eat whale blubber for the rest of their lives. Yes, replies his wife, she would stay, but she adds that she hopes it never happens. Had the wife of Carrey's character been Faroese or Vincentian, the request might have sounded strange, perhaps even comical. What if you had to eat dark chocolate, 70 percent cacao, from an artisanal single-origin Belgian chocolatier every day? Would you stay with me then? Yes, dear, but only because I love you.

8

Culturally Embedded Conservation Strategies

One rainy Sunday morning in Tórshavn I met up with a German couple with whom I'd become friends, Hannes Lesch and Eleonora Flach, with the plan to survey some beaches. We were halfway through a small project, investigating the claim that the beaches approved by the government to be used for whaling are smoother and less steep than other beaches in the Faroes. (Our conclusion: they aren't.) Hannes and Eleonora brought along their friend Birgit Johannessen, a young Faroese woman who was living in Germany but had come home for a visit. We loaded the waders, dry suits, ranging poles, and survey instruments into Hannes's car. I slipped my preprinted spreadsheets for recording measurements into plastic bags to try to delay their inevitable saturation. Eleonora had packed a delicious vegan lunch for the entire group. How did she find this food in the Faroes? The Faroese have long made the argument to anti-whaling activists that their archipelago is not sufficiently productive, agriculturally speaking, to warrant their giving up the grindadráp. Though it was obvious that Eleonora's garbanzo beans, tempeh, and tahini were not locally produced, it did speak to the changing of the times that they were found in the Faroe Islands at all. It also tended to undermine the so-called necessity argument for Faroese whaling.

With Hannes at the wheel, we entered the subsea tunnel to the island of Vágar. Although I had been through this tunnel many times before, it never gets old: driving under the ocean from one island to another. Faroese engineers are master tunnel-builders. There is talk of connecting Sandoy to Tórshavn, which would be the longest undersea tunnel in the Faroes yet—at least until Suðuroy is connected. People debate whether the Sandoy tunnel would aid in that island's inclusion into the Faroese transportation system or if it would simply speed up the already-in-progress abandonment of Sandoy.

Faroese tunnels are diverse. Some pass under water, others through mountains. One is said to be haunted; Matthew Workman, director of *The Faroe Islands Podcast,* recorded what sounds like the moan of a ghost while standing in that tunnel with his audio equipment. Tunnels that pass under the sea are wide, ventilated by ducts and fans, and well lit. The color of the lights changes from green to blue to indicate the shift from underground to underwater. Older tunnels that pass through mountains but not underwater are smaller, darker, and often one lane. Can you picture driving in an unlit tunnel under a thousand feet of basalt, with only minimal clearance between the sides of your vehicle and the rock walls to your right and left? If you aren't feeling claustrophobic yet, now imagine a set of headlights appearing in front of you. You share the same lane as this interloper. The small pullouts are spaced randomly along the sides of the road inside the tunnels. *Will they pull over, or should I? Will I even come to one before we meet? How would the rescue crews deal with a head-on collision in a tunnel?* These are the thoughts that come to mind while driving in the tunnels of the Faroe Islands.

We emerged, safe and relieved, on the island of Vágar. We looked back at Streymoy across the water; there is barely any indication of a route between the two islands, with the road simply disappearing into a hillside near the coast. On Vágar, there were four villages with beaches that we'd come to measure: Miðvágur, Bøur, Sandavágur, and Sørvágur. From 1709 until the present, the beach at Miðvágur has seen more whales driven ashore and killed than any other place in the Faroe Islands. This is due to some combination of geography and luck.

Bøur is no whaler's favorite beach for whaling—it's rocky—but it was there that a Swiss photographer named Marco Paoluzzo took a series of extraordinary photographs of a grindadráp that soon, without Marco's permission, were publicized by anti-whaling protesters in a series of spam emails. Maybe you've seen one in your inbox. The messages vary to some degree, but all share the common elements of a headline in bad English declaring something along the lines of "Denmark is a big shame" and several paragraphs of misinformation, usually discussing "Denmark" hunting the endangered "Calderon dolphin" interspersed with Marco's stunning photographs. Once or twice a year, a colleague, student, friend, or family member forwards an email to me asking something like, *Isn't this what you research? It sounds horrible! Please clarify!* My responses to these pleas, efforts to simply correct some misinformation, were some of the initial seeds of this book.

Sandavágur is unremarkable as a whaling beach, except for the fact that it stands in as something of an understudy to Miðvágur. If ocean currents are making it difficult to drive a pod of whales into Miðvágur, Sandavágur offers an alternative. The two beaches sit within the same bifurcated inlet, which looks, on the map, something like a pilot whale's fluke—Miðvágur at the end of the left fork and Sandavágur at the end of the right. It's apparently easier to get a pod of driven whales to make a left turn in this inlet than a right, so Miðvágur has historically been the first choice.

Whaling is not allowed at Sørvágur. Local residents know that the seafloor extends from the beach broad and flat for several hundred meters before dropping off precipitously. This landform, called a *marbakki* (mar-BA-chee) in Faroese, is thought to offer a reflecting surface for the whales' echolocation signals.[1] Their clicks and whistles bounce back, alerting the pod that land is approaching. Beaches with marbakki are not good for whaling. On better beaches, the absence of a marbakki means that the echolocation signals have nothing to bounce back from. To a whale, according to the theory, the lack of a return signal indicates open ocean ahead—not the reality of a gradually shallowing beach.

In older literature about the grindadráp, authors had advanced the belief that "there is a clear correlation between the effective whaling bay sites and seabed topography" and specifically that "a good whale bay should have a sandy shoreline inclining evenly upwards."[2] To investigate this supposed relationship between coastal geography and whaling potential, we needed to measure the smoothness and steepness of the beaches, then run a statistical analysis on the data alongside the whaling records to see if any correlation existed. Since the underwater part of a beach is what matters most to whaling, we had to wade out as deep as possible to take the measurements. I timed our surveying excursions to coincide with low tide. This allowed us to wade farther from shore than if we had arrived at high tide. It also meant that we got to do more of our surveying on dry land. We did try to reach as far out to sea as we could, though, so for this purpose we brought chest waders—the type that fly fishermen wear—and dry suits. Both leaked, by the way.

Hannes and I took turns at either end of the survey line. One of us would wade into progressively deeper water, holding a ranging pole still so that the other, on shore, could take a measurement with the clinometer. Eleonora recorded the slight changes in angle. When it was my turn to go deep I would take cautious steps, watching small flatfish scurry away from my footfalls through the clear water. We went as far out as we could without letting our heads go under; the edge of the marbakki was always our farthest limit.

After surveying Sørvágur we continued to Bøur. After Bøur we were done for the day, so we decide to drive through the mountain tunnel to Gásadalur. This tunnel, built in 2004, links this formerly remote village to Bøur by road. Before its construction, Gásadalur residents relied on a steep hiking trail as their main connection to Bøur, and thence to the rest of the Faroes. So remote was Gásadalur in its pre-tunnel years that there was once a Faroese reality television show that contrasted the life of a woman living there—making butter from her own cows, spinning wool from her own sheep—with another woman living a modern life in Tórshavn. I never saw the program, but apparently the differences were striking.

Gásadalur has one of my favorite landscape features in the world: a waterfall that drops directly into the ocean. This waterfall has an individual name, just like every other Faroese waterfall. It is called Múlafossur. Nearly every geographical feature in the Faroe Islands, no matter how small, has its own name. I've seen a rock about the size of a microwave oven with a blue-and-white plastic nameplate duly bolted to its face. The rock has a name, and that name needed to be made known. Jimmy Buffett, the musician so known for incorporating his world travels into song lyrics that the Department of Geography and Anthropology at Louisiana State University once offered a course titled "The Geography of Jimmy Buffett," mentioned his own fascination with waterfalls that fall directly into the sea in his book *A Pirate Looks at Fifty*.[3] Jimmy, if you haven't been to Gásadalur already—and I wouldn't be surprised if you have—I'd suggest you check out Múlafossur sometime. Maybe even write a song about it.

As we were exploring the area near the top of the waterfall my phone rang. In the Faroes I always carry a local cell phone, mainly so my friends and colleagues can alert me to a grindaboð. Whenever I hear the ring, I immediately think that it's time to rush off to a grindadráp. This time, though, there were no whales, just my friend David—the one who thinks stopping to chat in traffic is "redneckish"—laughing so hard that he was barely able to speak English. "You're on the beach at Sørvágur at church time!" David finally managed to get out. "They caught you on the beach at church time! No one cares—well, maybe some old people—but it's a tradition. People don't work at church time. Well, they do, but they work inside, where the old people can't see them." I tried to understand what David was talking

Múlafossur, below the village of Gásadalur

about. Was it taboo to work on Sunday—or, at least, to work out-doors on Sunday? And how did David, sitting in his living room in Tórshavn, know what we were doing?

When Hannes, Eleonora, Birgit, and I arrived back in the capital later that evening, I opened my laptop and found an email from David. It contained a link to a website called Vagaportal. *Portal* means "website" and *Vaga* is the combinatory form of the name of the island where we had been surveying, Vágar. It's basically an online tabloid. There aren't many celebrities in the Faroe Islands, so even ordinary people are the targets of tabloids. There, on the opening screen, was a grainy photo of the four of us standing on the beach with our survey equipment: Hannes and I in our waders, everyone wearing rain jackets. Birgit held a clipboard and glanced over her shoulder in the direction of the photographer, who must have been using a telephoto lens. A series of pictures followed—testament to the fact that any scene can look dubious when photographed from a sufficient distance. Above the photo spread was the headline "Ókend fólk á Sørvágs sandi í kirkjutíð," foreigners on Sørvágur's beach at church time. We'd been caught.

The article, broken into paragraphs interspersed between several similarly vague photos of us working, made a number of conjectures about what business we might have been up to. Hypotheses ranged from the benign (a possible expansion of the runway at the airport) to the sinister (a CIA-driven plot to spy on—and possibly assassinate!—a certain Faroese government official who resides in Sørvágur). I called the tabloid's editor to try to clear up the story—and he did publish a follow-up piece in which he explained my research, incorrectly, as having something to do with measuring the temperature and flow of the Gulf Stream—but the joke had already been played. I was a foreigner on the beach at church time and would hear about it for the rest of my season in the Faroes. From that day forward, I took Sundays off: a tradition, apparently, kept by all Faroese people, except, of course, photographers and tabloid journalists.

Culture and Morphology

Eventually we were able to measure a sufficient sample of Faroese beaches to run a statistical analysis. The result, which I published as an article titled "Coastal Geomorphology and Culture in the Spatiality of Whaling in the Faroe Islands," showed no correlation between the measurements of slope and steepness of a beach, on the one hand, and, on the other, that beach's history as a site for grindadráp.[4] Of course, a lack of correlation does not equate to a lack of success. Science doesn't start out seeking a particular outcome. The success of the study was that it produced reliable data that addressed the long-held belief regarding the connection between whaling and physical geography. While it may be the case that, subjectively, whalers prefer to conduct grindadráp on sandy shorelines that incline evenly upward, as opposed to steep, rocky beaches—who wouldn't?—statistically there is no correlation between a beach's smoothness and slope and either the likelihood of that beach being approved for whaling or its historical whaling success. Instead, the marbakki is probably the most important physical determinant of whether a beach will be approved for whaling or not. None of the approved beaches we surveyed had a marbakki. Of the eleven non-approved beaches that we surveyed, seven did.

As the title of the article hints, in addition to the beach's physical characteristics, culture plays a role in the selection and approval of whaling beaches. But what are these approved beaches all about in the first place? Throughout the Faroe Islands, twenty-four bays have been designated as *hvalvágir*, or whaling bays (sing. *hvalvág*). One of these, Gøta, has two separate beaches, each of which can be used for the grindadráp, which raises the total number of approved whaling beaches to twenty-five.[5] The Faroese government forbids whaling on non-approved beaches and confiscates any whale carcasses obtained through very rare instances of flouting this law. The list of approved hvalvágir was seeded in 1832 with the names of the most productive whaling beaches in use at that time. These original productive beaches were as much a result of Faroese culture and history as they were dependent on beach morphology. To illustrate the importance of these human factors to the approval of hvalvágir, let's consider three Faroese villages: Tjørnuvík, Vestmanna, and Klaksvík.

Tjørnuvík was the site of the grindadráp that my students witnessed in 2012. It is also one of the most recent permanent additions to the list of hvalvágir. Before Tjørnuvík's listing, older villagers remembered a single whale having been driven ashore in 1934 and the occasional pod of whales stranding on the beach without being driven.[6] These memories were enough to convince many that grindadráp could be practical there. After a petition led by local residents, the Faroese government added Tjørnuvík to the approval list at the beginning of 2007. That year, 143 whales were killed on Tjørnuvík's beach.

In Klaksvík, the Faroe Islands' second-largest village after Tórshavn, shoreline development has grown to the point that grindadráp are very difficult to conduct there. This large village maintains its status as a hvalvág, though, owing mainly to the influence of its relatively large and wealthy population. I once received a grindaboð while in Tórshavn, telling me that whales were being driven into Klaksvík. Unable to find a ride, I resorted to taking the slow public bus, nearly certain that I would miss the action.

When I arrived in Klaksvík, though, the boats and whales were still circling the fragmented bay. It was clear that the grindaformann was having a hard time keeping the whales in front of the flotilla. I stood on shore, one foot on the slippery, algae-covered concrete of a boat ramp and the other on the mud and gravel of a small section of beach. Shore-based whalers ran from spot to spot—hooks, ropes, and whaling knives in hand—unsure of where the beaching would take place. Finally, a dorsal fin rose close to shore, and a man with a hook leapt from a rock into waist-deep water and secured the whale. A small team tugged at the rope until the whale was pinned against a rock, and one man made the cut with his grindaknívur. Almost simultaneously two other whales from the pod were dragged ashore some fifty meters away. These would be the only three caught from the pod, which turned out not to be pilot whales after all but Risso's dolphins—the same species I had first seen harpooned off St. Vincent.

Faroese law does not permit the killing of Risso's dolphins, so the sýslumaður immediately stopped the grindadráp. According to a government notice issued soon after the aborted killing, the Risso's dolphin is "an unfamiliar species in Faroese waters. A large group was driven into the bay of Klaksvík on 16 September 2009. After three animals had stranded and it was confirmed that this was not a familiar species, the local authorities stopped the drive and ordered the rest of the group to be driven out again."[7] The government confiscated the carcasses of the three dolphins that had already been killed for necropsies and other laboratory analyses. The whalers claimed to have mistaken the pod for pilot whales, or possibly another permitted species, which is believable considering the rarity of Risso's dolphins in Faroese waters. Still, because of the mistaken identity, all that work,

Men scrambling along Klaksvík's rocky shore
during an attempted *grindadráp*

made doubly difficult by the unforgiving Klaksvík coastline, along
with the deaths of three dolphins, was for nothing.

The village of Klaksvík sits upon an isthmus between two bays:
one also called Klaksvík that fronts the village, and the back bay,
called Borðoyarvík. According to Ólavur Sjúrðarberg, president of the
Grindamannafelagið, or Faroese Pilot Whalers' Association, Klaksvík
will probably be the next Faroese bay to lose its approval status, with
Borðoyarvík being listed in its place. In early 2017, Borðoyarvík was
approved—provisionally—as a hvalvág. If it proves successful as a site
for grindadráp, it will likely be added permanently to the list of
approved bays and Klaksvík will be removed. Such a trade-off seems

to be the only way that the influential residents of Klaksvík would countenance their bay being removed from the list, although with its marbakki and muddy bottom conditions, Borðoyarvík is not likely to be as successful a whaling bay as Klaksvík has been.

Bays can also be added to the list if they are made suitable for whaling through landscape-altering engineering projects. Most of these projects involve only what is known as "beach nourishment," or the mechanical transport of sand from the seabed to the beach. The largest and costliest alteration to the landscape in the name of the grindadráp, though, occurred in the village of Vestmanna in 1992. When the former whaling beach there was developed into a harbor and fish-processing facility, the residents did not want to give up their status as a hvalvág. To remain on the list, the local council of Vestmanna funded the creation of a completely new and artificial beach on the seaward side of a rocky breakwater. This new beach has been the successful landing place for fifteen grindadráp, totaling 832 whales, since its construction.

The artificial whaling beach at Vestmanna

The case of Vestmanna illustrates the fact that the only insurmountable physical determinant of a beach's unsuitability as a hvalvág seems to be the marbakki—although even this "rule" may be challenged if Borðoyarvík is permanently added to the list in place of Klaksvík. The Faroese economist Árni Olafsson wrote that "the most fundamental factor behind Faroese whale and whaling policy is geography."[8] His statement is true, not only with regard to physical geography but with regard to the full range of human geography as well.

By limiting the places where grindadráp are allowed to occur, the Faroese government legitimizes whaling conducted on its terms, on its chosen beaches. While the physical environment presents a set of beaches upon which grindadráp may be possible, cultural and historical factors such as Vestmanna's ability to finance the construction of an artificial beach, Klaksvík's economic influence as the Faroe Islands' "second city," and Tjørnuvík's assertion of its own history as a whale-stranding beach are decidedly more influential in the development of a Faroese whaling and whale conservation regime.

Conservation indeed lies at the heart of the hvalvágir system. It is the codification of a long-standing tradition to drive whales only on certain beaches. In a 1985 Humane Society article condemning the grindadráp, ecologist Campbell Plowden wrote, "Unlike the killing of large whales, which is subject to the scrutiny of the IWC, tradition is the only regulator of the grisly slaughter of thousands of pilot whales occurring every year in the Faroe Islands."[9] Plowden is, of course, correct that the International Whaling Commission does not regulate the grindadráp. As "small cetaceans," pilot whales and the other species taken by the Faroese do not fall under the IWC's authority. While he neglects to recognize the existence of written Faroese whaling laws, he correctly identifies that traditional forms of regulation constitute a major force in the control of Faroese whaling. His implication, however, that "tradition" may be an inadequate form of regulation deserves further investigation. Indeed, in both the Faroe Islands and St. Vincent, tradition is the primary driver of whale and dolphin conservation. In the Faroes, many traditions either have been codified explicitly as law or have influenced the development of whaling laws. In St. Vincent, the regulation of whaling remains almost wholly governed by informal and unwritten tradition still today.

Scholars debate the ability, foresight, and willingness of people whose lives and livelihoods are directly dependent upon the exploitation of natural resources to conserve those resources.[10] Views range from Garrett Hardin's classic "tragedy of the commons" to wildlife biologist Kent Redford's "ecologically noble savage."[11] In St. Vincent and the Faroe Islands, though, we see societies that have, at least thus far, managed to conserve a resource using primarily cultural, traditional, and customary regulations—codified or not—with little to no policy imposed from outside. These societies are not unique in the world, of course. Anthropologists and other scholars have identified many examples of effective culturally embedded conservation strategies elsewhere.[12] Societies in which these strategies achieve the greatest success are those that exhibit "relatively constant group membership, long-term residence in an area, and heavy reliance on natural resources," a description that applies well to both the Faroese and Vincentian whaling communities and would predict the effectiveness of the culturally embedded conservation strategies at work there.[13]

In any discussion of conservation issues related to a whaling operation, records of the take are essential. In the Faroe Islands, continuous annual whaling records chronicle the number of whales killed, along with the date and location of each grindadráp from 1709 to the present, providing more than 300 years of data for spatial and historical analysis.[14] Records go back even further—to 1587—but include gaps. Some Faroese whaling researchers believe that even older records, predating the Protestant Reformation, might be archived at the Vatican.[15] By contrast, in St. Vincent, detailed whaling records, those containing more data than simple annual totals of whales and dolphins caught, exist only from 2007—and even then must be extrapolated from the records of only one boat. Less specific but still useful records of St. Vincent whaling, though, can be obtained from previous research publications.

The Knowledge Is Only Here

Worldwide, whaling does not have a good environmental track record. Certainly, sustainable examples do exist, primarily within the category of aboriginal subsistence whaling—as identified by the IWC—such as the Iñupiat's reliance upon the bowhead whale in the waters off northern Alaska, which, despite its long and sustainable history, may now be threatened by climate change.[16] With these few exceptions, the global history of whaling is primarily defined by unsustainable consumption. "Global" is indeed a fitting descriptor. One leading pair of researchers has called whaling "the world's most spatially extensive form of exploitation of wild living resources."[17] Mere spatial extent, of course, does not necessarily mean unsustainability. Rather, it was the way in which whaling became a global phenomenon that best exemplifies its irresponsibility. The history of commercial whaling is defined by an oft-repeated scenario in which whalers would deplete the targeted species in one area, then move on to another location and begin the cycle of depletion there.

Whaling in St. Vincent, like several current or recent whaling operations, began with influence from commercial whalers—both in technique and in philosophy. In these cases, when a whaling operation ceased, often due to the commercial extinction of the target species, the local whalers would be returned to their home islands with little to show for their efforts besides a new skill set. The departure of foreign whalers from a region often left open a niche for these newly trained local whalers to pursue whatever remnant of cetacean populations remained, using the techniques they had learned through association with the foreign whalers, usually for local subsistence rather than on an industrial scale. The Vincentian whalers, not having the luxury of being able to simply move on to another ocean basin, have had to adapt the philosophy of whaling they learned from the Yankee whalers to become more sustainable.

It's important to note that in the absence of any population estimates for the targeted species in the Caribbean, discussion of sustainability in the Vincentian whaling operation is necessarily speculative.[18] The best gauge of sustainability may come from the records of take and effort, specifically the number of whales and dolphins caught versus the number of boats—or, more precisely, boat-days—involved in the operation. If Vincentian whaling ever depletes the populations of resident whales and dolphins, the operation will necessarily cease. Before this catastrophic finale, we might expect to see an increase in the amount of effort expended, relative to the size of the take. The data, estimated and interpolated as they are, don't seem to bear this out. While the take records do show major fluctuations, especially in terms of species composition, the overall take does not seem to have declined, nor has the effort markedly increased to maintain a steady take. This suggests to me that the culturally embedded conservation strategies at work in St. Vincent are at least somewhat effective in conserving local cetacean populations.

Similar to the Faroe Islands, the primary culturally embedded method of whale conservation used in St. Vincent is the spatial limitation of the whaling operation itself. While the Faroe Islands maintain twenty-five separate beaches that are approved for the grindadráp, the spatial limitation in St. Vincent is far more extreme: specifically, the entire Vincentian artisanal whaling effort exists only in Barrouallie. This is the only village from which boats set out in the morning in pursuit of whales and dolphins, the only port to which they return, and the base of operations for all of the island's vendors. There is no intrinsic quality about Barrouallie that predisposes it to be St. Vincent's "Blackfish Town." In fact, pilot whales are most often sighted to the north and east of St. Vincent, far from Barrouallie and much closer to the fishing village of Owia and the population center of Georgetown. Upstart whaling operations that have arisen in other villages, though—such as Rose Bank, Wallilabou, and Cumberland—did not last longer than a generation.[19] Anytime I mentioned to a Vincentian acquaintance that my research involved whaling, I was told that I must go to Barrouallie. At the Barrouallie Fisheries Cooperative, employee Prislet Francis simply explained to me that "the knowledge is only here."

The sole explanation that anyone could give as to why Vincentian whaling had remained in Barrouallie alone was "tradition." This tradition has effectively created a system of limited entry by which all of the island's whalers and vendors are concentrated in one village and certain aspects of the national pilot whale economy—price, competition, and supply—are reduced to the village level.[20] In this way, the blackfish operation at Barrouallie resembles a caste-based field of labor—only the distinction between those who may work in the occupation and those who may not is geographical, not familial. Even Samuel Hazelwood, the de facto leader of Vincentian whaling, moved to Barrouallie from the nearby village of Layou when he decided to take on the profession.

Because crowds gather at the dock when the whaling boats return each day and observe the wholesale transactions made openly, prices paid by vendors are public knowledge. Whalers, competing only with other local whalers, decrease their hunting pressure immediately when supply is high and prices are low. If there were whaling operations based in other villages, each might create its own local economy where the wholesale prices paid by vendors varied, like the disparate pricing of bundles of dried whale meat sold in the villages. In the multiple-village scenario, wholesale prices might be high in one village and low in another, prompting whalers to continue their efforts and sell to the vendors paying the highest price. As it is, there is only one village where vendors are based, and therefore only one local whaling economy, though the product is distributed nationally.

This geographical limitation in turn limits the hunting pressure and creates a form of market-driven conservation. This stands as a counterexample to the commonsense and historically supported argument that when the extraction of a living natural resource is conducted for profit in a free market, capitalist society, the destruction of the resource base is part of the system's "normal functioning."[21] In the context of Vincentian whaling, it seems that the capitalistic structure of the whaling operation—geographically limited to one village—may actually be conserving, not destroying, local cetacean populations.

Another way in which elements of Vincentian culture encourage conservation is through the unwillingness of the whalers to upgrade their technology to something more efficient. We have already seen that the whalers readily adopted motorboats and harpoon guns in the past. According to Jennifer Cruickshank-Howard of the government's Fisheries Division, however, there has been little to no impetus among whalers to develop the technology of their operation beyond the current level. Fisheries authorities would like to see the storage and processing facilities improved but thus far have made no efforts to alter the technology employed by the whalers themselves. Since the advent of the boat engine and harpoon gun, no further technological advances have been embraced by the Barrouallie whalers, save the occasional use of mobile phones to communicate with shore or other boats. Better storage facilities would allow whalers to continue whaling when wholesale prices fall, stockpile surpluses, and wait for prices to rise. As it is, the most common recourse when prices are low is to reduce whaling effort. When demand is high and prices rise, effort increases, but even operating at full capacity, with all available boats out whaling, the potential take is limited by the technology in use and by the skill and number of the whalers. Both the whalers and the vendors seem content that the technological status quo provides an adequate supply of whale meat and blubber and that it generates adequate revenues without overtaxing the resource.

The difficulty of judging the sustainability effects of the Vincentian technological and spatial limitations empirically is directly linked to the absence of take data. There is no central repository for whaling records in St. Vincent, nor do whalers keep their own records for very long. The best sources of whaling records are the various studies that have been conducted by academic researchers over the years. This underscores the importance of researchers publishing not only their results and analyses but their raw data as well.[22]

When researchers are present in St. Vincent, they have access only to the current records and the records dating back, at most, a few years. For example, the first researcher to publish whaling records from Barrouallie was C. F. Hickling, a fisheries adviser from England, who conducted a broad survey of fishing and whaling activities throughout the British Caribbean colonies in 1949 and reported the number of pilot whales taken in Barrouallie for that year only.[23] The next researchers to collect and publish Vincentian whaling records were David and Melba Caldwell from the University of Florida, who in 1975 presented the records from 1962 to 1974.[24] The next researcher in Barrouallie was William Price of the Ocean Research and Conservation Association in Vancouver, who included the Caldwells' records and added records he collected himself for the years 1975 through 1983. After Price's fieldwork in St. Vincent came to an end, no one visited to collect records until Nigel Scott, then a graduate student at the University of the West Indies in Barbados, arrived in the early 1990s and published records for the years 1990, 1991, and 1992.[25] A gap of six years remains in the dataset, representing the time that passed between the conclusion of Price's work and the beginning of Scott's. Another gap—this one for fourteen years—then appears in the records from the end of Scott's collection to the beginning of mine. I began my fieldwork in St. Vincent in the summer of 2008—at which time the available records dated back only to January 2007. Since then, every time I return to Barrouallie, I make the trek up to Samuel Hazelwood's hilltop house and photograph his handwritten record books back to the page where I left off the time before. With the image files carefully saved on my phone or laptop, I return home at the end of the field season to transcribe the figures into a database—its own special challenge—to add to the growing record.

A sample page from Samuel Hazelwood's whaling records

Even this is not enough to ensure a precisely accurate record of Vincentian whaling. Samuel Hazelwood is the only Barrouallie whaler that keeps thorough accounts of the whales and dolphins his boat takes. Samuel's scrawled and bled-through notebook pages record only a portion of the total Vincentian take, but based on that portion the entire Barrouallie take can be reasonably estimated. Samuel takes about twice as many cetaceans as the rest of Barrouallie's whalers. This is not only due to his skill and experience but also, in part, to his persistence. Samuel's is the only whaling boat that goes out six days a week. (He knows better than I do, apparently, that he should not work during "church time.") To extrapolate from Samuel's records to the records of the entire operation, I multiply Samuel's take by 1.5. Until the Vincentian government or some other entity initiates a universal record-keeping system, this is the best we can do.

Because the existence of a permanent Vincentian whaling record relies completely upon the presence of outside researchers in Barrouallie, we are left with gaps in the data indicating times when none were there. Even when researchers are actively engaged in data collection—as I have been since 2008—gaps can still appear. During my summer 2016 fieldwork I was disappointed to learn that Samuel had thrown out his 2013 and 2014 records before I was able to see them. I had not been able to make trips into the field during these years and, as a result, the data from those years are now lost. Unless the records unexpectedly resurface someday, all future researchers into Vincentian whaling will be faced with a gap in the data for 2013 and 2014—the legacy of my absence.

This isn't how scientific records should be kept. The details of one researcher's travel schedule ought not create gaps in important data such as these. The Vincentian government, through its Ministry of Agriculture, Forestry, Fisheries and Rural Transformation, is the logical clearinghouse and repository for Vincentian whaling data. If all local whalers, not only Samuel Hazelwood, had kept accurate records and this national authority had collected those records into an accessible archive, the past sixty years of Vincentian whaling would be better understood than they are today. As it is, the absences of researchers have resulted in the fragmented dataset we now have. St. Vincent & the Grenadines needs a national whaling statistical database akin to that kept in the Faroe Islands.

The total take in St. Vincent has always consisted of both pilot whales and other dolphins of a variety of species, but the ratio has changed dramatically over the fifty-year period for which statistics are available. While pilot whales once were the mainstay of the take, the recent trend has been toward other dolphins making up an increasing percentage. This shift took place during the 1980s, most likely in response to declining pilot whale numbers, as evidenced by two bookending statements: Edward Mitchell's in 1975 that "pilot

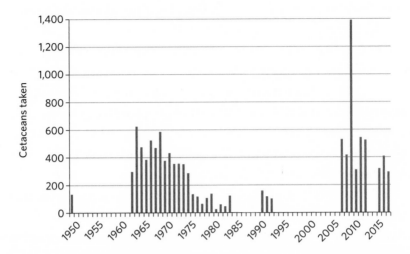

Estimated St. Vincent cetacean take, 1949–2017, by year. Gaps indicate missing data, not zero-catch years. *Data sources:* C. F. Hickling, *The Fisheries of the British West Indies: Report on a Visit in 1949,* Development and Welfare in the West Indies, Bulletin 29 (Bridgetown, Barbados: Cole's Printery, 1950); David K. Caldwell and Melba C. Caldwell, "Dolphin and Small Whale Fisheries of the Caribbean and West Indies: Occurrence, History, and Catch Statistics—with Special Reference to the Lesser Antillean Island of St. Vincent," *Journal of the Fisheries Research Board of Canada* 32, no. 7 (1975), 1105–1110; William S. Price, "Whaling in the Caribbean: Historical Perspective and Update," *Report of the International Whaling Commission* 35 (1985), 413–420; Nigel M. Scott, "The Current Status and Management Options for the Mammalian Fishery in Barrouallie, St. Vincent, West Indies," M.S. thesis, University of the West Indies, 1995; 2007–2012; and the financial records of Samuel Hazelwood.

whales ('blackfish') form the bulk of the catch," and Nigel Scott's in 1995 that "the blackfish (short-finned pilot whale) . . . is considered the main target of the fishery but at least 14 other species of marine mammals are also caught. The spinner dolphin . . . is the major contributor . . . of the entire mammalian catch of the fishery."[26] The operation has always been strongly associated with blackfish, or pilot whales. At some time between 1975 and 1995, however, the role of blackfish in the operation shifted from the actual mainstay to more of a symbolic portion of the take. According to my estimates, since

2007, Vincentian whalers have taken about five dolphins for every two pilot whales.

Considering all species together, the long-term average take in St. Vincent is 344 cetaceans annually. This accounts for all the years for which records exist, back to 1949. In studying the take composition, we again encounter the issue of sparse record-keeping, this time even more acutely. Recall that a researcher typically has access to take records going back, at most, a few years before their field season. These records, though, generally do not explicitly distinguish the species that make up the catch. In order to analyze the Vincentian cetacean take with more precision than just the vendors' categories of "blackfish" and "papas," the researcher must record the specifics of the take personally. Some have done this and some have not.

Nigel Scott provided a detailed inventory of the take during his three months of intensive fieldwork—September through November 1994—and I did the same for the months of June and July 2009. Later I engaged the services of Diallo Boyea, the local Barrouallie resident who laughed at his own unfamiliarity with his hometown's shanty tradition, to inventory cetaceans brought ashore for an entire year: August 2015 through July 2016. Although Boyea's record does not include every single cetacean taken during the year—he was sometimes unable to access a carcass before it was processed for food—it does offer a longer-term view of the species composition than any previous study. Taking the records collected during these three studies together, we begin to see a picture of the overall composition of the cetacean take brought in at Barrouallie.

Today Barrouallie retains its moniker, "Blackfish Town," but does so mainly because of its legacy of pilot whaling. If take statistics covering only the most recent decade were the determinant, Barrouallie would be called "Dolphin Town," or, to use the proper local term, "Papas Town."

So is the Vincentian artisanal whaling operation sustainable? It seems so, but it's difficult to say for sure. The total take of all cetaceans

Species composition of Vincentian cetacean take

Common name (standard English)	Common name (Vincentian Creole)	Scientific name	Count	Percentage of total take
spinner dolphin	rollover papas	*Stenella longirostris*	113	36%
short-finned pilot whale	blackfish	*Globicephala macrorhynchus*	81	26%
Atlantic spotted dolphin	gamin fish	*Stenella frontalis*	42	13%
killer whale	whitefish	*Orcinus orca*	28	9%
Fraser's dolphin	skipjack papas	*Lagenodelphis hosei*	10	3%
false killer whale	mongoose	*Pseudorca crassidens*	10	3%
Risso's dolphin	Americano	*Grampus griseus*	7	2%
melon-headed whale	black hardnocks	*Peponocephala electra*	7	2%
Clymene dolphin	speechy	*Stenella clymene*	3	1%
striped dolphin	speechy	*Stenella coeruleoalba*	3	1%
dwarf sperm whale	rat papas	*Kogia sima*	1	< 1%
rough-toothed dolphin	petty det	*Steno bredanensis*	1	< 1%
species unknown	papas	n/a	9	3%

Source: Based upon records collected by Nigel Scott, Russell Fielding, and Diallo Boyea, covering a cumulative seventeen months during 1994, 2009, 2015, and 2016.

remains relatively constant when adjusted for effort over the past half-century or so. But what about the individual species? The shift from pilot whales to other dolphin species probably indicates an increasing scarcity of pilot whales. Is the shift, then, to be interpreted as evidence of unsustainable whaling or as one of the strategies that makes Vincentian whaling sustainable? The answer depends crucially on the size of the population of each hunted species.

We need more information on cetacean population numbers in the Caribbean region, migratory patterns and year-round residence, and complete and official whaling records. Additional data on cetacean genetic diversity, the potential effects of climate change on habitat and prey availability, and the effects of environmental pollution on the health of the whales and dolphins would also help give a more complete view toward the sustainability of the operation. Without these, the best I can offer is to say that, considering the culturally embedded conservation strategies of spatial and technological limitations, the apparent lack of a decline in total take of all cetacean species when effort is held constant, and possibly the flexibility of the whalers to shift to another target species when one becomes temporarily scarce, the artisanal whaling operation in St. Vincent provisionally appears to be sustainable. More research is needed to say with any more certainty.

Homegrown Whaling Philosophy

It matters, in terms of sustainability, that the Faroese did not learn the techniques of the grindadráp through association with commercial whalers from abroad. Recall that the most likely historical scenario includes the grindadráp as "part of the common Norse culture which the first settlers brought with them to the Faroes."[27] This means that the Faroese, or their ancestors, developed not only the techniques but also the philosophy of drive-style whaling without outside influence. The grindadráp—always a community-based food production strategy—never had to modify the "hunt, deplete, and move on" approach of commercial whalers. A homegrown whaling philosophy developed in the Faroe Islands alongside the growth of the Faroese population and the evolution of the grindadráp itself. The resultant conservation strategies seamlessly permeate the institution in a way that quotas or other conservation efforts imposed from outside never would. The three main conservation strategies built into the grindadráp are the spatial limitation of whaling to certain bays and beaches, the prerogative of the authorities to instate a temporary ban on whaling in times of surplus, and the principle that the sighting of pilot whales must be a spontaneous event and not the result of a dedicated or systematic search.

First consider spatial limitations. How does the restriction of the grindadráp to twenty-five Faroese beaches promote conservation? This spatial limitation forces a major logistical decision during the initial moments after a pod of whales has been sighted and before the grindaboð is issued. The grindaformenn, upon learning of the sighting, must quickly evaluate the sea conditions, current and wind directions, advancing nightfall, and location of the nearest—or most convenient—hvalvág, or approved whaling bay. If any of these variables is not favorable to the grindadráp, the whales may not be pursued. Meteorologic and oceanic conditions are beyond anyone's control. The spatial limitation regime presented by the list of approved hvalvágir, however, is at least as much a human construct as it is a response to the physical realities of the natural environment.

Of course, whales *could* be driven onto non-approved beaches. The Faroese national whaling statistics are peppered with occasional examples of past grindadráp that happened on beaches not approved—or no longer approved—for whaling. Natural strandings occur on other beaches as well. In fact, the earliest known specific case of beached cetaceans being used for human consumption in the Faroe Islands was recorded in 1584 on the shores of Lítla Dímun, the smallest Faroe Island and the only one that is uninhabited. Because of this record, the year 1584 has often been cited as the beginning of the grindadráp's recorded history. It's almost certain, however, that this incident represents the stranding of four northern bottlenose whales—the species identification is based upon some biological details provided along with the record—and not the intentional beaching of a pod of pilot whales.

The first known reference to something approximating the modern grindadráp is found in a 1632 geography text. The Norwegian author, Peder Clausson Friis, undoubtedly described the grindadráp when he wrote that "in the year of our Lord, 1587, 300 small whales were harpooned and slaughtered and driven ashore in this one year in the islands, and such has occurred in ancient times, and usually happens every sixth or seventh year."[28] Several interesting points are worth drawing out from this short quote. First, the practice of whale-driving was already considered "ancient" by the early seventeenth century. This indicates that the date of 1587 is an extremely conservative estimate for the beginning of the grindadráp. Second, the frequency of grindadráp at the time was judged to be only about every six or seven years, compared with an average of about six grindadráp per year now. Has the increase been due to a growth in whale populations, a growth in human populations, or a more efficient system of sighting, driving, and slaughtering the whales? Finally, consider the mention of harpoons. The regulations limiting grindadráp tools to only the hook and the spinal lance were not initiated until the mid-1980s. Before this time, harpoons, spears, and all manner of fishing, hunting, or farming implements were part of a certainly more chaotic grindadráp.

When the list of approved hvalvágir was initiated in 1832, the Faroese government assumed geographical control of the grindadráp. From that time forward, whales would only be driven, legally, on the government's beaches and on the government's terms. This spatial limitation, while it was almost certainly originally established to retain control of whaling on the shores owned by those in power, now promotes conservation in much the same way that the limitation of Vincentian whaling activity to Barrouallie does: it restricts the activity to a finite set of locations and forbids whale drives that might have occurred elsewhere.

I have witnessed occasions when a pod of whales has been sighted but could not be driven into an approved hvalvág, owing to some combination of natural conditions and the relative locations of the sighting and the nearest whaling bays. Faroese friends and colleagues recall many more of these instances than I do. One could imagine that if there were no spatial restrictions dictating the list of beaches onto which whales may be driven, fewer grindadráp would have been called off and, over the centuries-long history of the activity, many more whales would have been killed. Essentially the system of hvalvágir adds a layer of non-arbitrary human geography to the challenges presented by nature itself. Faroese beaches that are not approved for whaling can be likened to no-take zones in fisheries management or wildlife refuges in the regulation of hunting. If hvalvágir are woodlots, non-approved beaches are forest preserves. In an insightful and subtle way, the Faroese government has limited the use of a resource by establishing a system of conservation geography based on its not quite environmentally determined selection of whaling beaches.

Second, the Faroese do not pursue every sighted pod of whales, even when an approved whaling beach is within reach. While no record exists, of course, of grindadráp that did not happen, anecdotal evidence indicates that the decision not to pursue a pod of whales that has been sighted is a common occurrence. The Executive Order on Pilot Whaling gives the Faroese government the right to institute "an emergency ban on pilot whaling" in one or more districts if, among other reasons, the food products that the grindadráp would make available are not currently needed.[29] If a pod of whales is too large to be driven into a chosen bay, or if the homes in the district are well stocked with whale meat and blubber, the sýslumaður can either call off the grindadráp entirely or negotiate a deal to give the meat and blubber to the inhabitants of another district in exchange for the payment of "municipal expenses" such as the loss or damage of property incurred during the grindadráp.[30]

One infamous and wasteful grindadráp more than a half century ago stands as the exception that proves this rule. On October 6, 1940, 1,200 pilot whales were driven into the whaling bay at Sandur in a single grindadráp. This large pod was more than could be handled by those present and many whales went to waste—they were killed but they spoiled before they could be processed for meat and blubber. Sandur is on Sandoy, the island still trying to get an undersea tunnel that would connect it to the rest of the nation. The remoteness of Sandur and its inaccessibility to much of the Faroese population resulted in a situation where the whalers were vastly outnumbered by the whales. Older Faroese people still speak of the shame of this event and praise the regulations that are now in place to avoid its repetition.

Some Faroese refer to pilot whales as a "gift from God," a term commonly used to describe the cultural understanding of the arrival of this free and unpredictable food source. With this worldview, it's obvious that to waste such a gift would be a sin, and the Faroese, through law and tradition, seek to avoid any wastage of the important resource and blessing that pilot whales are to them.

Third, grindadráp are made possible first by whale movements, not human intentionality. The term *grindadráp* is often translated into English as "pilot whale hunt." Some of the most learned Faroese experts on the subject have done so, and indeed, I have followed their example with the subtitle to this book.[31] While the translation is not entirely wrong, the use of the term *hunt* tends to connote an element of searching, seeking, or tracking on the part of the human participants. As Kate Sanderson points out, this connotation is misleading when one considers how grindadráp begin: "Grindadráp can be said to be a hunt in the sense that the target animal, as in other forms of hunting, is wild. But the inclusion of grindadráp in the general category of hunt is complicated by the fact that the whales are not sought out, as such, but are driven (like sheep) only when sighted a relatively short distance from land, and this only happens when a school is discovered, by chance, in the course of other activities such as coastal fishing. There is no particular season for grind, as the initiation of a drive depends upon the movement of the whales themselves and their proximity to land at any time, rather than any effort on the part of their exploiters to go out looking for them."[32]

As Sanderson makes clear, the Faroese do not actively seek whales outside of their coastal waters. If they did, the annual take would likely be much larger, as the Faroese economy would have developed a niche for professional whalers or whale-finders. As it is, with sightings made only by people who are in the process of doing other things—fishing, traveling aboard a ferry, working on shore—and the grindadráp themselves conducted by amateur whalers of a variety of professions, the number of whales killed varies drastically from year to year but stays lower than it would if the Faroe Islands supported a dedicated guild of whalers.

We know about this fluctuation thanks to the vast dataset of Faroese whaling records compiled by historians and scientists and dating back to the sixteenth century. These data represent, in the understated words of one whaling researcher, "surely . . . one of the longest runs of whaling statistics available anywhere in the world."[33] In fact, the Faroese grindadráp dataset likely represents the single longest and most scientifically reliable quantitative record of human interaction with wildlife in existence.

We don't know the exact date or location of the 1587 grindadráp, the first in the dataset, but we do know these precise details of time and place for most of the others. The first recorded grindadráp for which we know the time and place took ninety pilot whales in Klaksvík on November 14, 1599. When you know the exact date and location of an event, you can fill in a lot of the surrounding details.

Mid-November is late for a grindadráp. It was a Sunday, a day when most work—farming and fishing—would pause for "church time." Not that fish were in abundance then; the Little Ice Age was in full swing, meaning that sea surface temperatures were up to five degrees Celsius colder than today. Sea ice occasionally formed around and between the islands—something that hasn't happened since 1888.[34] Cod catches had declined. The year 1599 falls among the direst of the "famine years" as determined by the painstaking research of the Faroese historical geographer Rolf Guttesen.[35] This grindadráp, happening as it did late in the year during a cold climatic period, was probably very badly needed. On that date and at that latitude there would only have been about seven hours of daylight. Klaksvík—at the time not even a village, just a sparse collection of a few small settlements—sits at the base of a north-facing fjord with mountains to the southeast and southwest, shortening the day's length further still. We don't know the time of day when the grindaboð was sent out, but the whalers very likely would have either begun their work in the dark before sunrise or prolonged their activity well past the setting of the afternoon sun. Their first action, in response to the grindaboð, may well have been to beat a layer of ice off the oarlocks of their boats. We don't know for sure. But we do know, thanks to the meticulous whaling records kept by the Faroese, that November 14, 1599, ended with ninety pilot whales, their carcasses opened and steaming in the late autumn air, ready to be turned into much-needed food for the residents of Klaksvík.

Because of the sheer volume of data included in the Faroese National Whaling Statistics, the best way to approach a quantified history of the grindadráp is to consider the take by decade, rather than examining the numbers for individual whale drives or even annual take records as we do with Vincentian records. This summarization loses the fine detail preserved by the dataset but makes long-term trends more readily apparent. Over the three-century history of continuous records (1709 to the present), we see two distinct maxima, the mid-nineteenth century and the mid- to late-twentieth century, and two minima, the mid-eighteenth century and the late nineteenth century. The records appear to be rising out of another minimum currently—though we must remember that the last column represents less than a complete decade. The maxima—and to some degree, the minima—appear to be increasing as time progresses.

The apparently cyclical nature of the grindadráp over the centuries may indicate generational movements of whales, multigenerational movements of their prey, or changing levels of effort or efficiency on the part of the Faroese.[36] Pilot whales do not migrate in the long-range sense that, for example, humpback whales or California gray whales do, so scientists measure populations regionally rather than by ocean or worldwide. Marine biologist Boris Culik cites "North-Atlantic climatic variations" as the reason for the "cyclic variation" in Faroese

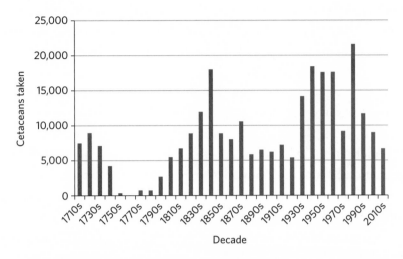

Faroe Islands cetacean take, 1710–2017, by decade. The gap at the 1760s indicates a zero-catch decade, not missing data. *Data source:* National Whaling Statistics, Føroya Náttúrugripasavn

take records.[37] If by this he means the North Atlantic Oscillation (NAO), an atmospheric and oceanic cycle similar, in some ways, to the El Niño/La Niña cycle in the Pacific, it would appear that his conclusion is not well founded. Together with a colleague, I conducted a statistical analysis of monthly grindadráp records and monthly NAO data, both sets spanning the period from 1865 to 2009, and found no correlation.[38] In general, it may be true that climate plays some role in grindadráp variation on a multi-decadal scale, though the exact mechanism remains unknown.

We understand the take composition in the Faroe Islands with far greater precision than that of St. Vincent. The national whaling statistics database contains not only the date, location, and number of cetaceans taken but also the species and—in many cases—the amount of meat and blubber obtained in each grindadráp. Records for each regularly-taken species begin at different years, the latest being Atlantic white-sided dolphins, for which the data go back "only" to 1872. Our species comparison will use the data from 1872 through 2017, then, the period for which records of the four most commonly

Species composition of Faroese cetacean take, 1872–2017

Common name (English)	Common name (Faroese)	Scientific name	Count	Percentage of total take
long-finned pilot whale	*grindahvalur*	*Globicephala melas*	154,861	93.21%
Atlantic white-sided dolphin	*skjórutur springari*	*Lagenorhynchus acutus*	10,404	6.26%
bottlenose dolphin	*hvessingur*	*Tursiops truncatus*	851	0.51%
Risso's dolphin	*rissospringari*	*Grampus griseus*	24	0.01%

Source: Data from National Whaling Statistics, Føroya Náttúrugripasavn.

caught species are available. It is apparent from these data that, unlike in St. Vincent, pilot whales make up the clear majority of the Faroese take. Thus, any discussion of sustainability in Faroese whaling must necessarily focus primarily upon the population and take of the long-finned pilot whale.

A 2011 shipboard sighting survey estimated the population of long-finned pilot whales in the waters surrounding Iceland and the Faroe Islands to be 128,093.[39] In 2004, using figures from an older, 1987 population survey that estimated 100,000 pilot whales in Faroese waters, Boris Culik determined that "the Faroese catch will not deplete the population."[40] His conclusion was based on a comparison of the average annual take to the estimated whale population size. The long-term average take since 1709 is 833 pilot whales per year.[41] The average annual take since 2000 has fallen to 636 whales. This is only half of 1 percent of the total pilot whale population, which actually rose by 28 percent between the 1987 and 2011 population surveys. At the current level of extraction, and with a definition of sustainability that simply indicates a rate of resource exploitation that will not deplete the resource in the foreseeable future, we can confidently say that the grindadráp is sustainable. This is attributable almost entirely to the culturally embedded conservation strategies used to regulate Faroese whaling.

Foreigners on the Beach in Black Hoodies

Recognition of their culturally embedded conservation strategies is of increasing importance in the Faroe Islands. It may reach equal importance in St. Vincent in the near future. In addition to viral social media posts, environmental activist organizations occasionally plan and conduct protests or other forms of on-site, direct action in the Faroe Islands. These activities are not common in St. Vincent, but it's likely that their absence there is due mainly to the obscurity of the Vincentian whaling operation and its perceived "subsistence" nature, as opposed to the grindadráp, which is frequently described as "unnecessary." According to Paul Watson of the Sea Shepherd Conservation Society, the grindadráp "is a cruel hunt conducted for sport in the name of tradition. There is no subsistence necessity to the slaughter and therefore it is an unjustified kill."[42] This sentiment is common among those fundamentally opposed to Faroese whaling. It's ironic, though, that the Vincentian whaling operation, capitalistic by nature, would be viewed through the lens of "subsistence whaling," even considering the disparity of wealth in the two countries, while the grindadráp, a free food source for the Faroese people, is not.

Throughout most of Faroese history, foreigners have observed the grindadráp and commented on it in their writings without weighing in on its morality. While these travelers may have mentioned their own feelings of shock or disgust at the sight, they rarely, if ever, ventured into value judgments. One of the first moments of international criticism of the grindadráp came in 1981, when Greenpeace representatives visited the Faroes to document the since-ceased commercial whaling operation targeting fin whales. Greenpeace's visit coincided with three large grindadráp. The representatives' final report focused primarily, and critically, on the grindadráp rather than upon the commercial whaling operation that was the original focus of the expedition.[43] Two years later, the Scottish branch of the Sea Shepherd

Conservation Society sent a small group with inflatable boats to observe the activity. In 1984, a Danish television company produced a documentary film about the grindadráp that increased its visibility within Europe.[44]

The commencement of broad public awareness of—and activism against—the grindadráp dates to 1985. That year, Sea Shepherd sent a larger crew aboard the *Sea Shepherd II* to attempt, physically, to interfere with Faroese whaling activities. At the annual meeting of the IWC that year in England, the topic of the grindadráp was brought up and the IWC maintained its stance that it would not regulate small cetacean operations. Also in 1985, the Humane Society of the United States published a short article calling "for the curtailment of the Faroe hunt."[45] In 1986, Paul Watson returned to the Faroe Islands with a BBC film crew, which produced a documentary film about the grindadráp.[46] That same year, the Faroese government changed the regulations regarding the grindadráp dramatically, with the goal of ensuring a more humane death for the whales.[47] This action was in direct response to concerns of cruelty and inhumane killing methods that the anti-whaling organizations raised.[48]

Shortly after this time, in 1993, the Grindamannafelagið was formed to recommend regulations for more-humane killing methods and to educate grindadráp participants in proper whaling techniques. At its 1995 meeting in Ireland, the IWC commended the improvements in killing methods that were instituted on the recommendation of the Grindamannafelagið and encouraged the Faroese government "to continue its work . . . monitoring the performance in the drive hunt and introducing training programmes in killing methods with a view to reducing times to death."[49] Some Faroese still reflect on the effects of the anti-grindadráp campaigns of the 1980s with some ambivalence. While the Sea Shepherd organization in general—and Paul Watson specifically—is almost universally opposed in the Faroes, some do recognize the positive effects that the increased attention had on the grindadráp. I've spoken with staunch grindadráp supporters in the Faroe Islands who thank Paul Watson—though they would never do so to his face and would not want me to even use their names—for his role in helping to reform the grindadráp into the practice that it is today: one that, they feel, takes conservation and humane killing methods seriously.

Throughout the 1980s, animal welfare organizations in Europe and North America continued promoting images and video of the grindadráp. Protests began. The Faroese government received thousands of postcards from abroad, urging an end to the killing of whales.[50] These campaigns receded by the late 1980s, only to resurge in the early twenty-first century. The renewed opposition to the grindadráp so far has culminated in the Sea Shepherd Conservation Society's 2012–2015 Operation Grindstop.[51] This campaign was featured in the Animal Planet television network's 2012 miniseries, *Whale Wars: Viking Shores,* and showed young activists wearing black hooded sweatshirts, Sea Shepherd's skull-and-crossbones logo emblazoned on the backs, attempting to physically block—with both their boats and their bodies—the confluence of humans and whales that is the grindadráp.

Operation Grindstop concluded in 2014 and was followed by Operation Sleppid Grindini, the name of which is an Anglicization of the Faroese *sleppið grindinni,* a command to "set the whales free." This imperative would be issued by a grindaformann or sýslumaður if a whale drive was going badly—owing to the weather, the conditions of the sea, or the behavior of the whales—and a decision was made to call off the grindadráp. While my personal views on what constitutes a proper form of international engagement with Faroese whaling certainly diverge from Paul Watson's, I have to applaud his good choice of a culturally relevant name for his anti-whaling operation.

While Sea Shepherd was doubling down on its efforts, some environmental organizations ceased to oppose Faroese whaling. The majority of scientific organizations involved in studies of whale populations in the North Atlantic have endorsed the sustainability of the grindadráp. The International Council for the Exploration of the

Sea, the North Atlantic Marine Mammal Commission, and the International Whaling Commission have concluded that, based upon population estimates and hunting pressure, the grindadráp will not deplete the whale population.[52]

Organizations that do continue to oppose the grindadráp on principle tend to concentrate most of their actual efforts on fighting other whaling operations, especially by Iceland and Japan. The World Wildlife Fund–Denmark (WWF) has prepared a standard response to inquiries that refers to the sustainability of the grindadráp, its long history in Faroese culture, and the efforts that Faroese authorities have made to reduce the suffering of individual whales that are killed. The statement concludes by noting that "WWF is a conservation organization and the question of cruelty of the pilot whale hunt is not a conservation issue."[53] The Faroese government continues to respond individually to all personally written protest letters. Complaints are occasionally sent to the Danish government, which has prepared a series of response letters. The standard Danish response acknowledges that the writer may have found images, video, or descriptions of the grindadráp disturbing but stresses that the practice is regulated, sustainable, and for the purpose of food production. It challenges the reader to consider how the grindadráp compares to other methods of food production more familiar to them.[54]

Some organizations continue to call for boycotts of Faroese products, mainly seafood but also tourism.[55] In the recent past, and especially during the late 1980s and early 1990s, it seemed to some Faroese that the international protests and threatened boycotts might require a cessation of the grindadráp. In August 2005, the Grindamannafelagið's president remarked that the protest was the biggest threat to the continuation of the grindadráp.[56] As recently as March 2008, Rolf Guttesen, a Faroese geographer at the University of Copenhagen, echoed this opinion.[57] The proposed boycotts have not had a major impact on the Faroese or Danish economies. Neither have the protests or boycotts ended—or even lessened—the occurrence of the grindadráp in the Faroe Islands. Rather, their effect was to call attention to some areas in which the grindadráp could be improved and to instigate the necessary improvements.

The only environmental activism campaign against whaling in St. Vincent came in 2001 when Sea Shepherd sent its ship *Ocean Warrior* (since renamed *Farley Mowat* after the Canadian author who wrote about the senseless killing of the fin whale in Newfoundland) to St. Lucia, to document and disrupt the activities of pilot whalers there and in St. Vincent.[58] This campaign did achieve its goal of documentation by making photographs of whalers returning to port in Castries with a pilot whale carcass onboard. But before the Sea Shepherd activists could proceed with their mission in St. Vincent, the St. Lucia Coast Guard, acting on reports of harassment of fishermen by the activists, escorted the *Ocean Warrior* out of Castries harbor and demanded that the crew restrict its activities to international waters.[59]

The relative obscurity of whaling in St. Vincent certainly plays some role in the unequal attention that the Faroes and St. Vincent receive from the international environmental activist community. In the ten years I've been conducting research there, the most common response I've received, by far, to an initial description of my work is something along the lines of, "Really? They hunt whales in the Caribbean? I had no idea." Ignorance may indeed play a role, but other, more nuanced, reasons also exist to explain this disparity.

The first reason that Caribbean whaling is more obscure than its Faroese counterpart is directly related to the method of whaling. The grindadráp, being conducted on the beach, usually in or near a village, occurs in full view of the Faroese public, foreign tourists, activists with cameras, and anyone else who happens to be on the scene. Additionally, though only a few grindadráp happen each year—the long-term average is about six—the scene of any one grindadráp is one of mass slaughter: many whales killed at once. This spectacle, dramatically enhanced by the reddening of the water, has served as the subject of many a shocking photograph in anti-whaling literature. By comparison, Vincentian whaling involves a much smaller number of individual whales per whaling event and most of the "action" takes place far from shore, under the eyes of the whalers alone. In the context of Vincentian whaling, the opportunities for obtaining subjects for visual display of spectacle are simply not as readily available. Thus, Faroese whaling has been the subject of a significantly greater amount of graphic visual anti-whaling literature.

But consider another way to think about the front-and-center nature of the grindadráp. While the locations are primarily selected out of practicality—physical geography limits the Vincentians to offshore whaling and permits drive-style whaling by the Faroese—the fact that so many approved whaling bays are found in or near population centers in the Faroe Islands indicates an openness, an unashamedness, and a willingness for grindadráp to be viewed, documented, and even participated in by the public. This difference has affected the relative volume of conflict over issues of whaling simply by making documentary evidence much easier to obtain in the Faroe Islands than in St. Vincent.

The second difference that has led to the disparity in foreign anti-whaling sentiment directed at St. Vincent and the Faroe Islands has more to do with the respective cultures, as wholes, within which these whaling operations are found. Scholars have shown, through survey data, that public perceptions of whaling are least supportive in predominately white, English-speaking, affluent societies such as the United States, the United Kingdom, and Australia.[60] Historian Richard Bulliet's identification of these areas as the heartlands of the postdomestic era—characterized by the physical and intellectual separation of consumers from most methods of food production—supports these findings.[61] Additionally, those who oppose whaling in general become more permissive of the activity when it occurs in societies most unlike their own.[62] Aboriginal subsistence whaling by Inuit peoples is less controversial than Japanese whaling, for example, because the former is perceived to be one of the few methods of food production available to those by whom it is practiced. Along this line of reasoning, whaling is something that is done by someone else, someone unlike the individual opposed to whaling, someone without access to Western methods of food production or commodity imports.

Perceptions of race also play a role. Vincentian whalers, in their poverty and blackness, can be perceived by white North Americans, Europeans, and Australians as having no other choice but to exploit nearby whale populations. The Faroese are white, European, and affluent—certainly not the model of a people that must whale to survive. Why, though, should a sustainable operation targeting a stable whale population be conducted only by a people without other options? Even assuming the logic of this argument, St. Vincent, with its tropical climate and comparatively more fertile soils, supports significantly more options for agriculture than do the Faroe Islands. Yet the Faroese are the recipients of far more anti-whaling protest than the Vincentians. The argument of necessity may be exposed as merely an argument of prejudice. The Vincentians, in their perceived otherness, can be excused for taking a few small whales each day in order to survive, while the Faroese, in their European sameness, are castigated as anachronistic practitioners of a mass slaughter that could easily be replaced by the importation of foreign foodstuffs.

The perception, then, is this: Vincentian whalers conduct an objectionable method of food production out of necessity and at least have the decency to do it out of sight of land. The Faroese, by contrast, immodestly slaughter entire pods of whales in full view of the public, turning their harbors to blood and allowing the events to be photographed. Although most species of Caribbean cetaceans remain uncounted, and thus sustainability can only be inferred through an analysis of historical take records and levels of effort, Vincentians are perceived to better fit the role of the "ecologically noble savage" and are thus not targeted as much as the Faroese by anti-whaling activists.[63] Under analysis, though, the differences in whaling and anti-whaling in St. Vincent and the Faroe Islands can be reduced to physical geography, history, and cultural prejudice.

People of higher socioeconomic classes are generally expected to produce food by relying to a higher degree on agriculture and the raising of livestock than on subsistence methods of food production such as hunting and foraging. If, like the Faroe Islands, these developed nations are located in places too small, steep, rocky, or otherwise unsuitable for large-scale agriculture, then importation on the globalized market stands as an acceptable alternative to self-sufficiency. Whaling is generally not viewed as an acceptable form of food production in developed nations. According to Paul Watson, Sea Shepherd opposes the grindadráp because "it is not done for subsistence. You cannot compare the materially wealthy communities in the Faeroes with subsistence communities in Greenland or Northern Canada."[64] He may well have included St. Vincent among those "subsistence communities" too. If the Faroese economy had remained undeveloped, as it was during the Danish trade monopoly, the grindadráp would be more acceptable internationally. Kate Sanderson, in her analysis of the Faroese experience with the anti-whaling movement, cites the former director of the Whale and Dolphin Conservation Society, who made a typical argument during a 1991 television interview: "If they want to kill whales in the traditional way, that's fine with us, if nothing else about their way of life, significantly anyway, has changed."[65] Of course, neither the Vincentians nor the Faroese require the permission of the Whale and Dolphin Conservation Society—nor must they meet anyone's conditions—to continue whaling. Still, this statement stands as an example of the notion that whaling is something anachronistic and can only be practiced by those who are yet to modernize.

Sanderson acknowledges the uniqueness of Faroese pilot whaling as "a subsistence hunt for food in what is now, in most other respects, a modern technological society."[66] She singles out this ambiguity for critical analysis, challenging scholars and other outsiders to reconsider their assumptions about the interactions of human societies and their natural environments and whether these interactions must necessarily change as a society modernizes: "Pilot whaling represents a meeting and merging of boundaries between land and sea, between the social and the wild, between culture and nature, between the pre-modern and the post-modern, between the historical continuity and modern function of a traditional form of food production and prevailing perceptions of modern society. As a result it also challenges us to rethink our all too rigid definition of what it is to be modern and civilised, and our increasingly artificial relationship with nature. Pilot whaling in the Faroes provides Faroe Islanders with food; for others, it may also provide some food for thought."[67]

The Faroese themselves often agree that the grindadráp represents a cultural anomaly, a vestige of subsistence that remains a part of their modern society, perhaps transformed and reclaimed from its original purpose, but still valued. Magni Garðalíð, expert maker of traditional grindaknívar, or whaling knives, considers the role of the grindadráp—and particularly of the food it produces—in modern Faroese society: "I don't think it's necessary today, but we like it. Here in the Faroe Islands we would not die of hunger. But we would have lost a very big tradition and identity. I believe we would feel like it was stealing from us because we use that which we kill. We don't kill for fun. We use it for living. But it is not true to say we *must* kill it for living. It's a delicacy for us. It is not necessary, but I must also say that it is not necessary to eat so much chicken."[68]

Garðalíð's reference to eating chicken raises an interesting question: can it truly be said that any one food product is necessary to the survival of a human population, especially in a developed economy with access to all the variety that the global market provides? Dorete Bloch, the longtime lead scientist studying Faroese pilot whales, emphasized the cultural value, pleasure, and sustainability of eating locally, even if that means eating food that is peculiar to your location: "Ask the Danes not to eat pork. Ask the Greenlanders not to eat seal. Ask the Italians not to eat pizza. You can eat other things, but why should you? You eat what you can get yourself from the country.

Magni Garðalíð, holding examples of his *grindaknívar*

It's also something if you are thinking about green economy: you take it directly off your beach here."[69]

So the grindadráp is not necessary in terms of human survival. Were it to cease, no Faroese would starve. Should it therefore be terminated? Who would enact that termination? Who would enforce it? This line of questioning exemplifies the notion that whaling is something done only by those without access to modern, Western methods of food production or commodity imports. The unspoken assumption here is that whales should be a food source of last resort and that in terms of the simple provision of food, the grindadráp is a choice, not a necessity.

The same is true in St. Vincent. While the standard of living and most other economic indicators there are noticeably lower than in the Faroe Islands, it could not be said that the Vincentians must whale to survive. Food is abundant. Fruit trees grow nearly everywhere and subsistence fishing is reliable, even from shore. In both St. Vincent and the Faroe Islands, whaling is but one of many available methods of food production and procurement.

So, what has been the effect of the protest in the Faroe Islands, and what might the Vincentians expect should Sea Shepherd or another group with similar tactics and ideology target their whaling operation? Ironically, actions against whaling from abroad may actually strengthen, not challenge, support for whaling at home. Domestic factions sometimes coalesce in the face of outside opposition.

Neither the consumption of whale and dolphin meat and blubber, nor even the approval of whaling, is universal in the Faroe Islands and St. Vincent. In both locations, local people oppose whaling for dietary, ideological, religious, and environmental reasons. In the Faroe Islands, the recent international opposition to whaling seems to have had the effect of quieting any nascent anti-whaling voices within Faroese national discourse and consolidating support for the grindadráp as an element of Faroese national identity and an important feature of Faroese sovereignty amid an emerging sense of "us versus them." The Vincentians might consider the experience of the Faroese, should their beaches ever be visited by teams of black-hoodie-wearing foreign protesters.

9

——

The Value of Seawater

Whaling is an improbable activity. Whales and dolphins live in the ocean, dive deep, and surface only to breathe or occasionally to feed, thus making them difficult for humans—land-dwelling and air-dependent—to reach. These difficulties are only alleviated, never completely removed, by the modern whaling technology seen more regularly in the practices of the commercial operations of Japan, Norway, and Iceland than among the artisanal whalers of the Faroe Islands and St. Vincent. To capture these huge animals requires bravery, technology, skill, and cooperation. The decision to pursue whales at sea is a difficult one, fraught with risk of personal injury or loss. These risks have been present for the vast majority of would-be whalers throughout history. Medievalist Vicki Szabo makes this point in her discussion of a tenth-century Anglo-Saxon text, *Ælfric's Colloquy,* in which a teacher questions various tradesmen about their work. The teacher's dialogue with a fisherman illuminates what may have been a dominant perception of whaling in medieval Europe. According to Szabo, "The master asks this ambitious fellow whether he would consider catching a whale, and the fisherman expresses horror at this notion, stating that, 'it is a risky business catching a whale. It's safer for me to go on the river with my boat, than to go hunting whales with many boats. . . . I prefer to catch a fish that I can kill, rather than a fish that can sink or kill not only me but also my companions with a single blow.'"[1]

When we think of the dangers of whaling today, our thoughts might return to the terrors of *Moby-Dick* or the ordeal depicted in *The Wreck of the Whaleship Essex*, initiated by an "enraged" sperm whale ramming and sinking a whaling vessel.[2] In the Faroe Islands and St. Vincent, the drawn-out suffering of these disastrous whaling voyages is generally absent since both operations are shore-based. It's replaced instead by acute dangers that occur during the time of whaling alone. (Although I recall once in Samuel's whaling boat slowly motoring toward a pair of sperm whales that were lolling on the surface, just to get a closer look. When the larger of the two whales awoke and began swimming, menacingly fast, directly toward our bow, Papas sprang into action at the tiller and quickly reversed course. I was relieved by his quick reflexes—having recently read the story of the whaleship *Essex*, I assumed I would be the first crewmember to be eaten if it came down to that.) In the Faroes, the very act of driving and then hauling living whales onto the beach presents dangers such as being struck with a thrashing fluke, accidentally cut or stabbed with an errant whaling knife or spinal lance, or pitched from a boat into the cold water. In St. Vincent, mechanical problems with outboard motors threaten to set whalers adrift, much like their sail-propelled forebears when the winds died down. It's not unheard of for Vincentian fishing or whaling boats to be lost to the west, drifting out of sight of land throughout the night. If lucky, crewmembers are picked up by a passing vessel or eventually make land alive. At least one whaling crew never returned to shore.

Why does whaling continue in the face of these difficulties and dangers? According to Szabo, the discussion of whaling in *Ælfric's*

Colloquy "concludes with the master's observation that those who are bold enough to hunt whales make great profit from this risky venture."[3] The profitability of whaling remains a major motivator for its continuation in both the Faroe Islands and St. Vincent today. Profit, though, means something different in each place.

In St. Vincent the term is straightforward: whalers sell their catch to vendors wholesale for cash; vendors in turn process the carcasses into food, which they sell to the public. The pay can be good. Samuel explained this to me in the universal language of middle-aged men—that is, by complaining about the sloth of today's youth. We sat together under the shade of the tarpaulin in his outdoor workshop, surrounded by power tools, half-finished harpoons, and even the ribs of a boat in progress. "Young people today feel that seawater has no value," Samuel said. He paused to look around, first taking stock of the whaling equipment, then, it seemed, letting his mind drift up the hill toward his home: Samuel has a large house and drives a late-model SUV. His family is well provided for. He continued, speaking slowly and intentionally, the way you talk when you want someone to remember what you're saying: "Everything I own is from seawater."

In the Faroe Islands the sale of whale products is discouraged, if not completely forbidden. The grindadráp is intended to be a source of free food for the public, and for the most part it achieves this goal. Despite the grindadráp's lack of commercialization, it plays an important role in the Faroese economy at a number of scales, and it also creates profit (though with a degree of nuance to the term). Both whaling operations, in fact, are vital components of economic systems, and the economics of both operations have evolved throughout their history. The general course of evolution experienced by whalers and consumers in both locations has been from exploitation toward empowerment, and it can best be understood by looking at the roles played by people of various socioeconomic classes throughout the history of Faroese and Vincentian whaling. In both places, whaling has become a means by which personal, local, and national value is

created and expressed, self-sufficiency is reinforced, and external influence is resisted at a variety of scales, from the interpersonal to
the international.

Landowners' Whales and Finders' Fishes

Although whaling began in the Faroe Islands within societies that
were based upon preindustrial agriculture and methods of subsistence food production, concepts of class and inequality can still
readily be found in the grindadráp's history. The most striking example is the *jarðarhvalur,* or landowner's whale. The jarðarhvalur
represented the portion of the total take that was claimed by the
owner of the beach onto which the pod of whales was driven. Portions ranged from one-fourth to three-fourths of the total take
throughout different historical periods. This system was a frequent
source of complaints from landless peasants to the authorities. For
centuries these complaints went unheeded, probably due to the fact
that many of the authorities were themselves landowners and had no
incentive to curtail their own source of free food and revenue.

For comparison, let's turn south briefly and consider again another North Atlantic whale drive. In the Shetland Islands, a drive-
style whaling operation similar to the grindadráp existed until the
early twentieth century. There, the total take was originally divided
into three unequal shares: one-half went to the landowner, one-fourth
was given to the head of the county government, and the remaining
one-fourth was to be divided among the whalers.[4] This structure
greatly favored members of the ruling and landowning classes, many
of whom were absentees and most of whom can be assumed never to
have had an active role in any whaling activities. If, by chance, a landowner did participate in a whale drive, he would undoubtedly make
every attempt to land the whales on his own shore, whether this was
a prudent choice for the success of the whale drive or not. The ensuing argument and diversion of attention from the matter at hand

would be unlikely to contribute to a successful drive. Drive-style whaling is a community activity and cannot be conducted with much hope of success without the collective effort of dozens of whalers—some distributed among multiple boats and others on the shore awaiting the arrival of the pod. This entire assemblage is spread over a large coastal area, making cooperation essential. The reward for the whalers' efforts, though, was less than ideal, as even a large pod of whales is quickly diminished when the whalers have only one-fourth to divide among themselves. In 1839, a Scottish Court of Session heard the case of a complaint against this unfair division. The land-owners settled before a court decision was reached, agreeing to lower their percentage to one-third. In the late nineteenth century, the system was abolished in the Shetlands and everything of value produced in a whale drive became property of the whalers themselves.[5]

The situation in the Faroes was even more exploitative than in the Shetlands. Here, according to the Seyðabrævi ð, or "Sheep Letter," of 1298, the landowner was entitled to three-fourths of the total value of any whale stranded on his shore.[6] Combined with other deductions—for the church or crown—this left even less meat and blubber for those who performed the work of whaling. Understandably, this highly unequal distribution scheme was the subject of much litigation and political wrangling. By the time of Jens Christian Svabo—the seventeenth- and early eighteenth-century Faroese scholar—the jarðarhvalur had been reduced to one-half of the total take.[7] By 1832, it had been reduced to one-fourth, and the practice was abolished altogether in the Faroes in 1934.

In the Faroe Islands, as well as in the Shetlands, an economy of whaling developed by which the landowning class benefited greatly while the peasant class performed most of the labor and saw little of the returns. Why then, did the peasant seamen continue whaling when the landowners appropriated the majority of their proceeds? Let's consider two reasons that show direct benefit to the whalers themselves and one that may have been influenced by the landowner class. The first reason relates to two simple biological and behavioral facts about pilot whales: they are physically large and they travel in large groups. Thus, the result of a successful whale drive is that a huge volume of food becomes available. Even when one-half, one-third, or one-fourth is taken by the landowner, there is still more food available to the whalers than there would have been after a comparable amount of work in any other available method of food production: fishing, fowling, or sheep slaughtering, for example. To be sure, the system of jarðarhvalur was exploitative and unfair. But it did not remove sufficient incentives from the work of whaling to warrant the abandonment of the grindadráp altogether.

The second reason is found in a practice related to the jarðarhvalur—that of the finningarfiskur, or "finder's fish." You'll recall that the finningarfiskur is the largest or best whale of the pod and it is allotted, in its entirety, to the person who first sighted the pod of whales. An entire whale is much more than one person or even one family can use. Therefore, the one who receives the finningarfiskur is in possession of a surplus. What is done with this surplus is the finder's own choice, but often the recipient trades with neighbors for other products and services or gives it away as part of a system of informal reciprocity, to be paid back at a later time. If the finder is feeling magnanimous, the surplus may be given to the poor, to a hospital, or to some other type of charity. The personal satisfaction of being able to provide for one's neighbors is evident in a verse from an 1835 ballad written about the grindadráp: "And I hope they die; it is an enormous flock, / And the poor can have my boat share; / I'll get plenty myself anyway."[8]

The third reason that whaling endured in the Faroe Islands despite inter-class exploitation could be that the landowners acted in specific ways to defend and protect the practice in order to keep their incentive. Whale-driving is an inherently dangerous activity. Whales become disoriented in the shallow water and begin thrashing violently. Their tail flukes are strong and have been known to injure whalers and destroy boats. Peasant whalers living in a subsistence economy would not have had the capital reserves to replace damaged vessels, nor could they have afforded to spend weeks or months con-valescing after suffering broken limbs or other injuries. Very early in the history of the grindadráp, another deduction from the total take was established—the *skaðahvalur*, or "damage whale." This represents one of the few instances in which products from the grindadráp were allowed to be sold, the proceeds from which were used to pay for the repair of boats or to compensate for the lost wages of injured whalers.[9] Today, a community tax has replaced the skaðahvalur, but the con-cept remains the same—the wealthy and ruling class establishes a means by which risk to the laboring class is mitigated and the likeli-hood of the grindadráp continuing is increased.

Guns and Labor

Class divide in St. Vincent reached its historical peak during the eigh-teenth century, in the era of plantation slavery. Following the intro-duction of sugarcane to the West Indies in the 1640s, the Atlantic slave trade—already in existence since 1505—increased dramatically in volume and economic importance. As is the case with most Caribbean islands, the major ancestry of St. Vincent's present-day population arrived through the Atlantic slave trade. To say that plan-tation economies, dependent upon forced labor, involved enor-mous class inequalities is a gross understatement. Far from consti-tuting a monolithic labor force, though, the slave class developed internal hierarchies based mainly upon the treatment of individuals by the planters and the ability to rise above the basic slave's level of economic access. Thus, enslaved laborers with skills in particular trades were able to form something of an elite sub-class.[10] While the treatment they received was uniformly deplorable, there were cer-tain realms of labor to which slaves could aspire that would increase their standing and improve their life conditions. One of these trades was fishing. Recall that slave fishermen not only developed skills that allowed them to earn a profit from the sales of their surplus production but also were among the very few of their class whose workdays were largely unsupervised and independent of their masters. These fishermen enjoyed a higher-quality diet than estate-based slaves and spent the majority of their workday away from the oppressive micromanagement and discipline to which their plantation-bound colleagues were subjected. Additionally, the possibility of escape was much more real for fishermen-slaves, as they were provided with boats and fishing gear—means of transportation and survival once free.

Slavery was abolished throughout the British Empire, including St. Vincent, in 1833, but vestiges of the class structure it left behind can still be found. Near the same time as emancipation, the Yankee whaling ships began to arrive in the Caribbean and take aboard local men who had experience at sea, perhaps those who had been fishermen when they were enslaved. As Yankee whaling declined, the rise of local whaling, based primarily on Bequia, arose to fill the niche. The largest Bequia whaling station employed nearly a hundred men in the capture and processing of humpback whales. Other whaling stations were established on St. Vincent and nearby islands. Their legacy lives on in the whaling operations of Bequia and St. Vincent today.

Because of the relative amount of freedom their predecessors enjoyed during slavery, the artisanal skills they developed, their entrepreneurial ability to provide employment and wages to their countrymen, and their association with foreign capital, travel, and adventure, Caribbean fishermen and whalers developed into something of an elite class of skilled labor during the nineteenth and twentieth centuries. Signs of this class division remain in place today on St. Vincent, where whalers enjoy a higher status than ordinary fishermen and laborers.

One way this plays out is the issue of gun ownership in St. Vincent. Every afternoon when the whaling is finished, the harpooner transports the gun to his house, where it must remain safely guarded until the next day's whaling begins. Within St. Vincent's strict laws regarding gun ownership, whaling is one of the few occupations that carries with it permission to own a firearm. As the harpooner walks home from the quayside in the afternoon, gun slung over his shoulder, villagers look on with respect reminiscent of that shown a Wild West sheriff—a status not unlike that held by a successful Caribbean whaler.

Whaling and Personal Reward

In the Faroe Islands and on St. Vincent, whaling provides an opportunity both for personal reward and for acts of generosity. The anthropologist Jonathan Wylie describes situations in the Faroe Islands and the Caribbean that result in an immediate abundance of food as "crises of glut."[11] How each of these "crises" is handled is based on the forms and traditions of the local culture. In the Faroe Islands, as we've seen, great personal reward is given to the person who first sighted the pod of whales. Usually all participants in the grindadráp receive large portions of meat and blubber, with much left over to distribute to the nonparticipating members of the community. In St. Vincent, a day's catch of whales or dolphins brings immediate cash reward to the boat owner and his crew, but it also provides food for the community. Crisps, the small pieces of fried blubber, are often given away to people who have queued near the cooking facility awaiting their handout.

In both locations, people in the local communities who have not participated in whaling activities are recipients of proceeds from the efforts of those who have. In both the distribution of whale meat and blubber in the Faroe Islands and the free handout of crisps on the beach at Barrouallie, all are welcome to take their portion: the poor and the better-off, the local and the outsider, those who helped with the catch and the processing and those who did not. I've stood in both lines myself, as have other foreign researchers, and we have taken our shares with thankfulness. These situations serve to reinforce the high status and popularity of the whalers as providers and also lead to good community relations, social activity, and feelings of mutual aid and interdependence.

In St. Vincent, the existence of a whaling operation as part of a cash economy means that there are some who earn their living directly from the whaling sector: the boat owners and the vendors, who control the wholesale and retail markets, respectively, and those whom they employ. Wholesale prices vary widely depending partially upon ordinary market factors such as the amount of meat in storage and times of increased demand but also upon social factors: some harpooners and vendors are related by kinship or marriage and give each other special deals. On some days when I arrived back in Barrouallie after whaling with Samuel's crew at about the same time as another boat, Samuel would wait to see which vendor the other boat sold to. To keep things fair, and to give everyone a chance, he would sell to another vendor.

Each vendor typically employs up to ten individuals who help with the processing, distribution, and sales of the product. One boat owner explained to me that he employs twelve crewmembers on a rotating basis, working on both his fishing and whaling boats. Other boat owners also rotate their similarly sized crews. Thus, the four whaling boats and ten vendors currently active in Barrouallie employ a workforce of about 124 on a part-time basis. Culturally, this system works well, given the norm of multiple part-time jobs in Vincentian society.[12]

At the end of each day, after receiving payment from the vendor, the boat owner must pay expenses and divide the income among the crew. First, the cost of fuel is taken from the total. If the fuel cost is more than the total value of the catch, the boat owner absorbs the difference; a crewmember will not lose money on a day of whaling. If there is a positive remainder, as there usually is if a catch was made, it is then divided in two—half going to "the boat" and half to the crew. "The boat," of course, means the boat owner, who must pay for the necessary whaling supplies. This portion of the income funds replacement harpoons and lines and repairs to the boat, engine, and gear. The other half is divided among four "crewmembers"—the harpooner, the sternman, the centerman, and the engine. "The engine is the fourth man," one boat owner told me after paying out the proceeds from a particularly good take. The money paid to the engine is used for repairs and upgrades when needed or simply adds to the boat owner's profit.

This payment made to the engine has an analogue in the distribution of meat and blubber in the Faroe Islands. Jóan Pauli Joensen cited a 1710 report that detailed the normal distribution of proceeds from the grindadráp. During this time each active participant in the grindadráp was awarded two shares of meat and blubber: one for himself and one for his "weapons." Those who did not participate got only one share each.[13] Today, whaling equipment (a term now preferred to *weapons*) receives no extra share. Its role in the grindadráp, however, is reacknowledged every time a sýslumaður decides to issue a drápspartur, or killers' share, either instead of or in addition to the more common heimapartur, or home share.

Back in St. Vincent, after the crewmember payments and as a gesture of good favor, the boat owner usually divides 10 percent from the boat's portion between the harpooner and the sternman. This extra payment—simply called the "percentage"—is given as a sign of appreciation for their skilled roles in the whaling activities. The centerman, my position aboard Samuel's boat, is the least skilled and therefore does not earn a percentage. After experiencing the job of the centerman and watching the harpooners and sternmen in their roles, I was fine with this.

It may appear, at first glance, that the distribution of payments in St. Vincent closely resembles the unfair Faroese practice of jarðar-hvalur, or landowner's whale. In fact, taking the amounts paid to the engine, the boat, and the harpooner in a hypothetical distribution shown in the figure following, we see that if the boat owner serves as harpooner on his own boat—a common practice—he stands to take home almost three-fourths of the net profit, a figure equivalent to the original, and most exploitative, amount that the jarðarhvalur gave to the landowners. Is the financial position of Vincentian crewmembers really as bad as those thirteenth-century non-landowning Faroese

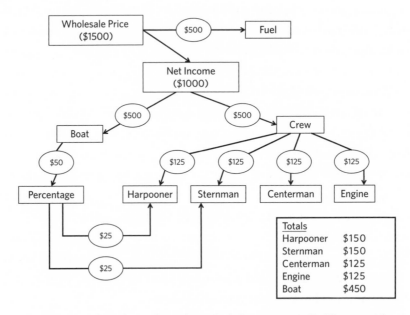

Payments resulting from a hypothetical whaling voyage in St. Vincent with amounts given in Eastern Caribbean dollars (EC$). The wholesale price, EC$1,500 (about US$555), and the fuel cost, EC$500 (about US$185), are typical for a successful day's whaling.

whalers? For two reasons I believe that the Vincentian whaling profit-sharing system is not as exploitative as the jarðarhvalur in the Faroe Islands was.

First, participants in the grindadráp must provide and maintain their own whaling equipment. The boats used in the drive are nearly always privately owned. Knives, hooks, and spinal lances belong either to the whalers themselves or to the community in which they live. In St. Vincent, the boat owner himself provides all the whaling equipment and absorbs all the cost of whaling. Any losses—whether financial, owing to unprofitable voyages, or physical, owing to damaged boats, engines, guns, or harpoons—are covered exclusively by the boat owner. Unprofitable voyages are quite common. In fact, of Samuel Hazelwood's 1,946 whaling days for which I have detailed financial records, 891 (46 percent) of them operated at a loss. For these voyages, while his crew received no pay, Samuel actually lost money. With greater risk comes greater reward.

Second, these profit-sharing payments, in the context of the broader Vincentian economy, provide a relatively good income for those directly employed in the whaling operation. For example, to achieve the average per capita gross national income level of US\$6,670, a centerman—the lowest-paid member of a blackfish boat's crew—would need to work 144 days with an average daily income of 125 Eastern Caribbean dollars.[14] This would certainly be attainable, according to Samuel's records from 2007 through 2017, which show whaling activity taking place on 59 percent of the days for which I have data during that period.

Vacations and Whale Dances

In addition to the supply of food and, in the case of St. Vincent, the monetary reward, whalers in both locations also enjoy a period of rest and relaxation after a large take. I remember meeting one St. Lucian whaler who had, the previous day, harpooned and sold a large pilot whale. He told me that the windfall would allow him to spend the next week "on vacation"—an aspect of labor not accessible to many of his compatriots. Similarly, according to Samuel's financial records, on 44 percent of the days after taking at least one pilot whale or orca, and on 46 percent of the days after grossing at least 1,000 Eastern Caribbean dollars (US\$372), the crew of the *Sea Hunter*, Samuel's whaling boat, took the day off. These non-whaling days provide the crewmembers and boat owners an opportunity for recreation or a chance to perform work that generates supplemental income. Either way, they represent a luxury afforded to few within their socioeconomic class.

In the Faroes, successful grindadráp were in the past followed by a community celebration. After the whales were brought ashore, while they were being counted and while the sýslumaður was calculating the shares, the whalers and other interested parties traditionally held a *grindadansur,* or pilot whale dance. Jonathan Wylie describes the grindadansur as part of the process of "recreating Faroese society" by reestablishing order after the excitement, drama, and disruption caused by the grindadráp.[15] Indeed, few dances exhibit the order, form, and restraint of the pilot whale dance. Wylie describes the scene: "Men and women link arms to form a long, twisting circle. Anyone may join the circle at any point. They dance with a rhythmically shuffling, kicking step to the singing of the ballads. There is no instrumental accompaniment. . . . When one ballad ends, the ring keeps moving round for a few moments until a new *skipari* [leader] starts up a new one. . . . The mood is high; the turning circle fills the room; the floor resounds to the beat as the dancers, backs straight and heads turned, 'tread the measure underfoot,' two steps forward and one, with a slight kick, back."[16]

The celebration of a community's good fortune, of which the grindadansur played a central role, constituted a welcome break from the mostly solitary life of farming or fishing. It is only the convenience of modern transportation—eliminating the need for everyone to remain in the whaling village while the sýslumaður tallies the whales and determines the shares—that has rendered the grindadansur obsolete in recent decades.

Whaling is dangerous and difficult work, and those who undertake it are rewarded for their skill and for their bravery. Like the culturally embedded conservation strategies, these incentives are constructed and maintained in the Faroe Islands and St. Vincent and have contributed to the establishment and endurance of whaling in these locations.

International Relations

With little locally driven opposition to whaling in either the Faroe Islands or St. Vincent, it is at the international scale that we see the majority of conflict about the activity. The Faroese grindadráp and the Vincentian blackfish operation are both, above all, food production methods. Each, however, also contributes to the cultural and national identity of the place where it occurs. In this way, international opponents of either whaling operation face cultural and nationalistic resistance to their simplistic assertions that if whaling ceased, an equivalent volume of food could be found from another source as a replacement. Whaling is for food, but it's not only for food.

The idea of an intentionally constructed "Faroese national identity" has been present since at least the mid-nineteenth century.[17] It was conceived as a base of resistance to Danish imperialism and as an expression of nationhood—even within a colonial political designation. The movement began as an effort to preserve the Faroese language, which at the time was perceived to be at risk of disappearing and being overwhelmed by the influence and prevalence of Danish, the written form of which had replaced written Faroese during the seventeenth century.[18] The movement that revived Faroese nationalism and placed political independence on the popular agenda officially began at the 1888 Jólafundurin, or Christmas Meeting, held in Tórshavn on December 26 of that year. This meeting was primarily intended to rally support "to defend the Faroese language," but Faroese cultural practices were also on the agenda.[19]

The Christmas Meeting began a national conversation that would last for more than sixty years, up until the establishment of home rule, and continues today in some circles toward the goal of total political independence from Denmark. It is within this discourse that the grindadráp and other traditions have been turned into Faroese national symbols—like the bald eagle in the United States, the *inuksuk* in Canada, or the *haka* in New Zealand. The Faroese ethnographer Jóan Pauli Joensen describes the grindadansur, or pilot whale dance, as "a national-romantic invention—invented as one of several cultural symbols in the creation of a Faroese identity."[20] The Faroese of the late nineteenth century, driven by this nascent cultural awareness, began a period of introspection, seeking symbols of their own culture in every aspect of their daily peasant lives. The first they found was the Faroese language, followed shortly by the grindadráp. The killing of pilot whales was elevated—or demoted?—from its position as a method of food production to a symbol of an emerging national identity. Joensen summarizes this transformation succinctly: "From being a part of the subsistence economy, the whale hunt became a tradition that conferred strength and substance to the developing Faroese identity and cultural awareness. The pilot whale became a Faroese symbol."[21]

Kenneth Williamson, a British soldier stationed in the Faroe Islands during the Second World War, described the grindadráp in 1948 as "an integral part of Faroese nationhood."[22] The innocence of this subsistence-strategy-turned-national-symbol was not to last, as the protests and threatened boycotts began during the 1980s and have continued to the present. The Faroese are probably now more attached to the grindadráp—or at least to the idea of the grindadráp—than ever, owing to their experience with the protests and the national solidarity that grew in response. What started as a movement toward national identity and language preservation has developed into a complex discourse about sovereignty, natural resource rights, food security, and the preservation of traditional ways of life. The grindadráp, according to plan, has been adopted as a symbol of what it means to be Faroese.

Prior to the anti-whaling protests of the 1980s, the grindadráp was seen as a unique yet largely unproblematic element of Faroese culture. Some even called it the "national sport" of the Faroe Islands.[23] The protests changed that. Anyone who remembers referring to the grindadráp as "sport" probably now regrets that choice of words. At first, the result of the protests was introspection among Faroese. This led to procedural changes to try to make the grindadráp more humane. Later, as the protests continued, the Faroese went through a period of reconsideration. Protesters were calling for boycotts of Faroese seafood, which makes up about 93 percent of the Faroe Islands' exports.[24] *If they boycott our fish, we'll have to stop whaling*—that was the common logic. As recently as 2008, multiple Faroese scholars stated that international protests would be the most likely cause of the grindadráp's cessation.[25] Today, though, intensified opposition to Faroese whaling has provoked a renewal of interest in the grindadráp among those who previously had been more ambivalent about its continuation. One Faroese contact remarked that the Sea Shepherd campaigns "have had the expected effect of giving the grind[adráp] massive support from the younger generations."[26] To distance themselves from Sea Shepherd and other anti-whaling organizations, the Faroese have largely consolidated what once was a spectrum of support for or opposition to the grindadráp into a monolithic—at least as it's presented to the outside world—culture that stands in opposition to the protesters and thus, by default, in favor of the grindadráp.

Additionally, the grindadráp could play a role in the future of Faroese-Danish relations, especially with regard to the possibility of Faroese independence. If the grindadráp ceased, the loss of its food products most likely would be made up through imports, bought on the cash economy. This would deepen the financial dependence of the Faroe Islands on Denmark. Danish subsidies totaled 630 million Danish kroner (US$94 million), or about 4 percent of Faroese gross domestic product, in 2013.[27] Many see these subsidies as an essential part of the Faroese economy, at least if the current standard of living is to be maintained. Political scientists have identified the Faroese reliance upon Danish financial subsidies as "one of the main obstacles toward independence."[28] Any economic changes that result in the Faroe Islands relying more heavily on the Danish subsidies could tend to weaken moves toward independence.

This is true not in spite of the noncommercial and nonprofessional nature of the grindadráp but instead precisely because it is an essentially free source of food. The Faroese prime minister's office pointed out in a 2002 report on sustainable development that "the economic value of pilot whales is measured against the economic value and environmental costs of importing the same amount of food."[29] Ragnheiður Bogadóttir and Elisabeth Olsen, a pair of Faroese social scientists, wrote in 2017, "In response to the powerful global forces challenging the grindadráp, Faroese people generally defend it as an alternative to deeper integration and dependence on the global food system."[30] Maintaining the grindadráp as a noncommercial, non-imported source of free, local food is a small but key part of a future Faroese economic and political independence.

Support for this view can be found in the past. During the Second World War, while British troops occupied the Faroe Islands, the national whaling records show frequent grindadráp. This is often attributed to the presence of patrol boats, which would have made sightings more frequent, but records from the late 1930s show that the annual take was already growing before the British arrived in April 1940, the same month Germany invaded Denmark. The increase in grindadráp during the war coincided with an increased need for food—not to feed the British, as they would have been well supplied from home, but to make up for lost imports, as the normal supply routes to Denmark were interrupted by the Nazi occupation. Recall Wylie's description of pilot whales as "an import, as it were, for which nothing had to be traded."[31] Danish support for the Faroe Islands, whether in the form of subsidies or commerce, contributes to the stability of the Faroese economy and society. When in the past this support has been cut off, the Faroese relied, at least in part, on the grindadráp to make up the shortfall. We might expect a similar need to arise should Danish support again be interrupted, this time by the establishment of a politically independent Faroese state.

International protests against whaling have not been as prevalent in St. Vincent as in the Faroe Islands, but they haven't been fully absent either. Those that have occurred have targeted the country's tourism industry. The major revenue-generating sector in most Caribbean countries is tourism. Some researchers and activists have pointed out the potential for the expansion of whale-watching tours in the Caribbean.[32] Whaling is often seen as incompatible with whale-watching for several reasons, including its potential to decrease the number of whales available, to change whale behavior and make the animals less likely to approach boats, and to cause negative perceptions of a place in the opinions of foreign tourists.[33]

The common assumption, supported by survey and interview data, that whale-watching tourists would be horrified if they were to actually see a whaling vessel in pursuit of a whale, or worst of all, making a kill, was put to the test in early 2017.[34] On a cloudy Thursday morning in March of that year, the crew of Samuel Hazelwood's whaling boat harpooned two orca from a pod that a whale-watching tour had recently been observing. Reports differ on whether tourists saw the whales killed or only heard the shots from the harpoon gun. What is not disputed is the fallout that the event caused. The international media picked up the story and publicized it with dramatic headlines like, "Whale-Watchers Horrified to Witness Fishermen Harpoon Two Orcas," and "Killing of Orcas in Front of Tourists Could Spell End of Whaling for Island Nation."[35] The Vincentian prime minister, Ralph Gonsalves, responded to the negative international attention by proposing a ban on the killing of orca, but he also defended Samuel—though he did not mention him by name—as "a very hard working fisherman."[36] The prime minister must navigate a narrow channel between the benefits that artisanal whaling brings to his country and the negative perception it can have on the world stage. He stated, in response to the orca hunt, "It is important for us to say that we have our traditions and we need to keep our traditions, but we can't keep traditions out of sync with the rest of the world or have those traditions continue in a manner which is injurious to us."[37] In St. Vincent, it is unclear whether the tradition of artisanal whaling can actually exist in sync with the rest of the world.

In other countries, such as Iceland, whaling and whale-watching industries do seem to coexist—the black whaling vessels and white whale-watching boats famously sharing a pier in Reykjavík's old harbor. Could this coexistence work in St. Vincent? Currently two tour operators offer whale- and dolphin-watching trips from St. Vincent. Their controversial encounter with Samuel's whaling boat in 2017 was the first of its kind. Ordinarily, when Vincentian whaling

and whale-watching vessels are at sea simultaneously, they are pursuing separate pods of cetaceans. If pilot whales and other dolphins become scarcer—or if whale-watching tourists become more
prevalent—will these conflicts increase? What about in the Faroe
Islands? Would a whale-watching excursion be granted an exception
to the law requiring that all pilot whale sightings be reported? If not,
would the trip turn into a grindadráp-watching cruise?

Worldwide, whale-watching generates higher revenues than
whaling.[38] While this economic statistic may be true in most specific cases as well, it is important to keep three important caveats in
mind. First, the tourist base must be large enough to support and
make profitable an upstart whale-watching business. Second, the
skills, connections, equipment, and capital needed to start a whale-
watching business are not necessarily available to whalers. In other
words, when a shift from whaling to whale-watching happens, those
individuals who lose their livelihoods are not always able to simply
start up a new business. If you were to go whale-watching in St. Vincent, wouldn't you expect a comfortable and reliable boat stocked
with familiar food and drink and well equipped with life preservers,
radios, and toilet facilities? Would you ride a "hot van" down to Barrouallie to arrange your tour, or would you prefer to visit a booking
office in Kingstown (or even inside your hotel lobby)? You would
probably rather just book the trip online from home and charge it to
your credit card. For Samuel Hazelwood and his colleagues to
stop whaling and start providing whale-watching tours, all of these systems would have to be created anew. It's far more likely that in a shift
from whaling to whale-watching in St. Vincent, those individuals currently whaling would not be the same ones to begin offering whale-
watching trips. That opportunity would be more accessible to new-
comers, probably from elsewhere, and to those local businesses
already involved in the tourism industry. The third caveat we must
remember is that the choice for whaling nations contemplating a
shift to whale-watching is really between the primary production of

food products and the generation of money. Of course, the money can be used to purchase food. The choice, then, is essentially a cultural one: is it preferable to produce or to buy food, and if to buy, from where?

The answer to the latter question is often the international import market, and in the context of the Caribbean, it is often the case that both the tourism revenue and the import commodities come from the same source—the United States. In a break from the Caribbean norm, the government of St. Vincent & the Grenadines has not acted to turn its back on whaling in favor of tourism, as have other island nations in the region, most notably Dominica.[39] Geographer Bonham Richardson explained the dominance of tourism in Caribbean regional politics and the associated racialized national expectations of behavior: "Billboards throughout the region remind (black) local residents to put on happy smiles for (white) tourists. . . . So groups of tourists can be typically loud and offensive while expecting deferential servility from their 'hosts.' Caribbean governments, with an eye on tourist profits, reinforce these expectations."[40] Part of the attraction of whaling as a Caribbean occupation traces back specifically to the opportunity to escape this sort of "deferential servility," first during the plantation era and now in today's neo-colonial, tourism-driven economy.

Whaling, then, can be seen as a form of national resistance to the reliance upon tourism and import commodity cycles that has become the standard economic procedure in many Caribbean nations. Not merely a method of food production, whaling is also a rejection of neocolonialism, an expression of national sovereignty, and a statement of political and economic autonomy. Tourism need not be the major—or only—economic activity, even in small, tropical island locations. In 2006, the BBC quoted Horace Walters of St. Lucia, the coordinator of the Eastern Caribbean Cetacean Commission, as saying, "We have islands which may want to start whaling again—it's expensive to import food from the developed world, and we believe there's a deliberate attempt to keep us away from our resources so we continue to develop those countries' economies by importing from them."[41]

The BBC story went on to quote an American tourist as saying, "If a country voted to bring back whaling it wouldn't affect my decision where to go on holiday. I'm just looking for a nice place to relax."[42] This tourist may not, however, constitute a representative sample. In 2001, Mark Orams, a New Zealand–based marine geographer, published the results of a questionnaire completed by 136 tourists in Tonga.[43] The Kingdom of Tonga supported a small-scale whaling operation, taking humpback whales for human consumption until 1978, when whaling was banned by royal decree. Tonga remains a constitutional monarchy and claims to be the only Polynesian country never colonized. Since at least the late 1990s, a pro-whaling international organization called the World Council of Whalers, with the support of some local Tongans, has been promoting a resumption of Tongan whaling. Stakeholders in the Tongan tourism industry are concerned about the effect this might have on tourism numbers. Based on the results of Orams's research, this concern seems justified. Sixty-five to 73 percent of foreign, whale-watching tourists who took the questionnaire reported that if whaling resumed in Tonga, they would be less likely to visit again. Considering that between 83 and 95 percent of Orams's respondents reported being opposed or strongly opposed to commercial whaling, it is likely that their reluctance to visit Tonga in a hypothetical future whaling era is due to their moral opposition to whaling and not simply the fact that there might be fewer whales to observe if some of them had been hunted.

The assumption that whaling and tourism cannot coexist, though, is not, and has not been, universally held. In the Faroe Islands, the grindadráp has long been viewed simply as a unique feature of Faroese folk society that exists alongside other subsistence activities such as fowling and sheep-rearing. Early visitors to the Faroe Islands certainly took note of the grindadráp and discussed it in their travelogues. Ac-

cording to the anthropologist Jonathan Wylie, "the grindadráp supports an immense literature."[44] The "largest body" of this literature,
according to Kate Sanderson, "consists of the many popular and general descriptions which have proliferated since the nineteenth
century, most of which are representative of the broad genre of travel
writing."[45] These "popular and general descriptions" rarely weigh in
on the grindadráp judgmentally. Rather, it was simply something to
observe, perhaps to participate in, and to describe. Even as recently
as 1990, a travel writer compared observing the grindadráp to other
iconic international experiences "like seeing the Great Wall in China
or the changing of the Guard at Buckingham Palace, though," the
author acknowledged, "the spectacle is a bit more bloody."[46] After
discussing select foreign impressions of the grindadráp from the
seventeenth to the twentieth centuries, Faroese ethnographer Jóan
Pauli Joensen explains that "only later in the descriptions of the pilot
whale kill does the focus fall on the whales."[47] This turn, Joensen explains, coincides with "the emergence of new environmental organisations" and signals the beginning of a new controversial era in the
history of whaling in the Faroe Islands and worldwide.[48]

Those who would take on the challenge of whaling, as acknowledged by the teacher in *Ælfric's Colloquy* and still evidenced by artisanal whalers today, expose themselves to great risk and stand to earn
great reward. While the decision to participate in whaling or not remains an individual choice, the potential for both gain and loss is
not limited to the scale of the individual. At scales based on occupation, economic class, geographic area, and international relations,
whaling continues to present extreme risks and rewards. Individual
whalers put their own lives and safety at risk in order to feed themselves and their families, to become financially secure, to earn
standing in their communities, to perform acts of generosity, or to
enjoy moments of comfort and leisure unknown to those in other
fields. Villages where whaling occurs enjoy the benefits of food and
economic security that others find more difficult to achieve, and they

invest both economic and human capital in the effort to maintain their status as whaling villages. Internationally, these whaling nations identify as such and acknowledge a lack of equivalence between whaling and other methods of food production. In the Faroe Islands and St. Vincent, the act of whaling provides more than a meal, an income, or a status; it contributes in a major way toward what it means to be Faroese or Vincentian.

10

The Mercurial Sea

Ólavur Sjúrðarberg, president of the Grindamannafelagið, and I stay in touch regularly by email. When he signs off, it is usually with some variant of the phrase "Not long now." This isn't—as far as I know—a translation of any normal Faroese valediction; it may just be Ólavur's style. I like the phrase because it looks forward with a sense of expectation. Ólavur probably uses it the way native English-speakers say "See you soon" at the end of a letter or phone call. The phrase takes on a sense of foreboding, though, in the context of most of my emails with Ólavur, which inevitably touch on the subject of the grindadráp. How long will the grindadráp continue? This is a question that the Faroese have been asking themselves for a long time. The answer has often sounded a lot like "Not long now."

One of the earliest predictions of the end of the grindadráp came during the late eighteenth century, when for twenty years, beginning in 1755, no pilot whales were killed in all the Faroes. This was not some intentional temporary moratorium; the whales simply didn't come in during those two decades. Jóan Pauli Joensen describes the situation as one in which "it was not possible to maintain the whaling tradition and the skills required to conduct a whale hunt correctly" and concludes that "correct hunting practice was lost for a number of generations."[1] In 1776, 743 whales were taken in two separate drives—one each in Miðvágur and Hvalvík—and for more than fifteen years thereafter, the grindadráp remained sporadic. During that time transportation was difficult and a grindadráp in Miðvágur would have been nearly impossible for someone from Suðuroy, for example, to attend. It was not until 1792 that the grindadráp started occurring regularly again. For many villages, then, that was thirty-seven years without whales. Think of how much knowledge can be lost in that amount of time!

Some Jugglery of Satan

It's no wonder that, in years past, some Faroese turned to religion to explain—and to try to reverse—periods of scarce whaling. The historian John West translated a 1720 letter from Diderik Marcussen, a provincial bailiff, to Peder Arhboe, a priest on the island of Vágar. In it, Marcussen appeals to the priest on behalf of the village of Skálabotnur, which he says "has formerly been one of the best pilot-whale beaching places in this country, but now for some years it has not been possible to drive the whales in, or on to the land, so that the inhabitants of that place are in the thoughts that some jugglery of Satan shall be there on the sand, hindering the entry of the whales, wherefore I together with all the inhabitants of that place, make the friendly request to you in case you know any means with God's help by which the enchantment may be dispelled." For good measure, Marcussen offered to pay Arhboe, both in money and in whales, if he was able to help.[2]

As for the priest's ability to reverse Satan's alleged jugglery, he appears not to have been successful: the decade of the 1720s saw only three grindadráp in Skálabotnur after Marcussen sent his letter—a total of sixty-six whales. When the list of hvalvágir was first established, Skálabotnur was not even included. What was lost there foretells what could be lost throughout the Faroe Islands if the grindadráp ever ceases completely. Marcussen, writing to the priest in 1720, was clearly concerned about his village's food supply. Today's concerns are no less practical: food is the one essential product of whaling in the Faroe Islands. The difference between then and now is that the residents of Skálabotnur still had access to whale meat and blubber from other villages. Sharing has long been integral to the grindadráp, but for the institution to continue there must be something to share. If the grindadráp were to cease completely throughout the Faroe Islands, then the food it produced would need to be replaced on a national scale from outside.

In early 2017, nearly 300 years after the village's bailiff wrote his desperate letter, the enchantment may finally have been dispelled. Skálabotnur was temporarily added to the list of approved hvalvágir. This provisional inclusion was meant to allow experts a chance to reassess its potential as a whaling beach. Then, in June of that year, a mixed-species pod of pilot whales and Atlantic white-sided dolphins was sighted near Nólsoy. The pod was split, the pilot whales were killed at Tórshavn, and the dolphins were driven up the long fjord to Skálabotnur and killed there. In terms of food production, the residents of Tórshavn clearly came out ahead: 164 large whales versus 8 small dolphins killed at Skálabotnur. But no one in Skálabotnur complained about the dearth of meat and blubber; the dolphins were worth much more than their skinn value. Their successful beaching proved that Skálabotnur could once again be included as a hvalvág.

Taking Our Time about Dying

Vincentian whaling, likewise, has been expected to fade away for decades now. When the journalist Ethel Starbird interviewed Griffith Arrindell, the de facto leader of Vincentian whaling at the time—referred to by Starbird as "the baron of Barrouallie"—for her 1979 article in *National Geographic,* Arrindell acknowledged that even then his trade was seen as being on its way out. "Doctor say I no live long," Starbird quotes the eighty-six-year-old Arrindell as saying, "same with blackfish fishing. But we both take our time about dying."[3] The major risk to the operation at the time was the decline in demand for pilot whale oil as an industrial lubricant. Since the whale oil market's collapse, we know, the demand for cetacean meat and blubber for human consumption has filled the void. Local demand for oil, not as a lubricant but as a health and grooming product, has contributed too. Vincentians recommend taking a spoonful—or a shot glass—of blackfish oil as a remedy against the common cold.

Later, during the 1970s and 1980s, the Barrouallie whaling operation "virtually collapsed" owing to a severe reduction in pilot whale takes, which reached its lowest point of only twenty-five whales during the entire year of 1979.[4] The operation was saved by increased catches of other, smaller species of dolphin, but as recently as 1994 it was considered to be "a relict industry" by one prominent researcher, hinting at its presumed imminent demise.[5] A relict is an anachronism, a holdover from a previous era, a thing destined to disappear. Barrouallie's whaling operation might have been a relict except for its adaptability. The trend of making up for a lack of pilot whales by pursuing smaller dolphins continued through the 1990s and is still evident today, with the pilot whale being "considered the main target" but other dolphin species actually constituting the bulk of the take during recent decades.[6]

In 2009, I surveyed more than 400 Vincentian and Faroese postsecondary students on their thoughts about whaling in their home countries.[7] The results indicated generally high levels of support for whaling and strong beliefs that it would continue throughout the students' lifetimes. This came as something of a surprise given that the demise of whaling has been predicted for so long in both places.

That demise has not happened yet, and it's difficult to talk about new threats, given each whaling operation's history of overcoming obstacles. Still, the state of today's marine environment presents a challenge to the continuation of whaling in both the Faroe Islands and St. Vincent that even the most adaptive of cultures may not be equipped to overcome. Rather than lost skills, fluctuating markets, or international protest, the greatest threat to whaling in both the Faroe Islands and St. Vincent today is the invisible presence of environmental contaminants in the ocean. The best-understood of these—and arguably the most concerning from a public health perspective—is mercury.

A traditional English shanty sings of the plight of the sailor aboard a whaling ship: "Sometimes we're catching whales, my lads, but mostly we get none."[8] Success in whaling depends, to a large degree, on something wholly out of the whaler's control: the sea itself. Poets refer to the ocean as "mercurial," a word used to emphasize the sea's volatile, temperamental, and unpredictable nature. But the word has another, more literal meaning: simply containing the element mercury. While the mercurial, unpredictable sea has brought times of abundance and times of dearth to the whaling communities of St. Vincent and the Faroe Islands, the mercurial, mercury-laden sea may prove to be a threat that neither whaling operation can overcome. In the Faroe Islands the contaminant issue is well known. In St. Vincent, the problem is just beginning to be understood.

A Fleet-Footed Messenger

Some mercury occurs naturally, released from the earth's crust slowly through the weathering of rocks or explosively during volcanic eruptions. It is also a component of air pollution, primarily from coal-burning power plants, and water pollution, either from industrial activities such as small-scale mining or as rainfall bringing down air pollution. Eventually, much of the atmospheric mercury finds its way to the ocean. Once in the ocean, the mercury, being much denser than water, sinks to the bottom, where it is methylated—that is, changed chemically from elemental mercury to methylmercury—by bacteria in the benthic, or ocean-floor, environment. Methylmercury is a far more dangerous form of the pollutant to humans.

The largest contributors of mercury to the environment are large, industrialized nations, which, unlike the Faroe Islands and St. Vincent, burn coal for energy. That's right: these two whaling nations, where an important food source is threatened by an industrial pollutant, do not themselves contribute directly to the pollution. Coal-burning areas often experience localized deposition of mercury in their soil and waterways but, true to its namesake, the fleet-footed Roman messenger god, mercury is quickly and widely dispersed in the upper atmosphere and deposited globally, including in otherwise pristine environments.[9]

Single-celled organisms living in the benthic environment absorb methylmercury. The tiny animals that feed on these organisms ingest the pollutant as well. As larger and larger animals feed on the smaller, polluted organisms, the concentration of methylmercury increases—a classic case of biomagnification. Because the oceans are natural sinks for pollution, high-trophic-level marine animals such as seabirds, sharks, and cetaceans are often found with high concentrations of methylmercury in their tissues—particularly the kidneys and liver, but also the muscles and other tissues. People who eat these animals are then claiming the apex position in the food web and ingesting the highest level of methylmercury of all.

The direct human health effects of methylmercury are largely neurological, but mercury and other toxins found in the tissues of cetaceans consumed in the Faroe Islands have been linked to diseases of the cardiovascular, immune, and reproductive systems as well.[10] The suite of conditions linked to mercury poisoning includes mental and physical impairments and is sometimes referred to as "Minamata disease," after the Japanese city where an early case of long-term mercury exposure was first discovered during the 1950s.[11] According to the World Health Organization (WHO), mercury poisoning causes symptoms that include "tremors, insomnia, memory loss, neuromuscular effects, headaches, and cognitive and motor dysfunction."[12] The WHO cautions that pregnant women should most strictly avoid methylmercury exposure, as the contaminant can affect developing fetuses through the placenta.

The suffering of the citizens of Minamata has been acknowledged and memorialized in the form of the Minamata Convention on Mercury—a United Nations treaty intended to "protect the human health and the environment from anthropogenic emissions and releases of mercury."[13] The United States was the first country to ratify the convention, in 2013, and it went into effect in 2017. If successful, the Minamata Convention will reduce the amount of mercury emitted annually, but the benefits will take a long time to be realized since so much already exists in the environment. In the near term, the Faroese and Vincentians will have to deal with the problem of mercury pollution on their own.

Since 1977, Faroese scientists have been aware of the problem of methylmercury and other environmental pollutants in the muscle and blubber tissue of pilot whales taken in the grindadráp.[14] Beginning in 1985, a joint Faroese-Danish-American research team selected nearly 2,000 children to participate in the Children's Health and the Environment in the Faroes (CHEF) Project, an ongoing, long-term study of the effects of chronic exposure to low doses of mercury on human development. The first cohort of participants are now young adults. Their mental and physical development has been monitored, along with their consumption patterns of pilot whale meat and blubber and the levels of methylmercury in their systems, for over thirty years.

Findings about the exposure to mercury and other environmental contaminants have led Faroese public health authorities to issue increasingly strict consumption guidelines to the population. The first recommendation was made in 1977 and advised people to limit their consumption of pilot whale meat and blubber to one meal per week, and to avoid the consumption of whale liver and kidneys altogether. This was a difficult recommendation for the Faroese people to accept. Pilot whale meat and blubber are otherwise healthy and popular food products: good sources of protein, A and B vitamins, and fatty acids.[15] Before the CHEF project began, Faroese doctors had regularly recommended that children be given more blubber to eat because of its high nutritional value.[16]

Then in 1980, because of the particular vulnerability of developing fetuses to mercury contamination, pregnant women were advised to further limit their consumption. In 1989, the discovery of high concentrations of polychlorinated biphenyls (PCBs), another kind of industrial pollutant, in pilot whale blubber, along with the increasing concentration of mercury in the lean muscle tissue, led Faroese health authorities to issue another guideline, this time suggesting the limit of no more than 200 grams each of pilot whale meat and blubber per month. Two hundred grams is about the size of a large chicken breast. A further revision to the guidelines took place in 1998, when adults were advised to eat pilot whale meat and blubber no more than twice per month. Additionally, the 1998 recommendations were the first to advise all girls and pre-menopausal women to avoid blubber completely, warning about the long-term accumulation of PCBs in the body. Women who absorbed PCBs through their food as young girls can still pass the toxins on to their children when they become pregnant as adults, either through the breastfeeding of infants or directly through the placenta to the developing fetus. After the issuance of the 1998 dietary guidelines there was a marked decrease in the consumption of pilot whale meat and blubber by women. Men continued to eat.

Finally, in 2008, citing data showing that "pilot whales today contain contaminants to a degree that neither meat nor blubber would comply with current limits for acceptable concentrations," the Faroese health authorities issued the landmark recommendation that "the pilot whale is no longer used for human consumption."[17] Consider the gravity of this recommendation. The advice of the Faroe Islands' top medical researchers was to discontinue the consumption of meat and blubber from pilot whales. Not to limit consumption;

to stop it. This was not a demand thrust upon the Faroese from abroad. Their own public health officials made this difficult call based upon the data they had been collecting for more than thirty years. They were not ignorant of what they were saying: without consumption of the food products it produces, the grindadráp becomes meaningless, unjustifiable. In 2008, the Faroese health authorities officially advocated ending the Faroe Islands' thousand-year history of whaling.

The Times and the Environment Are Changing

The issue of environmental contaminants, which could have had the potential to unify the concerns of those in favor of and those opposed to the grindadráp, has instead only served to distance the two positions. Ostensibly, both the organizations that strive to protect the ocean and the Faroese who draw their livelihoods from the ocean want to see a cleaner, healthier, less-polluted marine environment. Instead, environmental organizations have largely used the data related to marine pollution and its risks to Faroese public health not to decry the deterioration of marine ecosystems and to call for an abandonment of coal and a wider implementation of renewable energy production, but as further evidence that the grindadráp should cease, often ridiculing or castigating the Faroese for not immediately abandoning the grindadráp in light of the data on mercury contamination. For example, Paul Watson of Sea Shepherd states, "Considering that pilot whale meat is the reason that the Faeroese have the highest level of toxic mercury in their bodies of any people in the world, the intelligent thing would be to not eat whale meat. Tradition appears to outweigh common sense in the Faeroes."[18] The Environmental Investigation Agency's argument is similar. According to its director, Jennifer Lonsdale, "The Faroese Government is ignoring the terrifying health warnings of its own Chief Medical Officer. Allowing around 85 tonnes of toxic meat and blubber to be consumed by the islanders is astoundingly irresponsible."[19]

While these arguments contain some truth about the problem of mercury and other forms of industrial pollution in the marine ecosystem—Watson's superlative is likely hyperbole—they are most interesting in their apparently uncritical embrace of the pollution as an argument in their favor, a mere fact to be reconciled, mainly through the cessation of the grindadráp, and not as a problem in its own right. But organizations such as Sea Shepherd, Greenpeace, and the Environmental Investigation Agency—among others—exist specifically to advocate for whales, dolphins, marine ecosystems, and the natural environment more broadly. Are these organizations not concerned about the effects of mercury and other pollutants on the whales themselves? What about the presence of mercury in whale tissues as an indicator of the systemic deterioration of the marine environment? Marine biologists and other scientists have shown that cetacean health is compromised by the same contaminants now affecting human consumers of whales and dolphins in the Faroe Islands and St. Vincent.[20] Why do these organizations fail to decry the pollution that arguably affects more individual cetaceans than all the world's whaling operations combined? Probably because whales are large, endearing, recognizable animals, and mercury is essentially an invisible threat. Environmental organizations tend to focus on the charismatic, rather than the unseen, in their efforts to raise both awareness and funding.

Or this bias may actually be a case of cultural and geographical favoritism: excusing one's local method of energy production while finding fault in the food production methods employed somewhere else. Most international environmental organizations are based in large, developed, industrialized countries, many of which burn coal for energy and thus contribute directly to the problem of mercury in the ocean environment in general and in the tissues of pilot whales caught and consumed by the Faroese and Vincentians specifically. Most of these industrialized, often coal-burning, nations—countries that host international environmental organizations like Sea Shepherd, Greenpeace, and the Environmental Investigation Agency—

have extensive whaling histories but gave up whaling decades or more ago. For them, to argue against whaling is to implicate the whalers. To argue against mercury pollution is to implicate their own way of life. Thus, environmental organizations decry the grindadráp and strengthen their argument with findings related to their own countries' contributions toward environmental degradation.

To the Faroese, though, the presence of contaminants in the marine environment is an issue worthy of special consideration. For example, Ólavur Sjúrðarberg implored me during an interview to "tell the people from the distant countries, 'please, please do not put that much poison out in the oceans.'" Elin Brimheim Heinesen, a Faroese author, echoes this sentiment in an editorial: "The Faroese believe that they have the sovereign right to decide if or when they should stop pilot whaling. They think that whale-saving efforts should rather be concentrated on stopping the pollution that threatens the oceans and the maritime foods the Faroese live on, [including] the pilot whales."[21] The Faroese government makes a similar case in stating that, "the major focus of international efforts by governments, international bodies and environmental organisations must be to protect and promote the rights of coastal nations to the sustainable use of their marine resources. This is best achieved by adopting effective measures to reduce and eliminate, at its source, global industrial pollution, which can end up in the valuable food provided by the sea."[22]

In 2012, Pál Weihe, Chief Medical Officer of the Faroe Islands, principal investigator on the CHEF project, and the public health official who personally made the recommendations, first to reduce and then to cease the consumption of pilot whales, reflected on the issue in a paper for the *International Journal of Circumpolar Health*. In a departure from the ordinarily formal language of a medical research report, Weihe and his coauthor emotionally conclude their review by reiterating the recommendation that no pilot whale meat or blubber be consumed and by admitting, "It is with great sadness that this recommendation is provided. The pilot whale has served the Faroese well for many hundreds of years and has likely kept many

Faroese alive through the centuries. But the times and the environment are changing, and we therefore believe that this recommendation is necessary from a human health point of view."[23]

Appealing to the Faroe Islands' own innocence in the production of mercury as an environmental pollutant, Weihe reminds his readers that "we in the Faroe Islands are not responsible in regard to the marine pollution, which has been inflicted upon us from outside."[24] Weihe's exoneration of his own country with regard to the source of the marine pollution is correct, if only technically so. The Faroe Islands do not currently burn coal for energy on an industrial scale. But they have, since at least the early 1700s, mined coal on a small scale both for export and for domestic heating.[25] Small-scale coal production continues today.[26] Further, with regard to energy-based atmospheric pollution in general, the Faroe Islands rely on fossil fuels, all imported, for about 60 percent of their annual domestic energy production, and to power their many fishing vessels. Since 1992, the Faroese fishing fleet has used an average of more than 80,000 metric tons of oil per year—by far the biggest use of fossil fuels in the Faroe Islands.[27] Because of this heavy reliance on fuel and the small Faroese population, the former Faroese prime minister Kaj Leo Johannesen claimed that the Faroe Islands has the highest per capita oil consumption in the world.[28] Additionally, the Faroese have been exploring actively for oil in their territorial waters since 2001, inspired in part by the discovery of oil off the Shetland Islands during the 1970s.

The Faroese case against global atmospheric pollution would certainly be bolstered by a stronger commitment to renewable energy sources. The level of environmental awareness, especially among the politically engaged Faroese youth, is promising. Since I first began conducting fieldwork in the Faroe Islands in 2005, the sight of geothermal heating units in homes and electric cars on the streets has become noticeably more common. Indeed, in both the Faroe Islands and St. Vincent—as we shall soon see—an improved environmental record within the energy sector specifically, but also for other purposes such as heating or cooling, fisheries, and transportation, would

only make stronger the case against the polluting industries and nations of the world that are directly responsible for the contamination found in tissues of whales and dolphins they take for food. The
Faroese call on the world to reduce its contribution of mercury and
other pollutants to the atmosphere. The Vincentians are likely to add
their voices to that plea soon. As each of these two nations improves
its own environmental record, their collective pleas for sustainability
abroad grow more compelling.

Pál Weihe and other Faroese public health authorities remain
resolute that their findings suggest that the grindadráp will, and
should, cease. Already a reduction in consumption has been observed
in correlation with findings of higher mercury concentrations.[29] This
trend is likely to continue once the short-term increase in solidarity
against the environmental activist campaigns levels off.

St. Vincent is at least four decades behind the Faroe Islands in its
understanding of the public health risks presented by environmental
contaminants in cetacean tissues. Together with scientific colleagues
based in the United States and the Caribbean, I've been engaged in
the analysis of tissue samples collected from the edible parts of pilot
whales and other dolphins brought ashore at Barrouallie for the past
few years. We have found levels of mercury higher than those found
in the Faroe Islands at the beginning of the mercury studies there.
Mercury is normally measured in parts per million (ppm). The use of
such a precise unit indicates just how potent a contaminant mercury
is. Even tiny concentrations can be harmful. When Faroese scientists
first began studying mercury levels in pilot whales in the 1970s
they found an average methylmercury concentration of 0.77 ppm.
Our first study of Vincentian-caught cetaceans did not analyze tissues from pilot whales—Barrouallie whalers didn't take any during
the study period—but found an average concentration of 1.03 ppm in
the tissues of twenty-eight spinner dolphins and eleven Atlantic
spotted dolphins caught during 2009.[30] Our next Vincentian study
looked at a wider range of cetacean species, which included more
species of smaller dolphins and also both pilot whales and orca,

caught over the course of a year (August 2015–July 2016) and found even higher concentrations.

Various international health and environmental organizations offer different guidelines for determining when food is too contaminated for consumption. These range from the more conservative (0.22 ppm, recommended by the Biodiversity Research Institute) to the more permissive (1.0 ppm, suggested by the WHO and the U.S. Food and Drug Administration).[31] In the Faroe Islands during the late 1970s, 0.77 ppm was a concentration high enough to initiate a set of local dietary guidelines and a multi-decade longitudinal health study involving thousands of participants. With mercury found at higher concentrations now in St. Vincent, why should anything less be done there?

Vincentian journalist Paul Lewis was among the first to discuss the potential mercury problem there publicly. In a 2012 article, he called for both an end to Vincentian whaling and a reduction in pollution by industrialized countries.[32] Lewis's warning, however, may have an uphill battle toward public acceptance. In my surveys of Vincentian youths, I asked participants whether "blackfish meat" (using the local term) is a healthy food or not. Sixty-seven percent responded that it is. Another 19 percent said they didn't know. Only 8 percent answered that "blackfish meat" is not healthy. This result may not indicate ignorance as much as balance. Local, traditional foods often carry health benefits that are still available in spite of moderate loads of environmental contamination. In the Arctic, for example, the Arctic Monitoring and Assessment Programme (AMAP) has long studied the effects of environmental contaminants on both and human and ecosystem health. With regard to balancing the risks and benefits of traditional yet contaminated foods, AMAP's 1998 report stated, "Weighing the well-known benefits of . . . traditional food against the suspected but not yet fully understood effects of contaminants, it is recommended that . . . consumption of traditional food continues, with recognition that there is a need for dietary advice to Arctic peoples so they can make informed choices concerning the foods they eat."[33]

Like the AMAP scientists, the Vincentian youths I surveyed may have understood that the consumption of "blackfish meat" carries with it a certain degree of risk but that if it was abandoned, other risks would likely be present in whatever foodstuffs supplanted it as alternatives. Anytime a food product is discarded for reasons of health, safety, or environmental impact, it is important to consider these qualities of the replacement food. Magni Garðalíð, the Faroese knifemaker, put it succinctly: "If it was not a danger to eat whale meat, I would eat much more of that than junk food." The same alternative, "junk food," would likely be a popular choice in St. Vincent if dietary recommendations were introduced there. As the influx of international fast-food outlets to St. Vincent and throughout the Caribbean continues, finding food that is at once affordable, local, and healthy becomes increasingly difficult.

In both the Faroe Islands and St. Vincent, a strong reliance on the sea for sustenance is sure to continue, regardless of the specific products that constitute the mainstay of nutrition. Land area is simply too scarce in these archipelagic nations to provide all the necessary food. What both places lack in land is made up in offshore exclusive economic zones. St. Vincent & the Grenadines, as a recent United Nations report points out, controls a marine area 90 times larger than its terrestrial area.[34] In the Faroe Islands the ratio is even greater: almost 200 times more ocean territory than land area.[35] The nutritional future of both the Vincentians and the Faroese, good or bad, is inextricably tied to the sea.

The accumulation of marine pollution in cetacean tissue changes the discussion about whaling in an interesting way. Whaling is often seen, prima facie, as an assault upon the natural environment. Its opponents refer to whaling as a "crime against nature."[36] Here, though, we see data made available through whaling that give us an indicator of larger-scale patterns of ecological degradation. In their *Sierra Club Handbook of Whales and Dolphins,* first published in 1983, marine mammologists Stephen Leatherwood and Randall Reeves considered various threats to cetacean conservation, including whaling, and still concluded, presciently, that "the aspect of conservation that drives us closest to despair is pollution."[37] Marine pollution is a major threat to the ocean ecosystem and its cetacean inhabitants, as well as to humans who consume foods derived from fish, shellfish, and (in places where they are eaten) cetaceans.

The Faroese and Vincentians who are aware of—and concerned about—the presence of pollution in their food supply can, and do, speak out critically to the industrialized nations responsible for the pollution. It may seem ironic for whalers to criticize the environmentally destructive behavior of non-whalers. Maybe, rather than merely noting the irony, anti-whaling activists should consider what it means that the environmental effects of their own countries' actions are being called into question by small-island whalers and whale-eaters. Maybe this is a reminder that we all should consider the long-distance and long-term environmental effects of our lifestyles.

The End of Whaling

The grindadráp has existed in the Faroe Islands for centuries. The Vincentian blackfish operation is not nearly as old, but has come to play a role similar to that of the grindadráp in the creation and maintenance of a national identity. As one Vincentian government official told me, "Blackfish defines us as a nation."[38] Neither operation has exhausted its resource, the local cetacean populations, most likely because of their reliance upon culturally embedded conservation strategies in the regulation of their take. The problem of environmental contamination, though, may be too great a challenge for either whaling operation to withstand. If the Faroese public abides by the current dietary recommendations, it is likely that some of those alive today will witness the end of the grindadráp. This might occur within just a few years, or maybe, in an effort to balance the cultural connection to pilot whale meat and blubber with the health risks of its consumption, the food will be retained as something of a ceremonial meal, eaten only on special occasions such as weddings, birthdays, and the Faroese national holiday, Ólavsøka. Either way, it appears that the days of the grindadráp are numbered.

The Faroese, for now, hold their tradition and their health in tension. This leads to debates at the national level, with grindaformenn and other whaling advocates making public arguments against Pál Weihe and his medical colleagues on Faroese radio. It also spurs debate within households. The 2016 documentary *The Islands and the Whales* showed poignantly how families can be divided—along lines of both gender and generation—regarding the best way to respond to the evidence of environmental contaminants.[39] Pál Weihe himself views the findings from his research as the beginning of the end for the grindadráp. Still, he would rather see the end come gradually, naturally, and not through legislation. He told me in an email that "the reduction in the consumption of whale meat and blubber should be based on an understanding of the toxicological risks. Not a decision from the politicians. I think what will happen is that the women first will stop eating it and then the men will follow. However, my best prediction is that sporadic killings will take place over the next decade and then it will be a forgotten culture."[40] That email came in 2009. Weihe's decade-long timeline is nearing its end.

With the availability of the data from our ongoing mercury study in St. Vincent, when the Vincentian Ministry of Health, Wellness, & the Environment chooses a course of action, the public there is likely to react in a way similar to the Faroese. If international anti-whaling protests come to the Caribbean, whaling may be buoyed on for a few more years or decades in a show of solidarity and national sovereignty, but eventually the public response to the science will likely include a reduction in the consumption of whale meat and blubber. This will, in turn, result in a decrease in whaling effort, and an eventual end of whaling. In 2009, 78 percent of the postsecondary students I surveyed in St. Vincent expressed a belief that whaling there would continue indefinitely into the future. I expect this number to decrease as knowledge of the health risks posed by mercury and other environmental pollutants increases. A repeat of my 2009 survey would likely find fewer respondents who consider blackfish meat to be healthy, as well as a proportional decrease in the number who believe whaling will continue. The sustainable take rates in the Faroe Islands, and the likely sustainable numbers in St. Vincent, paired with the risks to the continuation of the operations themselves, may mean that the outlook for both of these artisanal whaling societies parallels a 2013 description of Norwegian minke whaling in *National Geographic* magazine: "With the North Atlantic minke whale population estimated at a healthy 130,000 animals, Norway's modest annual catch is considered highly sustainable. It's the whalers who are headed for extinction."[41]

If Faroese and Vincentian artisanal whalers become extinct, much will be lost. Along with the loss of a locally valued national tradition, the cessation of whaling will lead to a loss of an important food source in both places. In St. Vincent, whale and dolphin meat is affordable, "much cheaper than any other source of animal protein on the island," according to one researcher.[42] In the Faroes, whale meat and blubber are even more affordable: they're free. If the whaling operation in either place were to cease, these foods would need to be replaced—almost certainly by something more expensive. While there would likely be an economic effect, disproportionately felt—as is often the case—by the poor, the Vincentian and Faroese cultures will survive the end of whaling, for although a culture may produce a rich variety of materials and traditions, its existence is not dependent upon any single artifact.

The Contested Meal

While the Faroese and Vincentian cultures can certainly exist without whaling, attention must be given to the problem of identifying sustainable sources of food to replace the meat and blubber that would be lost. The solution will likely lie in a combination of increased imports, intensified local agriculture and livestock industries, and increased consumption of local fish—either wild-caught or farm-raised.[43] Flexibility and diversification will be key attributes of an economically successful and nutritionally balanced future for St. Vincent and the Faroe Islands. A dinner of grind og spik—wind-dried pilot whale meat and salted blubber—with boiled potatoes has long been considered the Faroese national dish. The presence of mercury and other contaminants, along with the pressure from international anti-whaling organizations, has turned what used to be a simple, unproblematic, local comfort food into what Faroese researchers Ragnheiður Bogadóttir and Elisabeth Olsen have called "the contested meal."[44] As the grindadráp fades away, another meal—one less contested than grind og spik—will rise to take its place, will be embraced by the culture, and will be enjoyed for years to come.

In my surveys, only 20 percent of Vincentian students identified blackfish as part of their concept of a Vincentian national dish. Most indicated that jackfish, usually served with breadfruit, was a more fitting culinary symbol of their country. With the evidence of the jackfish and the shorter whaling history—a century in St. Vincent versus a millennium in the Faroes—we can speculate that the Vincentians may not cling as tightly to their whaling traditions as the Faroese have. Still, the scientific findings on mercury and other environmental pollutants have taken almost forty years to make an impact on Faroese whaling. That impact is only beginning to be seen now in an increased level of awareness and, among some, a reduction in consumption. Starting as they are with a higher initial concentration of the pollutant, it's unlikely that the Vincentian people will have forty years to decide.

CONCLUSION

———

Foreignness and Familiarity

In September 2002, a thirty-two-year-old man named Erik Niclasen flew from his home in the Faroe Islands, through Copenhagen, to Port of Spain, Trinidad. He was traveling to volunteer aboard the M/V *Logos II,* a Maltese-registered ship making a two-year Christian missionary tour throughout Latin America and the Caribbean. Shortly before the trip commenced, Erik noticed a pretty young woman among the crew. Nelia Daize was born in Rose Hall, St. Vincent, a village just up the leeward coast from Barrouallie, and grew up both among family there and in Trinidad. On board the *Logos,* Erik and Nelia were both assigned to the engine room. When they met, Nelia had never heard of the Faroe Islands; Erik first told her that he came from Denmark. Their two-year volunteer term took them throughout the Caribbean and Central America, through the Panama Canal to the west coasts of North and South America, and finally back to Port of Spain. Somewhere along the way they fell in love.

When the voyage was completed in September 2004, the pair married in Trinidad and one month later moved to the Faroese village of Leirvík. When I met them at their home in 2009, Erik and Nelia had two young daughters, Anita and Victoria. Nelia stayed home with the girls and took Faroese language classes part-time. Erik, an expert mechanic, was the owner of a small rental car company. They are probably the only Faroese-Vincentian family in the world.

In May 2009, Nelia's mother, Anita Daize—her granddaughter's namesake—traveled from St. Vincent to the Faroe Islands to spend time with her daughter's family. During Anita's visit, there was a grindadráp: 188 whales killed at Hvalvík. Upon receiving the grindaboð, Erik rushed to drive his family from their village on Eysturoy across the bridge to Streymoy so they could witness this uniquely Faroese activity and procure meat and blubber for the next few months. He would have driven very fast, paying little attention to the posted speed limit. It's been said that if you're pulled over by the police for speeding in response to a grindaboð, rather than issuing you a citation, the officer is likely to simply ask, "Hvar?" and lead you to the whaling beach, lights flashing and siren blaring. Erik and his family, including his mother-in-law, Anita, made it to the grindadráp in time.

Standing among the crowd of onlookers that day in Hvalvík, Anita Daize must have watched with a certain degree of familiarity as the pilot whales were driven ashore, killed with simple tools, and processed into food on the beach. Of course, the number of whales was much greater than the largest catch she had ever seen landed at Barrouallie. She described the event to me one afternoon on her back porch in Rose Hall. "And the water was red with blood," she told me, echoing the descriptions made by generations of foreign visitors to the Faroe Islands. The actual killing process was unfamiliar to her, since in St. Vincent this normally happens out at sea rather than on shore in full view of the public. "They done stab a lot!" she recalled. Even if Anita had spent time on a Barrouallie blackfish boat, which she had not, the experience in no way would have prepared her for the grindadráp. Gone were the harpoons and gun, replaced with hooks and knives, with the whales coming ashore very much alive instead of dead or nearly so as they are in St. Vincent.

If she looked away from the action, even momentarily, Anita would have instantly known that she was far from her tropical home. Hvalvík is perched on the edge of Streymoy, with green cliffs, steep and treeless, rising behind the village. Without the enclosing vegetation of the leeward side of St. Vincent, you feel that you can see forever. The Faroese air is clean with a salty freshness that goes beyond smell and can actually be tasted.

The people performing the work of whaling would also have been unfamiliar: light-skinned and attired in wool, neoprene, and canvas, these Nordic men (and probably a few women) worked in methodical urgency to drag ashore and kill whales as quickly and efficiently as possible. Though, looking closer, Anita would have seen the same determination, excitement, and exhaustion on the blood-speckled faces of these Faroese whalers that she knew among the whalers of Barrouallie. If she had stayed until the end, and returned when the sýslumaður distributed the grindaseðilin—the tickets that detail each group's portion of the catch—she would have witnessed an entire community butchering the catch, not a specialized guild of vendors and their assistants. The cuts of meat and blubber would have been larger than Anita expected. "That's too big for blackfish portions!" she might have thought.

The whales themselves would have been slightly different too. Anita probably would not have noticed the difference in fin length between the long-finned pilot whales that the Faroese had driven in and the short-finned pilot whales landed at Barrouallie—you almost have to see two whales side by side to determine the species. She certainly would not have recognized the subtler differences such as skull morphology or number of teeth. The anatomical difference that would have been instantly apparent to Anita, though, is the blubber. As the first whale was cut behind its blowhole—this was 2009 and the mønustingari, or spinal lance, was not yet in regular use—a thick blanket of pure white blubber would have been exposed, a layer of warmth for these subarctic whales much thicker than that of their tropical cousins. *Oh, the crisps you could make from that!*

Anita might have felt sadness as she watched the whalers drag ashore and kill juvenile pilot whales. In St. Vincent, it's rarely worth the effort to harpoon such a small whale; in the Faroes you drive in the entire pod, old and young alike, to avoid the waste of whales stranding on some unpopulated beach.

Despite the technical, geographic, biological, and cultural differences that Anita witnessed during the grindadráp, the idea of capturing and killing large marine mammals for food was not at all foreign to her, as it would have been for nearly any other non-Faroese person standing in the crowd at Hvalvík that day. Anita would have understood the methodical urgency with which the whalers were working and their sense of the importance of what they were doing. She would have shared the celebratory spirit among the crowd who could already imagine the taste of that night's dinner, and recognized the glances of slight concern being directed at her, a foreigner and—*who knows?*—maybe an anti-whaling activist. She would have known the connections to history and the natural environment that were being reinforced by the activity that was happening along the shoreline in front of them and would have appreciated seeing her granddaughters learn a valuable lesson about the source of their food and the true cost of producing it. The crowd that gathered on the beach at Hvalvík must have reminded Anita of the crowds at Barrouallie, eagerly watching as the crew of the whaling boat unloads each day's catch. The entire scene would have blended foreignness with familiarity. As the whales were butchered and that oily, historical scent began to permeate the air, Anita might have momentarily closed her eyes, inhaled deeply through her nostrils, and thought of home.

Love and Apathy

In both the Faroe Islands and St. Vincent, pilot whales and other small cetaceans are turned to food in liminal spaces. As whalers and processors work in the swash zones, the ebb and flow of ocean waves washes the blood back to sea. Beyond this physical liminality, whaling today occurs in a space of cultural and historical liminality as well. Most of the world has given up not only whaling but the approval of whaling. Phil Clapham, a prominent marine mammal scientist, has referred to the present time as "a post-whaling world," in which "whaling continues at a modest level in various guises" but the majority of people and their governments fundamentally oppose the practice.[1] This attitudinal shift occurred in response to history and ecology: the unrestrained capitalistic hunting of large cetaceans for oil that drove several populations near—or beyond—the point of extinction.[2]

But whalers using traditional methods, guided by traditional philosophies and culturally embedded conservation strategies in their production of food have their own histories. If, as the historian and geographer David Lowenthal eloquently argued, "the past is a foreign country," then today's Vincentian and Faroese artisanal whalers are under an entirely different jurisdiction than the commercial whalers of previous centuries.[3] They have their own ecological histories separate from those of the commercial whalers. In the cases of the Faroe Islands and St. Vincent, the whalers appear to have struck equilibria with the local whale and dolphin populations. While both operations have room for improvement, neither should be cast equally alongside commercial whalers, whose very history answers the question posed by Melville in *Moby-Dick:* "whether Leviathan can long endure so wide a chase, and so remorseless a havoc; whether he must not at last be exterminated from the waters, and the last whale, like the last man, smoke his last pipe, and then himself evaporate in the final puff."[4]

Whaling operations like those in St. Vincent and the Faroe Islands are unlikely to ever cause the last whale to "evaporate." It is, however, uncertain whether whaling will continue in these places throughout young Anita and Victoria's lifetimes or whether these Faroese-Vincentians and others of their generation might witness the evaporation of their own whaling traditions.

If whaling ends during the twenty-first century in St. Vincent or the Faroe Islands—or both—most likely it will be in response to the environmental contaminants found in the tissues of the whales. While it pains me as an educator to say this, the problem of industrial contaminants in the marine environment can't be solved just by education. The Faroese public is fully aware of the problem of mercury and other toxins in their whale meat and blubber. As best I can tell, and to the best of Pál Weihe's expository ability, they understand the science. In St. Vincent, the knowledge isn't as widespread, but it's getting there. The data from our yearlong research program have been collected and communicated to the appropriate government ministries. We've moved from science to outreach.

The problem isn't a lack of knowledge. It's that there is no good course of action to prescribe after informing people of the risks. Even if all the world's polluting activities were to cease today, the methylmercury, PCBs, and other contaminants present in the environment would take decades or longer to dissipate. The Faroese and Vincentians need a plan for the present, not just for the future. You could, as AMAP did in the Arctic, weigh the health, economic, cultural, and environmental costs and benefits of the local, traditional foods against those of the available alternatives. The problem here is the trade-off. Whether your analysis results in advocacy for the traditional foods or for the alternative, you're replacing what once was good, local food with something that is, in one way or another, inferior. Or, like Sea Shepherd and other environmentalist organizations argue, you could simply tell the Faroese and Vincentians that the whale meat is polluted, so they should stop whaling. The problem with this approach is that the messengers are also the offenders. The majority of international environmental organizations are based in North America and Europe and participate fully in the fossil-fuel-based energy and industrial systems that delivered—and continue to deliver—mercury and other toxic substances to the marine environment. If I poisoned your well, I would not be in the best moral or ethical position to shame you into drawing your water somewhere else.

The controversy over whaling sometimes turns into an argument over who loves the whales and who does not. Sea Shepherd routinely refers to whalers as "murderers" and its own supporters as people "who love whales and our oceans."[5] Arne Kalland, the pro-whaling Norwegian anthropologist, wrote critically about the "dichotomization of mankind into whale-haters and whale-lovers."[6] In whaling, though, just as in human relationships, the opposite of love is not hate; we've learned from the late author and Holocaust survivor Elie Wiesel that it's indifference.[7] Love and hate are closely related; each involves a deep investment in someone else's life, though each provokes action in exactly opposite directions. Indifference, or apathy, is a lack of any concern at all.

Those like Paul Watson and Jennifer Lonsdale who hate whaling and others like Samuel Hazelwood or Liljan, the "pilot whale woman" from Klaksvík, and all the other Faroese and Vincentians who, it's fair to say, love it, share a common desire to see healthy populations of whales swimming freely in clean oceans, feeding, reproducing, and, at a rate lower than that of their reproduction, dying as a result of natural predation. The main difference, the only real difference, between those who hate whaling and those who love it is that the latter see themselves as part of the cycle of natural predation, while the former exclude themselves, along with all other humans, from this role.

An ocean devoid of whales is just as horrifying, if not more so, to the whalers as to the anti-whalers. To Paul Watson—and this is no trivial matter; in fact, it defines his life's mission—overhunting of whales means that a species could go missing from the planet. To Samuel Hazelwood, the repercussions are just as severe and just as personal: his livelihood, like Watson's, could disappear. Love and hatred of whaling can both save whales.

The apathetic, on the other hand, are neither for nor against the whales. These are the polluters, the destroyers, the turners of blind eyes, the mindlessly uninvolved. They see the ocean not as a habitat for creatures ranging from copepods and cod to whales and whalers, but rather as a sink, a sewer for all that is expelled from their industrial processes. If it's true that the solution to pollution is dilution, then no place dilutes like the ocean. Almost without exception, the commercial whalers were—and those few that remain still are—apathetic to the cause of the whales. When the Basques exhausted the Bay of Biscay, they moved to the North Sea. When the entire Atlantic had been laid waste by the American, British, and Norwegian whalers, they moved to the Pacific. The Japanese would not travel to the Southern Ocean Whale Sanctuary every austral summer for their so-called scientific whaling except that this is where the only commercially important populations of the whales they seek can be found. Especially in the latter period of large-scale commercial whaling, whales were understood as commodities rather than as creatures.

Industrial whalers did not and do not love whaling the way Samuel and Liljan do because their experiences bear so little resemblance to those of Faroese and Vincentian whalers.[8] Industrial processes are, by their nature, apathetic and insulated. An industrial whaler works impersonally. Each technological advance—from the cannon-fired, exploding harpoon to the stern slipway on a factory ship—lessens their direct, physical, hands-on engagement with the animals they take. Commercial whalers do not haul their catch over the gunwales of their boats by hand. They do not work in six-person teams to tug hooked whales ashore during a grindadráp. They do not use generations of cultural knowledge to put food on the table for their communities. The mutual respect demanded by the intimacy, challenge, and danger of artisanal whaling is absent. Industrial whalers may love the reward, paid out in money and adventure, as much as the "meanest mariners, and renegades and castaways" aboard Melville's *Pequod* did, but they do not love whales.[9] They don't love them because they have never truly known them.

Nor would it be accurate to say that one must choose between loving whales as living creatures and loving them as a resource. I recall several instances while out whaling with Samuel's crew when we saw sperm whales lolling on the surface; we cut the engine and drifted quietly to take a closer look. This was motivated only by curiosity and wonder, since Vincentians do not hunt sperm whales. Their attitude toward whales is more complex than Kalland's simple notion of "dichotomization" can capture. It is more accurately depicted by the science fiction novelist Robert Sawyer, whose parallel-universe-traveling Neanderthal character, Ponter Boddit, describes his affection for wooly mammoths, both as a food source and as an example of natural beauty: "'Oh,' said Ponter, softly. He looked out the window at the large backyard to Reuben's house. 'I am fond of mammoths,' he said. 'Not just their meat—which is delicious—but as animals, as part of the landscape. There is a small herd of them that lives near my home. I enjoy seeing them.'"[10]

I know a young Faroese man who does participate in the grindadráp, but at other times prefers to simply take photographs of living whales as he watches them from the porch of his seaside home, ignoring, for what it's worth, the requirement to report the sighting and initiate a grindaboð. One may love whales and work toward their complete protection from whaling, pollution, and everything else that may threaten their populations. Or one may love the food resources that can be derived from whales and work toward their conservation—their sustainable use as a resource. Crucially, one need not choose a single way in which to love whales or any other part of our natural environment. As postdomestic people, we may find it difficult to reconcile these seemingly contradictory feelings. You can love whales and still love—or at least tolerate—whaling. Perhaps this is why Sawyer had to use a transdimensional Neanderthal character to convey the idea in his novel. It seems foreign, unmodern, maybe unhuman. But it is human. We see no equivalent contradiction between the affection a small-scale farmer might have for the livestock she depends upon and devotes herself to and the necessity of selling some of her animals to slaughter, or serving them on her own table, when the time comes. The Faroese and Vincentian cultures provide evidence that a love of whaling can coexist with a love of whales.

Neither the whale-lovers nor the whaling-lovers are indifferent to the future of whales. Most of us, though, have proven by our actions—and especially by our inactions—to be somewhat more indifferent to the fate of the natural environment as a whole.

What is to be done about the indifference, the apathy, that permeates the world, pollutes the atmosphere and ocean, and confounds both whaling's lovers and its haters? The novelist John Dos Passos wrote that "the cure for apathy is comprehension."[11] If this is true, it should give hope to all of us who care about the ocean, the whales, and the whalers. It means that deep concern—whether expressed through love or through hate—can be learned, and that apathy is merely a result of ignorance. Comprehension, knowledge, learning: the cure for apathy can be taught. It's true that education alone will never solve the problem of mercury and the other environmental contaminants we're finding in whale and dolphin tissues. But these were never the core of the problem to begin with; they were merely symptoms. Of course, knowledge itself is neutral. One can teach another about the intricate, delicate, and resilient ecology of the ocean, its physical structure and dynamics, its role in the regulation of Earth's climate, its life and the human life it supports. After knowledge, either love or hate can develop. What cannot remain is apathy.

Appendix:
Whaling Records

Faroe Islands Whaling Records, 1587–2017

Year	Globicephala melas	Lagenorhynchus acutus	Tursiops truncatus	Grampus griseus	Year	Globicephala melas	Lagenorhynchus acutus	Tursiops truncatus	Grampus griseus
1587	300				1639–1663				
1588	115				1664	1,000			
1589–1598					1665–1708				
1599	90				1709	1,448			
1600	24				1710	1,430			
1601					1711	715			
1602	60				1712	385			
1603–1612					1713	1,090			
1613	80				1714	635			
1614	159				1715	625			
1615	507				1716	728			
1616	280				1717	720			
1617	120				1718	409			
1618	210				1719	726			
1619	155				1720	803			
1620	291				1721	905			
1621	1,000				1722	317			
1622	200				1723	1,320			
1623	32				1724	1,063			
1624	180				1725	1,359			
1625					1726	688			
1626	103				1727	835			
1627					1728	236			
1628	200				1729	1,423			
1629	20				1730	915			
1630	87				1731	2,188			
1631–1634					1732	277			
1635	400				1733	1,186			
1636					1734	696			
1637	60				1735	559			
1638	56				1736	391			

Faroe Islands Whaling Records, 1587–2017 (continued)

Year	Globicephala melas	Lagenorhynchus acutus	Tursiops truncatus	Grampus griseus	Year	Globicephala melas	Lagenorhynchus acutus	Tursiops truncatus	Grampus griseus
1737	350				1775	0			
1738	214				1776	743			
1739	313				1777	0			
1740	0				1778	0			
1741	1,460				1779	0			
1742	0				1780	0			
1743	622				1781	434			
1744	1,017				1782	50			
1745	0				1783	0			
1746	100				1784	0			
1747	647				1785	0			
1748	165				1786	0			
1749	212				1787	262			
1750	0				1788	0			
1751	0				1789	0			
1752	194				1790	0			
1753	0				1791	0			
1754	172				1792	152			
1755	0				1793	148			
1756	0				1794	288			
1757	0				1795	0			
1758	0				1796	545			
1759	0				1797	100			
1760	0				1798	91			
1761	0				1799	1,370			
1762	0				1800	53			
1763	0				1801	154			
1764	0				1802	752			
1765	0				1803	1,063		13	
1766	0				1804	953		0	
1767	0				1805	206		0	
1768	0				1806	550		0	
1769	0				1807	367		0	
1770	16				1808	1,145		0	
1771	0				1809	226		0	
1772	0				1810	429		0	
1773	0				1811	510		0	
1774	0				1812	834		35	

Faroe Islands Whaling Records, 1587–2017 (continued)

Year	Globicephala melas	Lagenorhynchus acutus	Tursiops truncatus	Grampus griseus	Year	Globicephala melas	Lagenorhynchus acutus	Tursiops truncatus	Grampus griseus
1813	281		0		1851	474		3	
1814	261		0		1852	2,230		0	
1815	543		0		1853	1,120		0	
1816	812		0		1854	794		9	
1817	652		0		1855	1,368		4	
1818	917		0		1856	411		2	
1819	1,448		0		1857	328		0	
1820	787		0		1858	757		44	
1821	263		0		1859	836		0	
1822	1,647		0		1860	640		0	
1823	1,098		0		1861	341		3	
1824	442		0		1862	1,129		1	
1825	1,935		0		1863	709		2	
1826	714		6		1864	574		0	
1827	711		0		1865	1,269		0	
1828	725		0		1866	1,758		4	
1829	556		0		1867	398		5	
1830	1,149		0		1868	478		0	
1831	695		0		1869	716		1	
1832	391		0		1870	842		4	
1833	1,455		0		1871	796		1	
1834	1,569		0		1872	2,315	26	41	
1835	1,338		0		1873	1,682	0	0	
1836	1,183		0		1874	652	0	0	
1837	1,221		0		1875	780	0	0	
1838	1,332		0		1876	802	0	0	
1839	1,614		0		1877	383	0	0	
1840	2,193		0		1878	329	0	0	
1841	1,651		0		1879	1,920	0	0	
1842	645		0		1880	628	0	0	
1843	3,142		0		1881	390	0	19	
1844	2,171		0		1882	521	0	0	
1845	2,541		0		1883	151	0	0	
1846	1,039		0		1884	368	0	32	
1847	2,675		5		1885	977	0	0	
1848	1,181		7		1886	734	0	0	
1849	769		0		1887	854	0	0	
1850	502		0		1888	476	0	0	

Faroe Islands Whaling Records, 1587–2017 (continued)

Year	Globicephala melas	Lagenorhynchus acutus	Tursiops truncatus	Grampus griseus	Year	Globicephala melas	Lagenorhynchus acutus	Tursiops truncatus	Grampus griseus
1889	695	6	1		1927	0	0	0	
1890	0	0	0		1928	480	335	0	
1891	0	0	0		1929	17	344	0	
1892	34	1	0		1930	266	80	0	
1893	840	0	0		1931	2,386	20	0	
1894	498	0	0		1932	1,282	172	0	
1895	542	0	0		1933	959	110	0	
1896	128	0	0		1934	178	30	0	
1897	342	0	0		1935	652	0	0	
1898	1,336	0	409		1936	1,633	37	0	
1899	2,377	0	0		1937	886	0	0	
1900	797	0	0		1938	2,094	0	0	
1901	0	0	2		1939	3,384	0	0	
1902	481	10	0		1940	2,847	226	0	
1903	212	0	0		1941	4,482	0	7	
1904	566	308	2		1942	1,864	0	0	
1905	221	143	0		1943	1,047	0	0	
1906	414	0	0		1944	1,386	156	0	
1907	242	27	0		1945	1,555	0	0	
1908	1,793	0	0		1946	1,040	0	0	
1909	985	0	0		1947	1,839	0	0	
1910	1,324	6	0		1948	587	440	0	
1911	1,650	237	0		1949	957	0	0	
1912	669	0	0		1950	569	0	0	
1913	168	0	0		1951	2,786	20	0	
1914	291	0	0		1952	1,242	0	0	
1915	1,203	0	0		1953	2,099	0	0	
1916	397	0	0		1954	2,015	0	0	
1917	263	0	1		1955	885	0	0	
1918	848	22	0		1956	1,843	0	0	
1919	153	0	0		1957	2,105	0	0	
1920	802	2	0		1958	2,619	0	0	
1921	1,076	0	0		1959	1,428	0	0	
1922	473	0	0		1960	1,783	137	40	
1923	1,047	0	1		1961	1,892	27	59	
1924	0	3	0		1962	1,764	0	0	
1925	468	0	0		1963	2,204	0	16	
1926	347	0	0		1964	1,364	0	17	

Faroe Islands Whaling Records, 1587–2017 (continued)

Year	Globicephala melas	Lagenorhynchus acutus	Tursiops truncatus	Grampus griseus	Year	Globicephala melas	Lagenorhynchus acutus	Tursiops truncatus	Grampus griseus
1965	1,620	176	4		1992	1,572	47	0	
1966	1,485	0	7		1993	808	377	16	
1967	1,973	0	0		1994	1,201	263	8	
1968	1,650	9	10		1995	227	157	0	
1969	1,394	0	0		1996	1,513	357	21	
1970	388	59	0		1997	1,162	350	0	
1971	1,015	50	0		1998	812	438	0	
1972	511	0	0		1999	607	0	0	
1973	1,050	0	0		2000	588	265	0	
1974	679	0	0		2001	918	546	13	
1975	1,086	5	0		2002	626	773	11	
1976	532	14	0		2003	503	186	3	
1977	897	30	2		2004	1,012	333	0	
1978	1,192	0	0		2005	302	312	0	
1979	1,674	0	14		2006	856	617	17	
1980	2,775	8	0		2007	633	0	0	
1981	2,909	0	2		2008	0	1	1	
1982	2,649	0	0		2009	310	171	1	3
1983	1,685	10	0		2010	1,107	14	0	21
1984	1,926	0	0		2011	726	0	0	0
1985	2,596	32	0		2012	714	0	0	0
1986	1,676	185	0		2013	1,104	430	0	0
1987	1,450	76	1		2014	48	0	0	0
1988	1,738	603	11		2015	501	0	0	0
1989	1,260	0	0		2016	296	0	0	0
1990	917	55	0		2017	1,203	530	0	0
1991	722	0	62						

Data source: National Whaling Statistics, Føroya Náttúrugripasavn. Blank cells indicate missing data.

St. Vincent Whaling Records, 1949–2017

Year	*Globicephala macrorhynchus*	*Orcinus orca*	Other dolphins	Year	*Globicephala macrorhynchus*	*Orcinus orca*	Other dolphins
1949	135			1980	9		17
1950–1961				1981	39		21
1962	97		200	1982	13		34
1963	425		200	1983	82		41
1964	275		200	1984–1989			
1965	183		200	1990	55		104
1966	323		200	1991	46		71
1967	269		200	1992	39		62
1968	387		200	1993–2006			
1969	176		200	2007	96	2	432
1970	232		200	2008	126	17	273
1971	153		200	2009	305	0	1,086
1972	155		200	2010	99	3	207
1973	151		200	2011	158	11	375
1974	86		200	2012	150	3	372
1975	135			2013–2014			
1976	117			2015	77	6	234
1977	65			2016	157	5	246
1978	52		55	2017	96	188	9
1979	25		113				

Data sources: **1949**: C. F. Hickling, *The Fisheries of the British West Indies: Report on a Visit in 1949*, Development and Welfare in the West Indies, Bulletin 29 (Bridgetown, Barbados: Cole's Printery, 1950); **1962–1974**: David K. Caldwell and Melba C. Caldwell, "Dolphin and Small Whale Fisheries of the Caribbean and West Indies: Occurrence, History, and Catch Statistics—with Special Reference to the Lesser Antillean Island of St. Vincent," *Journal of the Fisheries Research Board of Canada* 32, no. 7 (1975): 1105–1110. Note that Caldwell and Caldwell estimated the number of "other dolphins" taken during their study period; thus the records of 200 per year for this time span should be viewed as an approximation; **1975–1983**: William S. Price, "Whaling in the Caribbean: Historical Perspective and Update," *Report of the International Whaling Commission* 35 (1985): 413–420; **1990–1991**: Nigel M. Scott, "The Current Status and Management Options for the Mammalian Fishery in Barrouallie, St. Vincent, West Indies," MS thesis, University of the West Indies, 1995; **2007–2017**: An estimation extrapolated from the catch records kept by Samuel Hazelwood. Blank cells indicate missing data.

Notes

INTRODUCTION

1. Henry Labonne, *L'islande et l'archipel des Færœer* (Paris: Hachette, 1888), 345.
2. Ingvar Svanberg, "Vitunýra i färöisk folktradition," *Gardar: Årsbok för Samfundet Sverige-Island i Lund-Malmö och Samfundet Sverige-Färöarna* 37 (2007): 22–26.
3. Randall R. Reeves, "The Origins and Character of 'Aboriginal Subsistence' Whaling: A Global Review," *Mammal Review* 32, no. 2 (2002): 99.
4. Randall R. Reeves and Tim D. Smith, "A Taxonomy of World Whaling," in *Whales, Whaling, and Ocean Ecosystems,* ed. James A. Estes, Douglas P. DeMaster, Daniel F. Doak, Terrie M. Williams, and Robert L. Brownell Jr. (Berkeley: University of California Press, 2006), 82–101.
5. Seán P. Kerins, *A Thousand Years of Whaling: A Faroese Common Property Regime* (Edmonton, AB: CCI Press, 2010).
6. Finn Lynge, "Whaling: Samples from a Contemporary Debate," *North Atlantic Studies* 2, nos. 1–2 (1990): 138–144.
7. Ernest Hemingway, *Death in the Afternoon* (New York: Scribner, 1932), 1.
8. Paul Kalanithi, *When Breath Becomes Air* (New York: Random House, 2016), 43.

1. THE MOST EXCITING WORD IN FAROESE

1. Jonathan Wylie, "Grindadráp," in *Ring of Dancers: Images of Faroese Culture,* ed. Jonathan Wylie and David Margolin (Philadelphia: University of Pennsylvania Press, 1981), 95–132, quote on 95.
2. Thomas S. Traill, "Description of a New Species of Whale, *Delphinus melas.* In a Letter from Thomas Stewart Traill, M.D. to Mr. Nicholson," *Journal of Natural Philosophy, Chemistry, and the Arts,* February 1809, 81–83. Note that Traill's original taxonomic binomial, *Delphinus melas,* has since been modified. For a full listing of the scientific names by which this species has been known historically, as well as a list of its common names in many modern languages, see its entry in the World Register of Marine Species, http://www.marinespecies.org/aphia.php?p=taxdetails &id=137097.
3. Dorete Bloch, Martin Zachariassen, and Petur Zachariassen, "Some External Characters of the Long-Finned Pilot Whale off the Faroe Islands and a Comparison with the Short-Finned Pilot Whale," *Reports of the International Whaling Commission* 14 (1993): 117–136.

4. G. Storm, *Samlede Skrifter af Peder Claussøn Friis* (Kristiania: A. W. Brøgger, 1881), 67, translated in Kate Sanderson, "A Note on the Derivation of the Faroese *Grind*," *Fróðskaparrit* 43 (1995): 67–72.

5. Wylie, "Grindadráp," 103.

6. Jonhard Mikkelsen, ed., *Føroysk-Ensk Orðabók* (Tórshavn: Sprotin, 2007).

7. Wylie, "Grindadráp"; Dorete Bloch and Hans Pauli Joensen, "Faroese Pilot Whaling: Conditions, Practice, and Superstition," *North Atlantic Studies* 4, nos. 1–2 (2001): 57–67.

8. Bloch and Joensen, "Faroese Pilot Whaling."

9. Ibid.

10. "Statement from Government of the Faroe Islands on Grindalógin," Government of the Faroe Islands, news release, July 7, 2015, http://www.government.fo/news /news/statement-from-government-of-the-faroe-islands-on-grindalogin.

11. Ibid.

12. Lawrence Millman, *Last Places: A Journey in the North* (London: André Deutsch, 1990).

13. Jóan Pauli Joensen, *Pilot Whaling in the Faroe Islands: History, Ethnography, Symbol* (Tórshavn: Faroe University Press, 2009).

14. Örnólfur Thorsson, ed., *The Sagas of the Icelanders* (New York: Penguin, 2000).

15. Douglas Botting, *Island of the Dragon's Blood* (New York: Funk, 1959), 23–24.

16. Ibid., 24.

17. Wylie, "Grindadráp," 108.

18. The "layer cake" comparison is made frequently in travelogues and travel guides. See, for example, James Proctor, *Faroe Islands* (Guilford, CT: Bradt, 2016).

19. Venceslaus U. Hammershaimb, *Færøsk Anthologi* (Copenhagen: S. L. Møllers Bog-trykkeri, 1891), 401, translated in Kate Sanderson, "Grindadráp: A Textual History of Whaling Traditions in the Faroes to 1900," MPh thesis, University of Sydney, 1992, 102.

20. Richard W. Bulliet, *Herders, Hunters, and Hamburgers: The Past and Future of Human-Animal Relationships* (New York: Columbia University Press, 2005), 8.

21. See, for example, Wylie, "Grindadráp"; Arne Thorsteinsson, "Hvussu Gamalt er Grindadrápið?," *Varðin* 53 (1986): 65–66; Sanderson, "Grindadráp"; Joensen, *Pilot Whaling in the Faroe Islands;* Seán P. Kerins, *A Thousand Years of Whaling: A Faroese Common Property Regime* (Edmonton, AB: CCI Press, 2010).

2. OIL AND HISTORY ON A CARIBBEAN BEACH

1. John Steinbeck, *East of Eden* (New York: Penguin, 2002), 3.

2. Herman Melville, *Moby-Dick or the Whale* (New York: Harper & Brothers, 1851), 160.

3. Sebastian Junger, *Fire* (New York: W. W. Norton, 2001), 60.

4. Melville, *Moby-Dick,* 402.

5. Karen Pryor and Jon Lindbergh, "A Dolphin-Human Fishing Cooperative in Brazil," *Marine Mammal Science* 6, no. 1 (1990): 77–82; Danielle Clode, *Killers in*

Eden: the Story of a Rare Partnership between Men and Killer Whales (Sydney: Allen & Unwin, 2002).

6. Robert Pitman, ed., "Killer Whale: the Top, Top Predator," *Whalewatcher: Journal of the American Cetacean Society* 40, no.1 (special issue, 2011).

7. Chet van Duzer, *Sea Monsters on Medieval and Renaissance Maps* (London: British Library, 2013).

8. Thomas Thomason Perowne, *The Cambridge Bible for Schools and Colleges: Obadiah and Jonah* (Cambridge, UK: Cambridge University Press, 1905).

9. Cited in John K. B. Ford, Graeme M. Ellis, and Kenneth C. Balcomb, *Killer Whales: The Natural History and Genealogy of* Orcinus orca *in British Columbia and Washington* (Vancouver: University of British Columbia Press, 2000).

10. David Day, *The Whale War* (London: Routledge, 1987).

11. Ibid., 5.

12. Charlotte Epstein, *The Power of Words in International Relations: Birth of an Anti-Whaling Discourse* (Cambridge, MA: MIT Press, 2008).

13. "A Whale of a Business," *Frontline,* aired November 11, 1997, on PBS, http://www.pbs.org/wgbh/pages/frontline/shows/whales.

14. *Blackfish,* directed by Gabriela Cowperthwaite (Atlanta: CNN, 2013).

3. THE STONES OF FAROE

1. John W. Harshberger, "The Gardens of the Faeroes, Iceland, and Greenland," *Geographical Review* 14, no. 3 (1924): 404.

2. Jonathan B. Tourtellot, "111 Islands," *National Geographic Traveler* 24, no. 8 (2007): 108–127.

3. Kate Sanderson, "*Grind*—Ambiguity and Pressure to Conform: Faroese Whaling and the Anti-Whaling Protest," in *Elephants and Whales: Resources for Whom?,* ed. Milton Freeman and Urs P. Kreuter (Basel: Gordon and Breach, 1994), 187–201.

4. Ibid., 193.

5. Jóan Pauli Joensen, *Pilot Whaling in the Faroe Islands: History, Ethnography, Symbol* (Tórshavn: Faroe University Press, 2009), 113.

6. The "decapitation" charge is often repeated in anti-grindadráp literature. For a recent example, see Paul Watson, "Pilot Whales Dead at the Hands of Vicious Thugs," Sea Shepherd Conservation Society, June 29, 2015, https://seashepherd.org/2015/06/29/pilot-whales-dead-at-the-hands-of-vicious-thugs/.

7. Anne Morrow Lindbergh, *Locked Rooms and Open Doors* (New York: Harcourt Brace Jovanovich, 1974), 99.

8. M. Jules Michelet, *La Mer* (New York: Rudd and Carleton, 1861), 229.

9. Jonathan Burt, "Conflicts around Slaughter in Modernity," in *Killing Animals,* ed. Animal Studies Group (Champaign: University of Illinois Press, 2006), 120–144; International Whaling Commission, *Report of the Workshop on Humane Killing Techniques for Whales,* IWC/33/15 (Cambridge, UK: IWC, 1980); D. Bowles and

J. Lonsdale, "An Analysis of Behaviour and Killing Times Recorded during a Pilot Whale Hunt," *Animal Welfare* 3 (1994): 285–304.

10. Peter Singer, "Why the Whales Should Live," *Habitat* 6, no. 3 (1978): 9.

11. Jóan Pauli Joensen, "The Hunt and the Hunter," in *Hunters of the North*, ed. Birgir Kruse (Tórshavn: Forlagið & Sprotin, 2002), 26–79; Chie Sakakibara, "'No Whale, No Music': Iñupiaq Drumming and Global Warming," *Polar Record* 45, no. 4 (2009): 290.

12. Edith Turner, "American Eskimos Celebrate the Whale: Structural Dichotomies and Spirit Identities among the Inupiat of Alaska," *Drama Review* 37, no. 1 (1993): 101.

13. Michael Parnwell, "Regional Resonances: Vietnamese Whale Worship in Comparative Perspective," in *The Great Diversity: Trajectories of Asian Development*, ed. Camilla Brautaset and Christopher M. Dent (Wageningen, Netherlands: Wageningen Academic Publishers), 85.

14. Peter Harvey, *An Introduction to Buddhist Ethics: Foundations, Values and Issues* (Cambridge: Cambridge University Press, 2000); Rinjing Dorje, *Food in Tibetan Life* (London: Prospect, 1985).

15. Dorete Bloch, Geneviève Desportes, Kjartan Hoydal, and Patrick Jean, "Pilot Whaling in the Faroe Islands: July 1986–July 1988," *North Atlantic Studies* 2, nos. 1–2 (1990): 36–44.

16. M. Glover, *Faroese Fin Whale Campaign—1981* (London: Greenpeace, 1981); Jennifer Gibson, Allan Thornton, Dave Currey, and Rosalind Reeve, *Pilot Whaling in the Faroe Islands: A Third Report by the Environmental Investigation Agency* (London: Environmental Investigation Agency, 1987); Bowles and Lonsdale, "An Analysis of Behaviour and Killing Times."

17. Timothy Pachirat, *Every Twelve Seconds: Industrialized Slaughter and the Politics of Sight* (New Haven, CT: Yale University Press, 2013).

18. Justines Olsen, "Killing Methods and Equipment in the Faroese Pilot Whale Hunt," English translation of "Om avlivningsmetoder og udstyr for færøsk grindefangst" (NAMMCO/99/WS/2), presented to the NAMMCO Workshop on Hunting Methods, Nuuk, Greenland, February 9–11, 1999.

19. Ibid., 8.

20. Ibid.

21. Whale and Dolphin Conservation Society and the Humane Society of the United States, *Hunted Dead or Still Alive: A Report on the Cruelty of Whaling* (Chippenham, UK: WDCS, 2003), 13.

22. Paul Watson, email message to author, October 25, 2005.

23. Olsen, "Killing Methods," 5.

24. A historical photograph of the aftermath of a pilot whale drive in the Shetland Islands caused some amusement among my Faroese colleagues when they noticed that the whale carcasses had all been lined up on the beach with their tails pointing inland—perfectly acceptable in the Shetlands but considered odd in the Faroes.

The practical reason for the difference is the use of the blástrarongul to haul whales ashore in the Faroes and the use of ropes tied around the flukes in the Shetlands.

25. Jonathan Wylie, "Grindadráp," in *Ring of Dancers: Images of Faroese Culture,* eds. Jonathan Wylie and David Margolin (Philadelphia: University of Pennsylvania Press, 1981), 98.

26. Michael Pollan, *The Omnivore's Dilemma: A Natural History of Four Meals* (New York: Penguin, 2006), 360.

27. Sanderson, "Grindadráp," 27.

28. Jóan Pauli Joensen, "Pilot Whaling in the Faroe Islands," *Ethnologia Scandinavica* 6 (1976): 2.

29. Ibid., 3.

30. Ibid.

31. Irving Copi, *Introduction to Logic* (New York: Macmillan, 1953), 95.

32. Sanderson, "Grindadráp."

33. Joensen, "Pilot Whaling in the Faroe Islands," 6.

34. Wylie, "Grindadráp," 109.

35. Snorri Sturluson, *Heimskringla: History of the Kings of Norway,* trans. Lee M. Hollander (Austin: University of Texas Press, 1964).

36. Ibid., 61.

37. Ibid.

38. Ibid.

39. Ibid.

40. Carl O. Sauer, *Northern Mists* (Berkeley: University of California Press, 1968), 85.

41. Roberta Frank, "The Invention of the Viking Horned Helmet," in *International Scandinavian and Medieval Studies in Memory of Gerd Wolfgang Weber,* eds. Michael Dallapiazza, Olaf Hansen, Preben Meulengracht Sorensen, and Yvonne Bonnetain (Trieste: Parnaso, 2000), 199–208.

42. F. Donald Logan, *The Vikings in History* (New York: Routledge, 2013).

43. Mike J. Church, Símun V. Arge, Kevin J. Edwards, Philippa L. Ascough, Julie M. Bond, Gordon T. Cook, Steve J. Dockrill, Andrew J. Dugmore, Thomas H. McGovern, Claire Nesbitt, and Ian A. Simpson, "The Vikings Were Not the First Colonizers of the Faroe Islands," *Quaternary Science Reviews* 77 (2013): 228–232.

44. Tim Severin, *The Brendan Voyage* (New York: McGraw-Hill, 1978).

45. Sauer, *Northern Mists,* 83.

46. Pál Weihe and Høgni D. Joensen, "Dietary Recommendations Regarding Pilot Whale Meat and Blubber in the Faroe Islands," *International Journal of Circumpolar Health* 71 (2012): 18594–18598.

47. Joensen, *Pilot Whaling in the Faroe Islands.*

48. Ibid., 28.

49. Matthew Workman, "200," *Workman's Waste of Time* (blog), June 15, 2007, http://workman.blogspot.com/2007/06/200.html.

50. Matthew Workman, "Faroe Friday: Podcast Edition," *Workman's Waste of Time* (blog), February 6, 2009, http://workman.blogspot.com/2009/02/faroe-friday -podcast-edition.html.

51. Matthew Workman, "Faroe Friday: Føroyar, Her Komi Eg!," *Workman's Waste of Time* (blog), June 5, 2009, http://workman.blogspot.com/2009/06/faroe-friday -froyar-her-komi-eg.html.

52. Matthew Workman, Facebook message to author, October 15, 2015.

53. *The Faroe Islands Podcast,* "July 23" (podcast), October 10, 2015, http://www .faroepodcast.com/2015/10/podcast-252-july-23.html.

4. BARROUALLIE, ST. VINCENT'S BLACKFISH TOWN

1. The historical facts surrounding this shipwreck are contested. Major details such as the number of ships involved, the year and location of the shipwreck, and the possibility of Africans having arrived in St. Vincent earlier and by other means conflict in both the primary and secondary literature. For a thorough discussion of the competing theories, see Christopher Taylor, *The Black Carib Wars: Freedom, Survival, and the Making of the Garifuna* (Jackson: University Press of Mississippi, 2012).

2. I. A. Earle Kirby and Christian I. Martin, *The Rise and Fall of the Black Caribs of St. Vincent* (Kingstown: St. Vincent Archaeological and Historical Society, 1972).

3. Julianne Maher, *The Survival of People and Languages: Schooners, Goats and Cassava in St. Barthélemy, French West Indies* (Leiden: Brill, 2013), 29.

4. Taylor, *The Black Carib Wars.*

5. Lawrence S. Grossman, *The Political Ecology of Bananas: Contract Farming, Peasants, and Agrarian Change in the Eastern Caribbean* (Chapel Hill: University of North Carolina Press, 1998).

6. United Nations Environment Programme. *GEO-6 Regional Assessment for Latin America and the Caribbean* (Nairobi: UNEP, 2016).

7. Bonham Richardson, *Caribbean Migrants: Environment and Human Survival on St. Kitts and Nevis* (Knoxville: University of Tennessee Press, 1983), 40.

8. Ibid., 16.

9. Richard Price, "Caribbean Fishing and Fishermen: A Historical Sketch," *American Anthropologist* 68, no. 6 (1966): 1364.

10. Aldemaro Romero, "Yankee Whaling in the Caribbean Basin: Its Impact in a His-torical Context," in *New Approaches to the Study of Marine Mammals,* ed. Aldemaro Romero (n.p.: InTech, 2012), 223–232.

11. Edward Mitchell, *Porpoise, Dolphin, and Small Whale Fisheries of the World* (Morges, Switzerland: IUCN, 1975).

12. John E. Adams, "Historical Geography of Whaling in Bequia Island, West In-dies," *Caribbean Quarterly* 19, no. 4 (1971): 42–50.

13. Romero, "Yankee Whaling in the Caribbean."

14. Karl Brandt, *Whale Oil and Economic Analysis* (Redwood City, CA: Stanford Uni-versity Food Research, 1940), 54.

15. Adams, "Historical Geography of Whaling in Bequia"; Nathalie Ward, *Blows, Mon, Blows! A History of Bequia Whaling* (Woods Hole, MA: Gecko Productions, 1995).

16. John E. Adams, "Marine Industries of the St. Vincent Grenadines, West Indies," PhD diss., University of Minnesota, 1970.

17. Ward, *Blows, Mon, Blows!*

18. I compiled information about the historical geography of southeastern Caribbean whaling stations from a variety of sources, including Adams, "Marine Industries"; David K. Caldwell and Melba C. Caldwell, "Porpoise Fisheries in the Southern Caribbean—Present Utilizations and Future Potentials," *Proceedings of the Gulf and Caribbean Fisheries Institute* 23 (1971): 195–211; William S. Price, "Whaling in the Caribbean: Historical Perspective and Update," *Report of the International Whaling Commission* 35 (1985): 413–420; Nigel M. Scott, "The Current Status and Management Options for the Mammalian Fishery in Barrouallie, St. Vincent, West Indies," MS thesis, University of the West Indies, 1995; and Ward, *Blows, Mon, Blows!*

19. Sebastian Junger, *Fire* (New York: W. W. Norton, 2001), 57.

20. John E. Adams, "Last of the Caribbean Whalemen," *Natural History* 103 (1994): 64–72.

21. Tom Weston, *The Wind That Blows: A Portrait of the Last Yankee Whalers* (Bequia, St. Vincent & the Grenadines: Grenadines Motion Picture Company, 2014), DVD.

22. Alexander Gillespie, *Whaling Diplomacy: Defining Issues in International Environmental Law* (Cheltenham, UK: Edward Elgar, 2005), 222.

23. William Neufield, *The Last Whalers* (Plainfield, NJ: WBN Productions, 1973), 16 mm film, https://vimeo.com/36922756.

24. Roger Michael Johnson, "The Last Whale Hunters," *Maritime Life and Traditions* 8 (2000): 44–61.

25. Jan Olsen, "Faroe Islanders Continue Whale Hunts," *Los Angeles Times,* December 1, 1991.

26. Martin D. Robards and Randall R. Reeves, "The Global Extent and Character of Marine Mammal Consumption by Humans: 1970–2009," *Biological Conservation* 144 (2011): 2770–2786.

27. Gary Scharnhorst, ed., *Mark Twain: The Complete Interviews* (Tuscaloosa: University of Alabama Press, 2006), 315.

28. Price, "Whaling in the Caribbean."

29. Robert G. Cecil, "Geographical Characteristics of Fisheries in Selected Southeastern Caribbean Islands," PhD diss., McGill University, 1972.

30. Scott, "Current Status and Management Options."

31. Junger, *Fire,* 60; Adams, "Last of the Caribbean Whalemen," 65.

32. Caldwell and Caldwell, "Porpoise Fisheries."

33. Elizabeth Mohammed, Leslie E. Straker, and Cheryl Jardine, "St. Vincent and the Grenadines: Reconstructed Fisheries Catches and Fishing Effort, 1942–2001," *Fisheries Centre Research Reports* 11, no. 6 (2003): 95–116.

34. Adams, "Last of the Caribbean Whalemen," 67.

35. Price, "Whaling in the Caribbean," 415.

36. Adams, "Last of the Caribbean Whalemen"; Scott, "Current Status and Management Options."

37. Note that Bequia whalers make regular use of motorboats to locate, surround, and contain whales before harpooning as well as to tow whale carcasses ashore. The use of the sailboat in Bequia whaling is generally restricted to the act of harpooning alone.

38. Stan Hugill, *Shanties from the Seven Seas: Shipboard Work-Songs and Songs Used as Work-Songs from the Great Days of Sail* (London: Routledge, 1961).

39. Roger D. Abrahams, *Deep the Water, Shallow the Shore: Three Essays on Shantying in the West Indies* (Austin: University of Texas Press, 1974).

40. Daniel Lanier and Vincent Reid, "Whalers' Shanties of Barrouallie, St. Vincent: Observations on the Nature, Decline, and Revival of a Unique Caribbean Maritime Tradition," *International Journal of Intangible Heritage* 2 (2007): 70–80.

41. Ibid.

42. Ibid.

43. Jonathan Skinner, "License Revoked: When Calypso Goes Too Far," in *An Anthropology of Indirect Communication,* ed. Joy Hendry and C. W. Watson (London: Routledge, 2001), 181–200.

44. Lanier and Reid, "Whalers' Shanties of Barrouallie," 77.

45. Scott, "Current Status and Management Options."

46. Price, "Whaling in the Caribbean."

47. Scott, "Current Status and Management Options."

48. "Life in the Blackfish Town," *SVG News and Buylines,* February 6, 1999, 12–13.

49. Svein Jentoft and Håkan T. Sandersen, "Cooperatives in Fisheries Management: The Case of St. Vincent and the Grenadines," *Society and Natural Resources* 9, no. 3 (1996): 295–305.

50. Jonathan R. Strand and John P. Tuman, "Foreign Aid and Voting Behavior in an International Organization: The Case of Japan and the International Whaling Commission," *Foreign Policy Analysis* 8, no. 4 (2012): 409–430.

51. Barrouallie Fisheries Development Cooperative Society, Ltd., *BFDC and You,* pamphlet (Barrouallie: BFDC, 2007).

5. DRAWING OUT LEVIATHAN

1. Sang-Mog Lee and Daniel Robineau, "Les cétacés des gravures rupestres néolithiques de Bangu-dae (Corée du Sud) et les débuts de la chasse à la baleine dans le Pacifique nord-ouest," *L'anthropologie* 108, no. 1 (2004): 137–151.

2. C. B. Stringer, J. C. Finlayson, R. N. E. Bartond, Y. Fernández-Jalvo, I. Cáceres, R. C. Sabin, and E. J. Rhodes, "Neanderthal Exploitation of Marine Mammals in Gibraltar," *Proceedings of the National Academy of Sciences* 105, no. 38 (2008): 14319–14324.

3. Esbjörn Rosenblad and Rakel Sigurðardóttir-Rosenblad, *Iceland: From Past to Present*, trans. Alan Crozier (Reykjavík: Mál og Menning, 1993), 352.

4. Anne Brydon, *The Eye of the Guest: Icelandic Nationalist Discourse and the Whaling Issue* (Ottawa: National Library of Canada, 1992).

5. "Trout River Blue Whale Carcass Towed to Woody Point," CBC News, May 8, 2014, http://www.cbc.ca/1.2636049.

6. See, for example, David K. Caldwell, Warren F. Rathjen, and Melba C. Caldwell, "Pilot Whales Mass Stranded at Nevis, West Indies," *Quarterly Journal of the Florida Academy of Sciences* 33 (1971): 241–243.

7. Elizabeth S. Wing and Elizabeth J. Reitz, "Prehistoric Fishing Economies in the Caribbean," *New World Archaeology* 5 (1982): 13–32.

8. Vicki E. Szabo, *Monstrous Fishes and the Mead-Dark Sea: Whaling in the Medieval North Atlantic* (Leiden: Brill, 2008).

9. John Smith and John Kinahan, "The Invisible Whale," *World Archaeology* 16 (1984): 89–97.

10. Randall R. Reeves and Tim D. Smith, "A Taxonomy of World Whaling," in *Whales, Whaling, and Ocean Ecosystems,* eds. James A. Estes, Douglas P. DeMaster, Daniel F. Doak, Terrie M. Williams, and Robert L. Brownell Jr. (Berkeley: University of California Press, 2006), 82–101.

11. This narrative is entirely hypothetical but based upon the work of Reeves and Smith ("A Taxonomy of World Whaling") and the sources cited therein. The authors of this well-organized history of whaling name "Arctic Aboriginal" as the earliest confirmed "era" of whaling, while acknowledging the possible, yet unconfirmed, occurrence of whaling at a variety of sites around the world contemporary with, or even earlier than, Arctic whaling.

12. Kasey A. Stamation, David B. Croft, Peter D. Shaughnessy, Kelly A. Waples, and Sue V. Briggs, "Educational and Conservation Value of Whale Watching," *Tourism in Marine Environments* 4, no. 1 (2007): 52.

13. Chie Sakakibara, "*Kiavallakkikput Agviq* (Into the Whaling Cycle): Cetaceousness and Climate Change among the Iñupiat of Arctic Alaska," *Annals of the Association of American Geographers* 100, no. 4 (2010): 1003.

14. Job 41:1–2, 6–7 KJV.

15. Reeves and Smith, "A Taxonomy of World Whaling."

16. Alison DeGraff, email message to author, July 7, 2015.

17. J. L. Rathbone, "French Porpoise Fisheries," *Monthly Consular and Trade Reports* 33, no. 116 (1890): 361–363.

18. Ibid., 363.

19. Ibid.

20. Richard Ellis, "Azorean Whaling," in *Encyclopedia of Marine Mammals,* ed. William F. Perrin, Bernd Wursig, and J. G. M. Thewissen (San Diego: Academic Press, 2009), 64–67.

21. Reeves and Smith, "A Taxonomy of World Whaling," 89.

22. Ibid., 90–91.

23. Johan Nicolay Tønnessen and Arne Odd Johnsen, *The History of Modern Whaling* (Berkeley: University of California Press, 1982).

24. Klaus Barthelmess, "The Arts of Modern Whaling," Kommandør Chr. Christensens Hvalfangstmuseum Publication 32 (Sandefjord, Norway: Christensen's Whaling Museum, 2007).

25. Martin D. Robards and Randall R. Reeves, "The Global Extent and Character of Marine Mammal Consumption by Humans: 1970–2009," *Biological Conservation* 144 (2011): 2770–2786. This paper was invaluable in tallying the past and present whaling activities of the countries mentioned in this list. Many of the sources cited below were found here.

Brazil: William F. Perrin, *Dolphins, Porpoises and Whales: An Action Plan for the Conservation of Biological Diversity, 1988–1992* (Gland, Switzerland: IUCN, 1989); Rômulo R. N. Alves and Ierecê L. Rosa, "Use of Tucuxi Dolphin *Sotalia fluviatilis* for Medicinal and Magic / Religious Purposes in North of Brazil," *Human Ecology* 36 (2008): 443–447; V. Iriarte and M. Marmontel, "Insights on the Use of Dolphins (Boto, *Inia geoffrensis* and Tucuxi, *Sotalia fluviatilis*) for Bait in the Piracatinga (*Calophysus macropterus*) Fishery in the Western Brazilian Amazon," *Journal of Cetacean Research and Management* 13, no. 2 (2013): 163–173.

Cameroon: Monica Borobia, "Small Cetaceans of Eastern, Western and Central African Regions: A Summary Report," paper SC / 49 / SM48, presented to the IWC Scientific Committee, 1997).

Cape Verde: Francisco Reiner, Manuel E. dos Santos, Frederick W. Wenzel, and Allied Whale, "Cetaceans of the Cape Verde Archipelago," *Marine Mammal Science* 12, no. 3 (1996): 434–443; Pieter Lagendijk, "Report of a Study of the Present Status of Humpback Whales around the Cape Verde Islands," paper SC / 36 / PS16, presented to the Scientific Committee of the International Whaling Commission, Eastbourne, UK, 1984.

Côte d'Ivoire: J. Cadenat, "Rapport sur les petits cétacés ouest-africains," *Bulletin de l'Institut Français d'Afrique Noire* 21A (1959): 1367–1409; K. van Waerebeek, P. K. Ofori-Danson, and J. Debrah, "The Cetaceans of Ghana, a Validated Faunal Checklist," *West African Journal of Applied Ecology* 15 (2009): 61–90; Caroline R. Weir and Graham J. Pierce, "A Review of the Human Activities Impacting Cetaceans in the Eastern Tropical Atlantic," *Mammal Review* 43, no. 4 (2013): 258–274.

Dominica: Randall R. Reeves, "The Origins and Character of 'Aboriginal Subsistence' Whaling: A Global Review," *Mammal Review* 32, no. 2 (2002): 71–106.

Equatorial Guinea: Aurelio Basilio, *Caza y pesca en Annobon* (Madrid: Instituto de Estudios Africanos, 1957); Alex Aguilar, "Aboriginal Whaling off Pagalu (Equatorial Guinea)," *Report of the International Whaling Commission* 35 (1985): 385–386.

Florida: Silas Stearns, "The Fisheries of the Gulf of Mexico," in *The Fisheries and Fishery Industries of the United States,* ed. George Brown Goode (Washington, DC: Government Printing Office, 1887), 533–587.

France: Boris Culik, *Review of Small Cetaceans: Distribution, Behaviour, Migration and Threats* (Bonn: UNEP, 2004); R. Duguy and E. Hussenot, "Occasional

Captures of Delphinids in the Northeast Atlantic," *Report of the International Whaling Commission* 32 (1982): 461–462; R. Duguy, J. Besson, A. Casinos, A. Di Natale, S. Filella, A. Raduan, J. Raga, and D. Viale, "L'impact des activités humaines sur les cétacés de la Mediterranée occidentale," XXVIII Congres-Assemblée plenière de la CIESM, Monaco, December 2–11, 1982.

French Guiana: Koen van Waerebeek, "Preliminary Notes on the Existence of a Dolphin By-catch off French Guiana," *Aquatic Mammals* 16, no. 2 (1990): 71–72.

Martinique: Reeves, "Origins and Character."

Ghana: Joseph S. Debrah, "Taxonomy, Exploitation and Conservation of Dolphins in the Marine Waters of Ghana," MPh thesis, University of Ghana, 2000; Joseph S. Debrah, Patrick K. Ofori-Danson, and Koen van Waerebeek, "An Update on the Catch Composition and Other Aspects of Cetacean Exploitation in Ghana," report to the Scientific Committee of the IWC SC/62/SM10; Weir and Pierce, "Review of the Human Activities."

Gabon: F. C. Fraser, "Description of a Dolphin *Stenella frontalis* (Cuvier) from the Coast of French Equatorial Africa," *Atlantide Reports* 1 (1950): 61–83.

Gambia: Koen van Waerebeek, Ndiaye Edouard, Abdoulaye Djiba, Mamadou Diallo, Paul Murphy, Alpha Jallow, Almamy Camara, Papa Ndiaye, and Phillippe Tous, *A Survey of the Conservation Status of Cetaceans in Senegal, The Gambia, and Guinea-Bissau* (Bonn: UNEP/CMS, 2000).

Guinea: I. L. Bamy, K. van Waerebeek, S. S. Bah, M. Dia, B. Kaba, N. Keita, and S. Konate, "Species Occurrence of Cetaceans in Guinea, Including Humpback Whales with Southern Hemisphere Seasonality," *Marine Biodiversity Records* 3 (2010): e48.

Madeira: G. E. Maul and D. E. Sergeant, "New Cetacean Records from Madeira," *Bocagiana* 43 (1977): 1–8.

Mauritania: Fraser, "Description of a Dolphin"; R. Duguy, "Contribution à l'étude des mammifères marins de la côte nord-ouest Afrique," *Revue des Travaux de l'Institut des Pêches Maritimes* 39 (1976): 321–332.

Portugal: Cristina Brito, "Whaling on the Mainland of Portugal since the 13th Century: A First Approach," in *Proceedings of the ECS Workshop, Marine Mammal History, Held at the European Cetacean Society's 21st Annual Conference, The Aquarium, San Sebastián, Spain, 21st April 2007,* ECS Special Publication Series 50 (2009): 12–17; Cristina Brito and Nina Vieira, "Historical Accounts about the Occurrence and Capture of Common Dolphins in Portugal Mainland," report to the International Whaling Commission SC/61/SM17. 2009.

Senegal: A. R. Dupuy and J. Maigret, "Les mammifères marins des côtes du Sénégal 4, observations signalées en 1979," *Bulletin de l'Institut Fondamental d'Afrique Noire* 42A (1980): 401–409; J. Cadenat, "Rapport sur les petits cétacés"; van Waerebeek et al., *A Survey of the Conservation Status;* Weir and Pierce, "Review of the Human Activities."

Spain: Duguy et al., "L'impact des activités humaines."

St. Lucia: D. E. Gaskin and G. J. D. Smith, "The Small Whale Fishery of St. Lucia, W.I.," *Report of the International Whaling Commission* 27 (1977): 493; Price, "Whaling in the Caribbean"; Randall R. Reeves, "Exploitation of Cetaceans in St. Lucia, Lesser Antilles, January 1987," *Report of the International Whaling Commission* 38 (1988): 445–447.

St. Helena: William F. Perrin, "The Former Dolphin Fishery at St. Helena," *Report of the International Whaling Commission* 35 (1985): 423–428.

St. Vincent & the Grenadines: John E. Adams, "Shore Whaling in St. Vincent, West Indies," *Caribbean Quarterly* 19, no. 4 (1973): 42–50; Nathalie Ward, *Blows, Mon, Blows! A History of Bequia Whaling* (Woods Hole, MA: Gecko Productions, 1995).

Trinidad and Tobago: Aldemaro Romero, Ruth Baker, Joel E. Creswell, Anuradha Singh, Annabelle McKie, and Michael Manna, "Environmental History of Marine Mammal Exploitation in Trinidad and Tobago, W.I., and Its Ecological Impact," *Environment and History* 8 (2002): 255–274; Randall R. Reeves, Jalaludin A. Khan, Randi R. Olsen, Steven L. Swartz, and Tim D. Smith, "History of Whaling in Trinidad and Tobago," *Journal of Cetacean Research and Management* 3, no. 1 (2001): 45–54.

Venezuela: Aldemaro Romero, A. Ignacio Agudo, and Steven M. Green, "Exploitation of Cetaceans in Venezuela," *Report of the International Whaling Commission* 47 (1997): 735–746; Aldemaro Romero and Joel Cresswell, "In the Land of the Mermaid: How Culture, Not Ecology, Influenced Marine Mammal Exploitation in the Southeastern Caribbean," in *Environmental Issues in Latin America and the Caribbean,* ed. Aldemaro Romero and Sarah E. West (New York: Springer, 2005), 3–30.

26. Robert Sullivan, *A Whale Hunt: How a Native-American Village Did What No One Thought It Could* (New York: Simon & Schuster, 2000).

27. Rob van Ginkel, "The Makah Whale Hunt and Leviathan's Death: Reinventing Tradition and Disputing Authenticity in the Age of Modernity," *Etnofoor* 17, nos. 1 / 2 (2004): 58–59.

28. The intensity of air-conditioning in Caribbean offices is, according to St. Lucia's Nobel Prize-winning poet and playwright, Derek Walcott, "an assertion of power . . . the colder the offices the more important, an imitation of another climate." Derek Walcott, *The Antilles: Fragments of Epic Memory: the Nobel Lecture* (New York: Farrar, Straus and Giroux, 1993): n.p.

29. Aldemaro Romero and Kyla Hayford, "Past and Present Utilization of Marine Mammals in Grenada, W.I.," *Journal of Cetacean Research and Management* 2, no. 3 (2000): 223–226.

30. Judith Schalansky, *Atlas of Remote Islands: Fifty Islands I Have Not Visited and Never Will,* trans. Christine Lo (London: Particular, 2010).

31. Basilio, *Caza y pesca.*

32. Ibid., 79.

33. Bo Beolens, Michael Watkins, and Michael Grayson, *The Eponym Dictionary of Mammals* (Baltimore: Johns Hopkins University Press, 2009).

34. Aguilar, "Aboriginal Whaling off Pagalu."

35. Roger Michael Johnson, "The Last Whale Hunters," *Maritime Life and Traditions* 8 (2000): 44–61.

36. Richard H. Barnes, "Lamakera, Solor: Ethnographic Notes on a Muslim Whaling Village of Eastern Indonesia," *Anthropos* 91 (1996): 75–88.

37. Ibid., 79.

38. Tim Severin, *In Search of Moby Dick: the Quest for the White Whale* (New York: Basic Books, 2000), 151.

39. Reeves and Smith, "A Taxonomy of World Whaling," 87; Richard H. Barnes, *Sea Hunters of Indonesia: Fishers and Weavers of Lamalera* (Oxford: Clarendon Press, 1996), 336.

40. Heidi Dewar, "Preliminary Report: Manta Harvest in Lamakera," Pfleger Institute of Environmental Research, May 17, 2002, http://www.equilibrioazul.org /documentos/Dewar_Report.pdf

41. William H. Dawbin, "Porpoises and Porpoise Hunting in Malaita," *Australian Natural History* 15, no. 7 (1966): 207–211; Daisuke Takekawa, "The Method of Dolphin Hunting and Distribution of Teeth and Meat: Dolphin Hunting in the Solomon Islands," *Coastal Foragers in Transition, Senri Ethnological Studies* 42 (1996): 67–80.

42. Louie Psihoyos, *The Cove* (Santa Monica, CA: Lionsgate, 2001), DVD.

43. Farley Mowat, *Sea of Slaughter* (Toronto: McClelland & Stewart, 1984), 292.

44. Robert L. Brownell Jr., Douglas P. Nowacek, and Katherine Ralls, "Hunting Cetaceans with Sound: A Worldwide Review," *Journal of Cetacean Research and Management* 10, no. 1 (2008): 81–88.

45. Arctic: Robert McGhee, *Beluga Hunters: An Archaeological Reconstruction of the History and Culture of the Mackenzie Delta Kittegaryumiut* (St. John's, NL: Institute of Social and Economic Research, Memorial University of Newfoundland, 1974); C. V. Lucier and J. W. Vanstone, "Traditional Beluga Drives of the Inupiat of Kotzebue Sound, Alaska," *Fieldiana,* Anthropology New Series No. 25 [Publication 1468], (Chicago: Field Museum, 1995); Milton M. R. Freeman, *Whitefish (= White Whale) Hunting at Kakuk,* unpublished English translation of a Greenlandic textbook of hunting and fishing, on file with the author.

   Basque: J. T. Jenkins, *History of the Whale Fisheries* (Port Washington, NY: Kennikat Press, 1921); Michael Graham, "The Harvest of the Seas," in *Man's Role in Changing the Face of the Earth,* ed. W. L. Thomas Jr. (Chicago: University of Chicago Press, 1956), 487–503.

   Japan: Edward Mitchell, *Porpoise, Dolphin, and Small Whale Fisheries of the World* (Morges, Switzerland: IUCN, 1975); Brownell et al., "Hunting Cetaceans with Sound."

   North Atlantic: Lowrens Hacquebord, "'There She Blows': A Brief History of Whaling," *North Atlantic Studies* 2, nos. 1–2 (1990): 11–21; Szabo, *Monstrous Fishes.*

   Pacific: T. R. Peale, "United States Exploring Expedition during the Years 1838–42, under the Command of Charles Wilkes," *Mammalia and Ornithology*

8A, no. 25 (1848): 17–338; Charles Hedley, "General Account of the Atoll of Funa-futi," in *The Atoll of Funafuti, Ellice Group*, ed. Charles Hedley (Sydney: Australian Museum, 1896), 1–73; E. S. C. Handy, "The Native Culture in the Marquesas," *Bernice P. Bishop Museum Bulletin* 9 (1923); Arthur Grimble, *A Pattern of Islands* (London: John Murray, 1952); Gladys Zabilka, *Customs and Culture of Okinawa* (Rutland, VT: Bridgeway Press, 1959); Dawbin, "Porpoises and Porpoise Hunting in Malaita"; Kenneth P. Emory, *Material Culture of the Tuamotu Archipelago*, Pacific Anthropological Records 22 (Honolulu: Bernice Pauahi Bishop Museum, 1975); Anne Lavondès, *Le tahitien et la mer* (Paris: Nouvelles Editions Latines, 1979); Lyall Watson, *Sea Guide to the Whales of the World* (Boston: Dutton, 1981); M. W. Cawthorn, *Meat Consumption from Stranded Whales and Marine Mammals in New Zealand: Public Health and Other Issues,* Conservation Advisory Science Notes no. 164 (Wellington: Department of Conservation, 1997); Cara E. Miller, *Current State of Knowledge of Cetacean Threats, Diversity and Habitats in the Pacific Islands Region* (Adelaide: Whale and Dolphin Conservation Society, Australasia, 2007).

46. Arne Thorsteinsson, "Hvussu Gamalt er Grindadrápið?," *Varðin* 53 (1986): 65–66.
47. Connecticut: Charles F. Holder, "Among the Florida Keys," *St. Nicholas: An Illustrated Magazine* 16, no. 2 (1889): 674–684.

   Denmark: Mitchell, *Porpoise, Dolphin, and Small Whale Fisheries;* C. Kinze, "Exploitation of Harbour Porpoises (*Phocoena phocoena*) in Danish Waters: A Historical Review," *Report of the International Whaling Commission* 16 (1995): 141–153.

   England: Margaret Klinowska, "Catches, Live Strandings and Sightings of the Pilot Whale (*Globicephala melaena*) in the British and Irish Islands," IWC SC/39/SM2, 1987.

   Faroe Islands: Jóan Pauli Joensen, "Pilot Whaling in the Faroe Islands," *Ethnologia Scandinavica* 6 (1976): 1–42.

   Greenland: Milton M. R. Freeman, *Inuit, Whaling, and Sustainability* (Walnut Creek, CA: Altamira, 1998); Freeman, *Whitefish.*

   Hebrides: Alexander Fenton, *The Northern Isles: Orkney and Shetland* (Edinburgh: John Donald, 1978).

   Iceland: Mitchell, *Porpoise, Dolphin, and Small Whale Fisheries;* Trausti Einarsson, *Hvalveiðar við Ísland 1600–1939,* Sagnfræðirannsóknir/Studia Historica, Sagnfræðistofnun Háskóla Íslands, vol. 8 (Reykjavík: Bókaútgáfa Menningarsjóðs, 1987); Ole Lindquist, *Peasant Fisherman Whaling in the Northeast Atlantic Area: ca. 900–1900 AD* (Akureyri, Iceland: Háskólinn á Akureyri, 1997).

   Ireland: Thomàs Ó Criomhthain, *The Islandman* (Dublin: Talbot Press, 1937); C. E. O'Riordan, "Long-Finned Pilot Whales, *Globicephala melaena,* Driven Ashore in Ireland, 1800–1973," *Journal of the Fisheries Research Board of Canada* 32, no. 7 (1975): 1101–1102.

   Maine: E. P. Morris, "Along the Maine Coast," *Geographical Review* 2, no. 5 (1916): 325–333.

   Manitoba: "Catching Porpoises at Hudson's Bay," *The Friend* 61 (1888): 222–223.

Massachusetts: Henry David Thoreau, *Cape Cod* (New York: Crowell, 1908); Mitchell, *Porpoise, Dolphin, and Small Whale Fisheries.*

New Jersey: Mitchell, *Porpoise, Dolphin, and Small Whale Fisheries.*

Newfoundland and Labrador: Anthony B. Dickinson and Chesley W. Sanger, *Twentieth-Century Shore-Station Whaling in Newfoundland and Labrador* (Montreal: McGill-Queen's University Press, 2005); Willis P. Martin, *Two Outports: A History of Dildo and New Harbour* (St. John's, NL: Flanker Press, 2006); Russell Fielding, "The Whale Drivers of Newfoundland," *Focus on Geography* 52, no. 3 (2009): 1–8; A. J. Howell, "Autopsy of a Whale," *The Eclectic Medical Journal* 38, no. 1 (1878): 9–13.

North Carolina: Frederick W. True, "The Porpoise Fishery of Cape Hatteras," *Transactions of the American Fisheries Society* 14, no. 1 (1885): 32–38.

Norway: Mitchell, *Porpoise, Dolphin, and Small Whale Fisheries;* R. Anderson, *Norwegian Small Type Whaling in Cultural Perspectives* (Tromsø: Norwegian College of Fisheries, 1991).

Orkneys: John R. Tudor, *The Orkneys and Shetland: Their Past and Present State* (London: Edward Stanford, 1883).

Quebec: John Horden, "A Great Fishery," *Chatterbox* 16 (1866): 126–127.

Scotland: Klinowska, "Catches, Live Strandings, and Sightings of the Pilot Whale."

Shetlands: A. Sandison, "Whale Hunting in the Shetlands," *The Saga Book of the Viking Club* 1 (1896): 42–53; Brian Smith, "Whale Driving in Shetland and the Faroes," *Sea Mammal Report,* 2003, 8–16.

Sweden: A. C. Strubberg, ed., *Dansk Fiskeristat* (Copenhagen: Danske Erhvervs Forlag, 1936); Ingvar Svanberg, "Fångst av tumlare (*Phocoena phocoena*) i Sverige," *Svenska Linnésällskapeta årskrift* (2004–2005), 87–100.

48. Dorete Bloch and Lena Lastein, "Biometrical Segregation of Long-Finned Pilot Whales off Eastern and Western North Atlantic," *ICES Conference and Meeting Documents* N21 (1992).

49. Fielding, "The Whale Drivers of Newfoundland."

50. A. T. Pinhorn, "Living Marine Resources of Newfoundland-Labrador: Status and Potential," *Bulletin of the Fisheries Research Board of Canada* 194 (1976): 1–64.

51. Alan G. Abend and Tim D. Smith. *Review of Distribution of the Long-Finned Pilot Whale (Globicephala melas) in the North Atlantic and Mediterranean,* NOAA Technical Memorandum NMFS-NE-117 (Woods Hole, MA: NOAA, 1999).

52. Calculated from the national whaling statistics maintained by Føroya Náttúrugripasavn (the Faroese Museum of Natural History).

53. Smith, "Whale Driving in Shetland and Faroes."

54. Fenton, *The Northern Isles,* 549.

55. Smith, "Whale Driving in Shetland and Faroes," 16.

56. Thoreau, *Cape Cod,* 132.

57. Freeman, *Inuit, Whaling, and Sustainability;* Marion Nestle, "Animal v. Plant Foods in Human Diets and Health: Is the Historical Record Unequivocal?," *Proceedings*

of the Nutrition Society 58 (1999): 211–218; Nancy Shoemaker, "Whale Meat in American History," *Environmental History* 10, no. 2 (2005): 269–294.

58. Mark P. Simmonds and Paul A. Johnston, "Whale Meat: A Safe and Healthy Food?" *British Food Journal* 96, no. 4 (1994): 26–31.

59. Tønnessen and Johnsen, *The History of Modern Whaling.*

60. Hacquebord, "'There She Blows,'" 17.

6. LAWS AND TRADITIONS

1. International Union for the Conservation of Nature, "About," https://www.iucn.org/about. Accessed March 28, 2018.

2. Kurkpatrick Dorsey, *Whales and Nations: Environmental Diplomacy on the High Seas* (Seattle: University of Washington Press, 2013).

3. International Agreement for the Regulation of Whaling, "The International Whaling Conference, Washington, DC, November 20-December 2, 1946, Final Act": 39.

4. Harry N. Scheiber, "Historical Memory, Cultural Claims, and Environmental Ethics in the Jurisprudence of Whaling Regulation," *Ocean and Coastal Management* 38 (1998): 14.

5. Robert Gambell, "International Management of Whales and Whaling: An Historical Review of the Regulation of Commercial and Aboriginal Subsistence Whaling," *Arctic* 46, no. 2 (1993): 101.

6. Ibid., 106.

7. Dorsey, *Whales and Nations.*

8. Ibid.

9. International Whaling Commission, "Aboriginal Subsistence Whaling," https://iwc.int/aboriginal. Accessed March 28, 2018.

10. Ibid.

11. Despite the geographical proximity and cultural and historical ties between humpback whaling based in Bequia and small cetacean hunting based in Barrouallie, St. Vincent, these two operations hold starkly different legal statuses, owing to the species targeted in each.

12. Isao Miyaoka, *Legitimacy in International Society: Japan's Reaction to Global Wildlife Preservation* (New York: Palgrave Macmillan, 2004).

13. International Agreement for the Regulation of Whaling, "The International Whaling Conference"

14. S. B. Reilly, J. L. Bannister, P. B. Best, M. Brown, R. L. Brownell Jr., D. S. Butterworth, P. J. Clapham, J. Cooke, G. P. Donovan, J. Urbán, and A. N. Zerbini, "*Balaenoptera bonaerensis*," *The IUCN Red List of Threatened Species* (Cambridge, UK: IUCN, 2008); S. B. Reilly, J. L. Bannister, P. B. Best, M. Brown, R. L. Brownell Jr., D. S. Butterworth, P. J. Clapham, J. Cooke, G. P. Donovan, J. Urbán, and A. N. Zerbini, "*Balaenoptera edeni*," *The IUCN Red List of Threatened Species* (Cambridge, UK: IUCN, 2008); Shiro Wada, Masayuki Oishi, and Tadasu K. Yamada, "A Newly Discovered Species of Living Baleen Whale," *Nature* 426 (2003): 278–281; Salva-

tore Cerchio, Boris Andrianantenaina, Alec Lindsay, Melinda Rekdahl, Norbert Andrianarivelo, and Tahina Rasoloarijao, "Omura's Whales (*Balaenoptera omurai*) off Northwest Madagascar: Ecology, Behaviour and Conservation Needs," *Royal Society Open Science* 2 (2015): 150301.

15. Alexander Gillespie, "Small Cetaceans, International Law and the International Whaling Commission," *Melbourne Journal of International Law* 2, no. 2 (2001): 257–303.

16. Steinar Andresen, "The Effectiveness of the International Whaling Commission," *Arctic* 46, no. 2 (1993): 108–115.

17. David D. Caron, "The International Whaling Commission and the North Atlantic Marine Mammal Commission: The Institutional Risks of Coercion in Consensual Structures," *American Journal of International Law* 89, no. 1 (1995): 154–174; Alf H. Hoel, "Regionalization of International Whale Management: The Case of the North Atlantic Marine Mammals Commission," *Arctic* 46, no. 2 (1993): 116–123.

18. Wendy Elliott, Heather Sohl, and Valerie Burgener, *Small Cetaceans: The Forgotten Whales* (Gland, Switzerland: World Wildlife Fund, 2009).

19. Simon Winchester, *Outposts: Journeys to the Surviving Relics of the British Empire* (London: Penguin, 2003).

20. Consolidated version of the Treaty on the Functioning of the European Union, October 26, 2012, Part Seven, Article 355.5.a, http://eur-lex.europa.eu/legal-content /en/ALL/?uri=CELEX:12012E/TXT. Note that *Faeroe* is a common variant spelling.

21. Ibid.

22. Gunnar Karlsson, *The History of Iceland* (Minneapolis: University of Minnesota Press, 2000).

23. Einar Kallsberg, "The Faroes Today," in *The Atlantic Islands: A Study of Faeroe Life and Scene,* ed. Kenneth Williamson (London: Routledge, 1970), 305–321.

24. Ibid., 305.

25. Maria Ackrén, "The Faroe Islands: Options for Independence," *Island Studies Journal* 1, no. 2 (2006): 223–238.

26. Sea Shepherd Conservation Society, "Sea Shepherd Challenges Denmark at the European Commission," https://seashepherd.org/news/sea-shepherd-challenges-denmark-at-the-european-commission/; Convention on the Conservation of European Wildlife and Natural Habitats, September 19, 1979, Chapter 3, Article 6.a, http://www.coe.int/en/web/conventions/full-list/-/conventions/rms /0900001680078aff.

27. Árni Olafsson, email message to author, February 24, 2010.

28. John Petersen and Kai P. Mortensen, *Executive Order on Pilot Whaling* (Torshavn: Faroese Representative Council, 1998), translated in Jóan Pauli Joensen, *Pilot Whaling in the Faroe Islands: History, Ethnography, Symbol* (Tórshavn: Faroe University Press, 2009), 272.

29. Jens C. Svabo, *Om den Færøsk Marsviin-Fangst* (Copenhagen: Det Almindelige Danske Bibliothek, 1779), 51, translated in Joensen, *Pilot Whaling in the Faroe Islands,* 66.

30. Petersen and Mortensen, *Executive Order on Pilot Whaling.* Translated in Joensen, *Pilot Whaling in the Faroe Islands,* 274.

31. Russell Fielding, "Coastal Geomorphology and Culture in the Spatiality of Whaling in the Faroe Islands," *Area* 45, no. 1 (2013): 88–97; Petersen and Mortensen, *Executive Order on Pilot Whaling,* translated in Joensen, *Pilot Whaling in the Faroe Islands.*

32. Virginia Heyer Young, *Becoming West Indian: Culture, Self, and Nation in St. Vincent* (Washington, DC: Smithsonian Institution Press, 1993), 183.

33. Wallace W. Zane, *Journeys to the Spiritual Lands: The Natural History of a West Indian Religion* (New York: Oxford University Press, 1999), 7.

34. Lord Ashcroft Foundation, "President Obama Needs Our Help to Save the Whales" [advertisement], *Searchlight,* June 5, 2009, 13.

35. St. Vincent and the Grenadines, *Statutory Rules and Orders: The Fisheries (Fish and Fish Products) Regulations* (Kingstown: Government Printing Office, 2001); St. Vincent and the Grenadines, *Fisheries (Fish and Fish Products) Regulations: Arrangement of Regulations* (Kingstown: Government Printing Office, 2006). St. Vincent & the Grenadines has a separate set of policies regarding the take of IWC whales, which primarily sets the quotas and establishes restrictions on whaling methods for the Bequia humpback operation.

36. UNEP, "Protocol Concerning Specially Protected Areas and Wildlife in the Wider Caribbean Region—A Regional Legal Framework for Biodiversity," January 18, 1990. http://www.cep.unep.org/cartagena-convention.

37. Ibid.

38. Ibid.

39. UNEP, "Final Act of the Conference of Plenipotentiaries for the Adoption of the Annexes to the Protocol Concerning Specially Protected Areas and Wildlife in the Wider Caribbean Region," March 2017, http://www.cep.unep.org/cartagena-convention.

40. UNEP, "Protocol Concerning Specially Protected Areas and Wildlife."

41. "St. Vincent to Outlaw Killing of Sea Turtles," *iWitness News,* November 3, 2016, http://www.iwnsvg.com/2016/11/03/st-vincent-to-outlaw-killing-of-sea-turtles.

42. UNEP, "Protocol Concerning Specially Protected Areas and Wildlife."

43. Ibid.

44. Ibid.

45. Aldo Leopold, *A Sand County Almanac, and Sketches Here and There* (New York: Oxford University Press, 1989), 204.

46. Stan Stevens, ed., *Conservation through Cultural Survival: Indigenous Peoples and Protected Areas* (Washington, DC: Island Press, 1997); Karl S. Zimmerer and Kenneth R. Young, eds., *Nature's Geography: New Lessons for Conservation in Developing Countries* (Madison: University of Wisconsin Press, 1998).

47. Carl O. Sauer, "The Morphology of Landscape," *University of California Publications in Geography* 2, no. 2 (1925): 19–53.

48. Mark Bonta, *Seven Names for the Bellbird: Conservation Geography in Honduras* (College Station: Texas A&M University Press, 2003), 3.
49. Milton M. R. Freeman, "The Nature and Utility of Traditional Ecological Knowledge," *Northern Perspectives* 20, no. 1 (1992): 9.
50. Claude Lévi-Strauss, *The Savage Mind* (Chicago: University of Chicago Press, 1966), 13.
51. Jared Diamond, "This-Fellow Frog, Name Belong-Him Dakwo," *Natural History* 98, no. 4 (1989): 16–23.
52. Owing to the relatively short history of today's Vincentian culture, some researchers prefer to use the term "local ecological knowledge" (LEK), instead of TEK, to acknowledge that valuable knowledge of one's environment need not be based upon generations of tradition.
53. Stevens, *Conservation through Cultural Survival*, 2.
54. Ibid.
55. Carl O. Sauer, "The Agency of Man on the Earth," in *Man's Role in Changing the Face of the Earth*, ed. William L. Thomas Jr. (Chicago: University of Chicago Press, 1956), 68.
56. Clark S. Monson, "Indigenous Resource Taboos: A Practical Approach towards the Conservation of Commercialized Species," PhD diss., University of Hawai'i, 2004, 5.

7. THE FRAGILE LINK

1. George Perkins Marsh, *Man and Nature* (New York: Scribner, 1864), 549.
2. Farley Mowat, *A Whale for the Killing* (Boston: Little, Brown, 1972), 204.
3. Dorete Bloch and Martin Zachariassen, "The 'Skinn' Values of Pilot Whales in the Faroe Islands: An Evaluation and Corrective Proposal," *North Atlantic Studies* 1, no. 1 (1989): 39–56.
4. Jóan Pauli Joensen, *Pilot Whaling in the Faroe Islands: History, Ethnography, Symbol* (Tórshavn: Faroe University Press, 2009).
5. The legal historian Graham Burnett describes a fascinating 1818 New York court case in which the fish-or-mammal question was put to a jury in his entertaining and informative, *Trying Leviathan*. The case involves an oil merchant who refused the pay the fee for the state-required inspection of "fish oils" on three barrels of whale oil that he had imported. His reasoning? Simple: the law clearly stated that it applied to fish oils and whales are not fish. The ensuing court case questioned not only the law and taxonomy but, as Burnett puts it, "the whole order of nature." D. Graham Burnett, *Trying Leviathan: The Nineteenth-Century New York Court Case That Put the Whale on Trial and Challenged the Order of Nature* (Princeton, NJ: Princeton University Press, 2007).
6. Joensen, *Pilot Whaling in the Faroe Islands*, 125.
7. Árni Olafsson, "Faroese Whale and Whaling Policy," *North Atlantic Studies* 2, nos. 1–2 (1990): 130–137; Kate Sanderson, "Grindadráp: The Discourse of Drama," *North Atlantic Studies* 2, nos. 1–2 (1990): 196–204.

8. Herman Melville, *Moby-Dick, or the Whale* (New York: Harper & Brothers, 1851).

9. Brent Berlin, Dennis E. Breedlove, and Peter H. Raven, "Folk Taxonomies and Biological Classification and Nomenclature," *Science* 154, no. 3746 (1966): 273–275.

10. Victor Turner, *The Forest of Symbols: Aspects of Ndembu Ritual* (Ithaca, NY: Cornell University Press, 1967); Victor Turner, *The Ritual Process: Structure and Anti-Structure* (Chicago: Aldine, 1969); Arnold van Gennep, *The Rites of Passage* (London: Routledge, 2004).

11. For a more thorough discussion of the concept of liminality as it applies to the processing of Vincentian-caught whales and dolphins, see Russell Fielding, "The Liminal Coastline in the Life of a Whale: Transition, Identity, and Food-Production in the Eastern Caribbean," *Geoforum* 54 (2014): 10–16.

12. Greg Dening, *Islands and Beaches: Discourse on a Silent Land: Marquesas, 1774–1880* (Belmont, CA: Dorsey Press, 1980).

13. Dorete Bloch and Hans Pauli Joensen, "Faroese Pilot Whaling: Conditions, Practice, and Superstition," *North Atlantic Studies* 4, nos. 1–2 (2001): 66.

14. Joensen, *Pilot Whaling in the Faroe Islands,* 43. It should be noted that Taylor herself seems to have been allowed to view the grindadráp, as her descriptions appear to be based on firsthand observations.

15. Kenneth Williamson, *The Atlantic Islands: A Study of the Faeroe Life and Scene* (Glasgow: Collins, 1948), 115.

16. Venceslaus U. Hammershaimb, *Færøsk Anthologi* (Copenhagen: S. L. Møllers Bogtrykkeri, 1891), 401, translated in Kate Sanderson, "Grindadráp: A Textual History of Whaling Traditions in the Faroes to 1900," MPh thesis, University of Sydney, 1992, 102; Hammershaimb, *Færøsk Anthologi,* 401, translated in Joensen, *Pilot Whaling in the Faroe Islands,* 198.

17. Ragnheiður Bogadóttir and Elisabeth Skarðhamar Olsen, "Making Degrowth Locally Meaningful: The Case of the Faroese *Grindadráp,*" *Journal of Political Ecology* 24 (2017): 508. For more on traditional gender roles in Faroese society, see Elisabeth Vestergaard, "Space and Gender at the Faroe Islands, or an Explanation of Why 'Kúgv er Konu Lík,'" *North Atlantic Studies* 1, no. 1 (1989): 33–37.

18. Liljan's surname was intentionally left out of this narrative at her request.

19. "Ein grind," *Føringatíðindi* 7, no. 15 (August 6, 1896): 2, translated in Jonathan Wylie, "Grindadráp," in *Ring of Dancers: Images of Faroese Culture,* ed. Jonathan Wylie and David Margolin (Philadelphia: University of Pennsylvania Press, 1981), 111.

20. This anecdote was originally cited in Williamson, *The Atlantic Islands,* and was retold by Wylie in "Grindadráp."

21. Sally Price, "When Is a Calabash Not a Calabash?," *New West Indian Guide / Nieuwe West-Indische Gids* 1/2 (1982): 69–82.

22. National Broadcasting Company—St. Vincent & the Grenadines, on-air interview with Samuel Hazelwood, March 4, 2009.

23. John E. Adams, "Last of the Caribbean Whalemen," *Natural History* 103 (1994): 69.

24. Sanderson, "Grindadráp: A Textual History"; Joensen, *Pilot Whaling in the Faroe Islands.*

25. Russell Fielding, "Whaling Futures: A Survey of Faroese and Vincentian Youth on the Topic of Artisanal Whaling," *Society and Natural Resources* 26, no. 7 (2013): 810–826.

26. This is not to be confused with the name of the volcano on St. Vincent, La Soufrière. *Soufrière* derives from the French *soufre,* meaning "sulfur," and is a common name in the Caribbean for volcanoes and villages near volcanoes. Examples include the Vincentian volcano and St. Lucian village already mentioned as well as the villages of Soufrière and Petit Soufrière on Dominica; La Grande Soufrière, a volcano on Guadeloupe and that island's highest point; and Soufrière Hills, the Montserratian volcano that erupted violently, beginning in 1995, causing the destruction of that island's capital and evacuation of its population.

27. Rufus George, letter to author, June 2, 2009.

8. CULTURALLY EMBEDDED CONSERVATION STRATEGIES

1. Arne Thorsteinsson, "Land Divisions, Land Rights, and Landownership in the Faroe Islands," in *Northern Landscapes: Region and Belonging on the Northern Edge of Europe,* ed. Michael Jones and Kenneth R. Olwig (Minneapolis: University of Minnesota Press, 2008), 92.

2. Dorete Bloch and Hans Pauli Joensen, "Faroese Pilot Whaling: Conditions, Practice, and Superstition," *North Atlantic Studies* 4, nos. 1–2 (2001): 57–67; Jóan Pauli Joensen, *Pilot Whaling in the Faroe Islands: History, Ethnography, Symbol* (Tórshavn: Faroe University Press, 2009), 101.

3. Jimmy Buffett, *A Pirate Looks at Fifty* (New York: Random House, 1998).

4. Russell Fielding, "Coastal Geomorphology and Culture in the Spatiality of Whaling in the Faroe Islands," *Area* 45, no. 1 (2013): 88–97.

5. Joensen, *Pilot Whaling in the Faroe Islands,* 281–282. The list of whale bays has been updated several times. The most current version of the list is maintained online.

6. Jonathan Wylie, "Grindadráp," in *Ring of Dancers: Images of Faroese Culture,* ed. Jonathan Wylie and David Margolin (Philadelphia: University of Pennsylvania Press, 1981).

7. Bjarki Gyldenkærne Dalsgarð, "*Springarar:* Dolphins Killed in the Faroe Islands," 2017. Unpublished report on file with the author.

8. Árni Olafsson, "Faroese Whale and Whaling Policy," *North Atlantic Studies* 2, nos. 1–2 (1990): 132.

9. J. Campbell Plowden, "Pilot Whale Hunt Attacked," *Humane Society News,* Fall 1985, 13.

10. Fikret Berkes, Johan Colding, and Carl Folke, "Rediscovery of Traditional Ecological Knowledge as Adaptive Management," *Ecological Applications* 10, no. 5 (2000): 1251–1262; Janis B. Alcorn, "Noble Savage or Noble State? Northern Myths and Southern Realities in Biodiversity Conservation," *Etnoecológica* 2, no. 3 (1994): 7–19; Kent H. Redford and John G. Robinson, "Hunting by Indigenous Peoples

and Conservation of Game Species," *Cultural Survival Quarterly* 9, no. 1 (1985): 41–44.

11. Garrett Hardin, "The Tragedy of the Commons," *Science* 162 (1968): 1243–1248; Kent H. Redford, "The Ecologically Noble Savage," *Orion Nature Quarterly* 9 (1990): 24–29.

12. Johan Colding and Carle Folke, "Social Taboos: Invisible Systems of Local Resource Management and Biological Conservation," *Ecological Applications* 11, no. 2 (2001): 584–600.

13. Julia P. G. Jones, Mijasoa M. Andriamarovololona, and Neal Hockley, "The Importance of Taboos and Social Norms to Conservation in Madagascar," *Conservation Biology* 22, no. 4 (2008): 977.

14. Dorete Bloch, Kjartan Hoydal, Jákup S. Joensen, and Petur Zachariassen, "The Faroese Catch of the Long-Finned Pilot Whale: Bias Shown of the 280 Year Time-Series," *North Atlantic Studies* 2, nos. 1–2 (1990): 45–46.

15. Dorete Bloch, personal communication, 2005.

16. Milton M. R. Freeman, *Inuit, Whaling, and Sustainability* (Walnut Creek, CA: Altamira, 1998); Chie Sakakibara, *"Kiavallakkikput Agviq* (Into the Whaling Cycle): Cetaceousness and Climate Change among the Iñupiat of Arctic Alaska," *Annals of the Association of American Geographers* 100, no. 4 (2010): 1003–1012.

17. Randall R. Reeves and Tim D. Smith, "A Taxonomy of World Whaling," in *Whales, Whaling, and Ocean Ecosystems,* ed. James A. Estes, Douglas P. DeMaster, Daniel F. Doak, Terrie M. Williams, and Robert L. Brownell Jr. (Berkeley: University of California Press, 2006), 82.

18. Randall R. Reeves, "Insights on Marine Mammals of the Wider Caribbean Sea Region (Including the Gulf of Mexico) Derived from Whaling Documents," paper presented at the Regional Workshop of Experts on the Development of the Marine Mammal Action Plan for the Wider Caribbean Region, Bridgetown, Barbados, July 18–21, 2005.

19. David K. Caldwell and Melba C. Caldwell, "Porpoise Fisheries in the Southern Caribbean—Present Utilizations and Future Potentials," *Proceedings of the Gulf and Caribbean Fisheries Institute* 23 (1971): 195–211.

20. R. E. Johannes, "Traditional Marine Conservation Methods in Oceania and Their Demise," *Annual Review of Ecology and Systematics* 9 (1978): 351.

21. Noel Castree, "Nature, Economy and the Cultural Politics of Theory: The 'War Against the Seals' in the Bering Sea, 1870–1911," *Geoforum* 28, no. 1 (1997): 11.

22. The data I collected and compiled for both field sites are provided in the appendix to this book.

23. C. F. Hickling, *The Fisheries of the British West Indies: Report on a Visit in 1949,* Development and Welfare in the West Indies, Bulletin 29 (Bridgetown, Barbados: Cole's Printery, 1950).

24. David K. Caldwell and Melba C. Caldwell, "Dolphin and Small Whale Fisheries of the Caribbean and West Indies: Occurrence, History, and Catch Statistics—

with Special Reference to the Lesser Antillean Island of St. Vincent," *Journal of the Fisheries Research Board of Canada* 32, no. 7 (1975): 1105–1110.

25. Nigel M. Scott, "The Current Status and Management Options for the Mammalian Fishery in Barrouallie, St. Vincent, West Indies," MS thesis, University of the West Indies, 1995.

26. Edward Mitchell, *Porpoise, Dolphin, and Small Whale Fisheries of the World* (Morges, Switzerland: IUCN, 1975), 18; Scott, "Current Status and Management Options," 6.

27. Arne Thorsteinsson, "Hvussu Gamalt er Grindadrápið?," *Varðin* 53 (1986): 66.

28. Kate Sanderson, "Grindadráp: A Textual History of Whaling Traditions in the Faroes to 1900," MPh thesis, University of Sydney, 1992, 52.

29. John Petersen and Kai P. Mortensen, *Executive Order on Pilot Whaling* (Torshavn: Faroese Representative Council, 1998), translated in Joensen, *Pilot Whaling in the Faroe Islands,* 272.

30. Dorete Bloch, *Pilot Whales and the Whale Drive* (Tórshavn: H. N. Jacobsens Bókahandil, 2007), 45.

31. Joensen, *Pilot Whaling in the Faroe Islands;* Justines Olsen, "Killing Methods and Equipment in the Faroese Pilot Whale Hunt," English translation of "Om avlivningsmetoder og udstyr for færøsk grindefangst" (NAMMCO/99/WS/2), paper presented to the NAMMCO Workshop on Hunting Methods, Nuuk, Greenland, February 9–11, 1999.

32. Sanderson, "Grindadráp: A Textual History," 18.

33. Mitchell, *Porpoise, Dolphin, and Small Whale Fisheries of the World,* 77.

34. Hubert H. Lamb, *Climate: Present, Past and Future,* vol. 2 (New York: Routledge, 2013).

35. Rolf Guttesen, "Food Production, Climate and Population in the Faeroe Islands 1584–1652," *Geografisk Tidsskrift, Danish Journal of Geography* 104, no. 2 (2004): 45.

36. The long-finned pilot whale's primary prey species in Faroese waters, as determined by stomach content analysis, are the European flying squid (*Todarodes sagittatus*) and boreoatlantic armhook squid (*Gonatus fabricii*). See Geneviève Desportes and R. Mouritsen, "Preliminary Results on the Diet of Long-Finned Pilot Whales off the Faroe Islands," *Report of the International Whaling Commission* 14 (1993): 305–324.

37. Boris Culik, *Review of Small Cetaceans: Distribution, Behaviour, Migration and Threats* (Bonn: UNEP, 2004), 76.

38. Jay Arnett and Russell Fielding, "Whaling in the Faroe Islands: A Climate Study," unpublished report on file with author, 2014.

39. North Atlantic Marine Mammal Commission, *NAMMCO Annual Report 2011* (Tromsø, Norway: NAMMCO, 2012).

40. S. T. Buckland, D. Bloch, K. L. Cattanach, T. Gunnlaugsson, K. Hoydal, S. Lens, and J. Sigurjónsson, "Distribution and Abundance of Long-Finned Pilot Whales in the North Atlantic, Estimated from NASS-1987 and NASS-89 Data," *Report of the International Whaling Commission* 14 (1993): 33–50; Culik, "Review of Small Cetaceans," 77.

41. The standard deviation on the 1709–2017 dataset, however, is 742, indicating the high degree of variability in the annual catch.
42. Paul Watson, email message to author, October 25, 2005.
43. M. Glover, *Faroese Fin Whale Campaign—1981* (London: Greenpeace, 1981).
44. Sanderson, "Grindadráp: A Textual History."
45. Plowden, "Pilot Whale Hunt Attacked," 13.
46. Jeff Goodman, dir., *Black Harvest: The Fight for the Pilot Whale* (London: British Broadcasting Company, 1987), documentary film.
47. Sanderson, "Grindadráp: A Textual History"; Olsen, "Killing Methods."
48. Joensen, *Pilot Whaling in the Faroe Islands.*
49. *Report of the International Whaling Commission* 46 (1996): 43.
50. For a thorough analysis of the discourse surrounding this letter and postcard campaign, see Kate Sanderson, "Grindadráp: The Discourse of Drama," *North Atlantic Studies* 2, nos. 1–2 (1990): 196–204.
51. Sea Shepherd Conservation Society, "Grindstop 2014 Update," 2014, https:// seashepherd.org/news/grindstop-2014-update/.
52. Culik, *Review of Small Cetaceans.*
53. Christina Sabinsky, email message to author, September 15, 2009.
54. Thanks to Árni Olafsson, specialist on Faroe Islands affairs at the Danish Foreign Ministry, for sharing several versions of this protest letter response with me.
55. Sea Shepherd Conservation Society, "Hollywood Stars Demand Costco Stop Its Purchase and Sale of Faroe Islands' Salmon," July 7, 2016, https://seashepherd.org /news/hollywood-stars-demand-costco-stop-its-purchase-and-sale-of-faroe-islands-salmon/; "Faroe Islands: Cruise Boycott Hits Tourism," Deutsche Welle, July 13, 2016, http://www.dw.com/en/faroe-islands-cruise-boycott-hits-tourism /a-19397715.
56. Ólavur Sjurðarberg, personal communication, 2005.
57. Rolf Guttesen, personal communication, 2008.
58. Sea Shepherd Conservation Society, "Master and Commander: Complete List of Sea Shepherd Voyages, 1979–2012," http://archive.seashepherd.org/who-we-are /master-and-commander.html.
59. "'Ocean Warrior' Asked to Stay in International Waters," news release, Government of St. Lucia, July 24, 2001, http://www.govt.lc/news/ocean-warrior-asked-to -stay-in-international-waters.
60. Arne Kalland, *Unveiling the Whale: Discourses on Whales and Whaling* (New York: Berghahn Books, 2009).
61. Richard W. Bulliet, *Herders, Hunters, and Hamburgers: The Past and Future of Human-Animal Relationships* (New York: Columbia University Press, 2005).
62. Freeman, *Inuit, Whaling, and Sustainability;* Milton M. R. Freeman, "The International Whaling Commission, Small-Type Whaling, and Coming to Terms with Subsistence," *Human Organisation* 52, no. 3 (1993): 243–251.
63. Redford, "The Ecologically Noble Savage."
64. Paul Watson, email message to author, October 25, 2005.

65. Kate Sanderson, *"Grind*—Ambiguity and Pressure to Conform: Faroese Whaling and the Anti-Whaling Protest," in *Elephants and Whales: Resources for Whom?,* ed. Milton Freeman and Urs P. Kreuter (Basel: Gordon and Breach, 1994), 187.

66. Ibid., 195.

67. Ibid., 199.

68. Magni Garðalíð, personal communication, 2005.

69. Dorete Bloch, personal communication, 2005.

9. THE VALUE OF SEAWATER

1. Vicki E. Szabo, *Monstrous Fishes and the Mead-Dark Sea: Whaling in the Medieval North Atlantic* (Leiden: Brill, 2008), 57.

2. Herman Melville, *Moby-Dick, or the Whale* (New York: Harper & Brothers, 1851); Owen Chase, *The Wreck of the Whaleship Essex* (San Diego: Harcourt Brace, 1993).

3. Szabo, *Monstrous Fishes,* 57.

4. A. Sandison, "Whale Hunting in the Shetlands," *Saga Book of the Viking Club* 1 (1896): 42–53; Thomas Henderson, "The Whale Hunt," *Scots Magazine* 42, no. 4 (1945): 249–253.

5. Sandison, "Whale Hunting in the Shetlands."

6. Jóan Pauli Joensen, "Faroese Pilot Whaling in the Light of Social and Cultural History," *North Atlantic Studies* 2, nos. 1–2 (1990): 179–184.

7. Jóan Pauli Joensen, "Pilot Whaling in the Faroe Islands," *Ethnologia Scandinavica* 6 (1976): 1–42.

8. Kate Sanderson, "Grindadráp: A Textual History of Whaling Traditions in the Faroes to 1900," MPh thesis, University of Sydney, 1992, 91.

9. Joensen, "Faroese Pilot Whaling in the Light of Social and Cultural History."

10. Bonham C. Richardson, *Caribbean Migrants: Environment and Human Survival on St. Kitts and Nevis* (Knoxville: University of Tennessee Press, 1983).

11. Jonathan Wylie, "Too Much of a Good Thing: Crises of Glut in the Faroe Islands and Dominica," *Comparative Studies in Society and History* 35, no. 2 (1993): 352–389.

12. Virginia Heyer Young, *Becoming West Indian: Culture, Self, and Nation in St. Vincent* (Washington, DC: Smithsonian Institution Press, 1993).

13. Jóan Pauli Joensen, *Pilot Whaling in the Faroe Islands: History, Ethnography, Symbol* (Tórshavn: Faroe University Press, 2009), 129.

14. The World Bank, *St. Vincent and the Grenadines,* 2016, http://data.worldbank.org /country/st-vincent-and-the-grenadines.

15. Jonathan Wylie, "Grindadráp," in *Ring of Dancers: Images of Faroese Culture,* ed. Jonathan Wylie and David Margolin (Philadelphia: University of Pennsylvania Press, 1981), 114.

16. Ibid., 99.

17. Jonathan Wylie, *The Faroe Islands: Interpretations of History* (Lexington: University Press of Kentucky, 1987).

18. Jonathan Wylie, "The Christmas Meeting in Context: The Construction of Faroese National Identity and the Structure of Scandinavian Culture," *North Atlantic Studies* 1, no. 1 (1989): 5–13.

19. Ibid.

20. Joensen, "Faroese Pilot Whaling in the Light of Social and Cultural History," 182.

21. Ibid.

22. Kenneth Williamson, *The Atlantic Islands: A Study of the Faeroe Life and Scene* (Glasgow: Collins, 1948), 96.

23. Sanderson, "Grindadráp," 1.

24. Hagstova Føroya, "Statistics Faroe Islands—Statbank," http://www.hagstova.fo. Accessed September 1, 2017.

25. Russell Fielding, "Environmental Change as a Threat to the Pilot Whale Hunt in the Faroe Islands," *Polar Research* 29 (2010): 430–438.

26. Bjarki Gyldenkærne Dalsgarð, email message to author, July 24, 2015.

27. Björn Lindahl, "Kaj Leo Johannesen: The Faroe Islands' Challenge Is to Keep Hold of Its Youths," *Nordic Labour Journal,* December 11, 2013, http://www.nordic labourjournal.org/artikler/portrett/portrait-2013-1/article.2013-12-10.6561116189.

28. Kimberly Cannady, "Dancing on Fissures: Alternative Senses of Crisis in the Faroe Islands," in *Crisis in the Nordic Nations and Beyond: At the Intersection of Environment, Finance and Multiculturalism,* ed. Kristín Loftsdóttir and Lars Jensen (Farnham, UK: Ashgate, 2014), 92.

29. Løgmansskrivstovan, *The Faroe Islands: A North Atlantic Perspective on Sustainable Development* (Tórshavn: Løgmansskrivstovan, 2002).

30. Ragnheiður Bogadóttir and Elisabeth Skarðhamar Olsen, "Making Degrowth Locally Meaningful: The Case of the Faroese *Grindadráp,*" *Journal of Political Ecology* 24 (2017): 507.

31. Wylie, "Grindadráp," 109.

32. Erich Hoyt and Glen T. Hvenegaard, "A Review of Whale-Watching and Whaling with Applications for the Caribbean," *Coastal Management* 30 (2002): 381–399.

33. J. E. S. Higham and D. Lusseau, "Urgent Need for Empirical Research into Whaling and Whale-Watching," *Conservation Biology* 21, no. 2 (2007): 554–558.

34. Hoyt and Hvenegaard, "A Review of Whale-Watching and Whaling."

35. Cleve R. Wootson Jr., "Whale-Watchers Horrified to Witness Fishermen Harpoon Two Orcas," *Washington Post,* April 6, 2017; Sarah Gibbens, "Killing of Orcas in Front of Tourists Could Spell End of Whaling for Island Nation," *National Geographic,* April 6, 2017.

36. Kenton X. Chance, "St. Vincent to Outlaw Killing of Orcas," *iWitness News,* April 5, 2017, https://www.iwnsvg.com/2017/04/05/st-vincent-to-outlaw-killing-of -orcas.

37. Ibid.

38. Hoyt and Hvenegaard, "A Review of Whale-Watching and Whaling."

39. Martin D. Robards and Randall R. Reeves, "The Global Extent and Character of Marine Mammal Consumption by Humans: 1970–2009," *Biological Conservation* 144 (2011): 2770–2786; Ronald Sanders, "Dominica: A Whale of a Pride," BBC Caribbean, March 30, 2009, http://www.bbc.co.uk/caribbean/news/story/2009/03/printable/090327_sanders_dominica.shtml.

40. Bonham C. Richardson, *The Caribbean in the Wider World 1492–1992: A Regional Geography* (Cambridge, UK: Cambridge University Press, 1992), 127.

41. "In Pictures: Spectrum of Opinion at Whaling Meeting," BBC News, 2006, slide 5, http://news.bbc.co.uk/2/shared/spl/hi/pop_ups/06/sci_nat_spectrum_of_opinion_at_whaling_meeting/html/5.stm.

42. "In Pictures: Spectrum of Opinion at Whaling Meeting," BBC News, 2006, slide 6, http://news.bbc.co.uk/2/shared/spl/hi/pop_ups/06/sci_nat_spectrum_of_opinion_at_whaling_meeting/html/6.stm.

43. Mark Orams, "From Whale Hunting to Whale-Watching in Tonga: A Sustainable Future?," *Journal of Sustainable Tourism* 9, no. 2 (2001): 128–146.

44. Wylie, "Too Much of a Good Thing," 353.

45. Sanderson, "Grindadráp," 15.

46. Lawrence Millman, *Last Places: A Journey in the North* (London: André Deutsch, 1990), 39.

47. Joensen, *Pilot Whaling in the Faroe Islands,* 54.

48. Ibid.

10. THE MERCURIAL SEA

1. Jóan Pauli Joensen, *Pilot Whaling in the Faroe Islands: History, Ethnography, Symbol* (Tórshavn: Faroe University Press, 2009), 70.

2. John F. West, *The History of the Faroe Islands, 1709–1816*, vol. 1, *1709–1723* (Copenhagen: Reitzels, 1985), 102.

3. Ethel A. Starbird, "St. Vincent, the Grenadines, and Grenada: Taking It as It Comes," *National Geographic*, September 1979, 410.

4. John E. Adams, "Last of the Caribbean Whalemen," *Natural History* 103 (1994): 72.

5. Ibid.

6. Nigel M. Scott, "The Current Status and Management Options for the Mammalian Fishery in Barrouallie, St. Vincent, West Indies," MS thesis, University of the West Indies, 1995, 6.

7. Russell Fielding, "Whaling Futures: A Survey of Faroese and Vincentian Youth on the Topic of Artisanal Whaling," *Society and Natural Resources* 26, no. 7 (2013): 810–826.

8. Peggy Seeger and Ewan MacColl, *The Singing Island: A Collection of English and Scots Folksongs* (London: Mills Music, 1960), 69.

9. Dean W. Boening, "Ecological Effects, Transport, and Fate of Mercury: A General Review," *Chemosphere* 40 (2000): 1335–1351.

10. Philippe Grandjean, David Bellinger, Åke Bergman, Sylvaine Cordier, George Davey-Smith, Brenda Eskenazi, David Gee, Kimberly Gray, Mark Hanson, Peter van den Hazel, Jerrold J. Heindel, Birger Heinzow, Irva Hertz-Picciotto, Howard Hu, Terry T.-K. Huang, Tina Kold Jensen, Philip J. Landrigan, I. Caroline Mc-Millen, Katsuyuki Murata, Beate Ritz, Greet Schoeters, Niels Erik Skakkebæk, Staffan Skerfving, and Pál Weihe, "The Faroes Statement: Human Health Effects of Developmental Exposure to Chemicals in Our Environment," *Basic and Clinical Pharmacology and Toxicology* 102 (2007): 73–75. See also the report from the National Research Council of the United States, *Toxicological Effects of Methylmercury* (Washington, DC: National Academy Press, 2000).

11. Timothy S. George, *Minamata: Pollution and the Struggle for Democracy in Postwar Japan* (Cambridge, MA: Harvard University Press, 2001).

12. World Health Organization, *Exposure to Mercury: A Major Public Health Concern* (Geneva: WHO, 2007), 3.

13. United Nations Environmental Programme, *Minamata Convention on Mercury* (Nairobi: UNEP, 2013), 6.

14. Kåre Julshamn, Allan Andersen, Ole Ringdal, and Jacup Mørkøre, "Trace Elements Intake in the Faroe Islands: I. Element Levels in Edible Parts of Pilot Whales (*Globicephalus meleanus*)," *Science of the Total Environment* 65 (1987): 53–62.

15. Dorete Bloch, *Pilot Whales and the Whale Drive* (Tórshavn: H. N. Jacobsens Bókahandil), 2007.

16. Pál Weihe and Høgni Debes Joensen, *Recommendations to the Government of the Faroe Islands Concerning the Pilot Whale. English Translation Released 1 December 2008* (Tórshavn: Landslægen, 1998).

17. Ibid.

18. Paul Watson, email message to author, October 25, 2005.

19. World Society for the Protection of Animals, "Animal Welfare Groups Condemn Faroese Pilot Whale Hunt," press release, 2009, 1.

20. Krishna Das, Virginie Debacker, Stéphane Pilletand, and Jean-Marie Bouquegneau, "Heavy Metals in Marine Mammals," in *Toxicology of Marine Mammals*, ed. Joseph G. Vos, Gregory D. Bossart, Michael Fournier, and Thomas J. O'Shea (New York: Taylor and Francis, 2003), 135–167.

21. Elin B. Heinesen, "Cultural Clashes Make Sea Shepherd Campaign Counterproductive," Heinesen.info, August 4, 2014, http://heinesen.info/wp/blog/2014/08/04/cultural-clashes-make-the-sscs-grindstop-campaign-counterproductive.

22. Kári Thorsteinsson, "Whaling in the Faroe Islands in Brief," *Heimabeiti,* 2014, http://www.heimabeiti.fo/default.asp?page=3&id=502.

23. Pál Weihe and Høgni D. Joensen, "Dietary Recommendations Regarding Pilot Whale Meat and Blubber in the Faroe Islands," *International Journal of Circumpolar Health* 71 (2012): 18594–18598.

24. Ibid.

25. Philip T. Wheeler, *The Faroe Islands: Fieldwork in 1975 with Background Information,* Regional Studies Series, no. 21 (Nottingham: Geographical Field Group, 1978);

G. A. Greener, "The Coal-Fields of the Faröe Islands," *Transactions of the Institution of Mining Engineers* 27 (1905): 331–342. Another author notes that the "first investigations" of coal in the Faroe Islands took place even earlier, in 1626; West, *The History of the Faroe Islands,* 164.

26. Petter Hojem, *Mining in the Nordic Countries: A Comparative Review of Legislation and Taxation* (Copenhagen: Norden, 2015).

27. Hagstova Føroya, "Statistics Faroe Islands—Statbank," http://www.hagstova.fo. Accessed September 15, 2017.

28. Kaj Leo Johannesen, personal communication, August 16, 2012.

29. Fielding, "Whaling Futures."

30. Russell Fielding and David W. Evans, "Mercury in Caribbean Dolphins (*Stenella longirostris* and *Stenella frontalis*) Caught for Human Consumption off St. Vincent, West Indies," *Marine Pollution Bulletin* 89 (2014): 30–34.

31. David C. Evers, D. G. Buck, S. M. Johnson, and M. Burton, *Mercury in the Global Environment: Understanding Spatial Patterns for Biomonitoring Needs of the Minamata Convention on Mercury* (Portland, ME: Biodiversity Research Institute, 2017).

32. Paul Lewis, "Commentary: Goodbye to the Whale Hunt!," *Caribbean News Now,* May 31, 2012, http://www.caribbeannewsnow.com/svg.php?news_id=11130.

33. AMAP, *AMAP Assessment Report: Arctic Pollution Issues* (Oslo: Arctic Monitoring and Assessment Programme, 1998), x.

34. United Nations Environment Programme, *GEO-6 Regional Assessment for Latin America and the Caribbean* (Nairobi: UNEP, 2016).

35. Darah Gibson, Kyrstn Zylich, and Dirk Zeller, "Preliminary Reconstruction of Total Marine Fisheries Catches for the Faroe Islands in Faroe Islands' EEZ Waters (1950–2010)," Working Paper #2015–36, University of British Columbia, 2015.

36. Roderick Frazier Nash, *The Rights of Nature: A History of Environmental Ethics* (Madison: University of Wisconsin Press, 1989), 182.

37. Stephen Leatherwood and Randall R. Reeves, *The Sierra Club Handbook of Whales and Dolphins* (San Francisco: Sierra Club Books, 1983), 29.

38. Neri James, Chief Environmental Health Officer, personal communication, March 20, 2018.

39. Mike Day, dir., *The Islands and the Whales* (North Berwick, Scotland: Intrepid Cinema, 2016), http://intrepidcinema.com/the-islands-and-the-whales.

40. Pál Weihe, email message to author, January 29, 2009.

41. Rolf Smith, "Last of the Viking Whalers," *National Geographic* 223, no. 6 (June 2013): 133.

42. Adams, "Last of the Caribbean Whalemen," 72.

43. Russell Fielding, "Environmental Change as a Threat to the Pilot Whale Hunt in the Faroe Islands," *Polar Research* 29 (2010): 430–438.

44. Ragnheiður Bogadóttir and Elisabeth Skarðhamar Olsen, "Making Degrowth Locally Meaningful: The Case of the Faroese *Grindadráp,*" *Journal of Political Ecology* 24 (2017): 508.

CONCLUSION

1. Phillip J. Clapham, "Managing Leviathan: Conservation Challenges for the Great Whales in a Post-Whaling World," *Oceanography* 29, no. 3 (2016), http://dx.doi.org /10.5670/oceanog.2016.70.

2. Philip J. Clapham, Alex Aguilar, and Leila Hatch, "Determining Spatial and Temporal Scales for Management: Lessons from Whaling," *Marine Mammal Science* 24, no. 1 (2008): 183–201.

3. David Lowenthal, *The Past Is a Foreign Country* (Cambridge, UK: Cambridge University Press, 1985).

4. Herman Melville, *Moby-Dick, or the Whale* (New York: Harper & Brothers, 1851), 432.

5. Paul Watson, "The Murder of the Whales, Courtesy of the Royal Danish Navy," Sea Shepherd Conservation Society, July 24, 2015, https://seashepherd.org/2015 /07/24/the-murder-of-the-whales-courtesy-of-the-royal-danish-navy/; "Thousands Around the World Support Sea Shepherd's 'World Love for Dolphins Day,'" Sea Shepherd Conservation Society, February 19, 2016, https://seashepherd.org /news/thousands-around-the-world-support-sea-shepherds-world-love-for -dolphins-day/.

6. Arne Kalland, "Management by Totemization: Whale Symbolism and the Anti-Whaling Campaign," paper presented at the Workshop in Political Theory and Policy Analysis, Indiana University, October 14, 1994, http://dlc.dlib.indiana.edu /dlc/bitstream/handle/10535/1437/Management_by_Totemization_Whale _Symbolism_and_the_Anti-Whaling_Campaign.pdf.

7. Alvin P. Sanoff, "One Must Not Forget," *U.S. News & World Report,* October 27, 1986, 68.

8. Robert B. Robertson, *Of Whales and Men* (New York: Knopf, 1954); Rolf Smith, "Last of the Viking Whalers," *National Geographic* 223, no. 6 (June 2013): 118–133.

9. Melville, *Moby-Dick,* 240.

10. Robert J. Sawyer, *Hominids: The Neanderthal Parallax* (New York: Tor, 2002), 319.

11. John Dos Passos, *The Theme Is Freedom* (New York: Dodd, Mead, 1956), 255.

Further Reading

THE FAROE ISLANDS AND WIDER NORTH ATLANTIC

The Faroe Islands Podcast, website. http://www.faroepodcast.com/

Guttesen, Rolf, ed. *The Faeroe Islands Topographical Atlas.* Copenhagen: Det Kongelige Danske Geografiske Selskab and Kort & Matrikelstyrelsen.

Millman, Lawrence. *Last Places: A Journey in the North.* London: André Deutsch, 1990.

Nansen, Fridtjof. *In Northern Mists: Arctic Exploration in Early Times.* New York: Frederick A. Stokes Company, 1911.

Sauer, Carl O. *Northern Mists.* Berkeley: University of California Press, 1968.

Williamson, Kenneth. *The Atlantic Islands: A Study of the Faeroe Life and Scene.* Glasgow: Collins, 1948.

Wylie, Jonathan. *The Faroe Islands: Interpretations of History.* Lexington: University Press of Kentucky, 1987.

Wylie, Jonathan, and David Margolin, eds. *Ring of Dancers: Images of Faroese Culture.* Philadelphia: University of Pennsylvania Press, 1981.

ST. VINCENT & THE GRENADINES AND THE WIDER CARIBBEAN

Grossman, Lawrence S. *The Political Ecology of Bananas: Contract Farming, Peasants, and Agrarian Change in the Eastern Caribbean.* Chapel Hill: University of North Carolina Press, 1998.

Kirby, I. A. Earle, and Christian I. Martin. *The Rise and Fall of the Black Caribs of St. Vincent.* Kingstown: St. Vincent Archaeological and Historical Society, 1972.

Maher, Julianne. *The Survival of People and Languages: Schooners, Goats and Cassava in St. Barthélemy, French West Indies.* Leiden: Brill, 2013.

Richardson, Bonham C. *Caribbean Migrants: Environment and Human Survival on St. Kitts and Nevis.* Knoxville: University of Tennessee Press, 1983.

——. *The Caribbean in the Wider World, 1492–1992: A Regional Geography.* Cambridge, UK: Cambridge University Press, 1992.

Taylor, Christopher. *The Black Carib Wars: Freedom, Survival, and the Making of the Garifuna.* Jackson: University Press of Mississippi, 2012.

Young, Virginia Heyer. *Becoming West Indian: Culture, Self, and Nation in St. Vincent.* Washington, DC: Smithsonian Institution Press, 1993.

WHALING IN THE FAROE ISLANDS

Bloch, Dorete. *Pilot Whales and the Whale Drive.* Tórshavn: H.N. Jacobsens Bókahandil, 2007.

Day, Mike. *The Islands and the Whales.* Documentary film. North Berwick, Scotland: Intrepid Cinema, 2016. http://intrepidcinema.com/the-islands-and-the-whales/

Føroya Landsstýri. "Whales and Whaling in the Faroe Islands." http://www.whaling.fo/

Goodman, Jeff. *Black Harvest: the Fight for the Pilot Whale.* Documentary film. London: British Broadcasting Company, 1987.

Huguet, Benjamin. *The Archipelago.* Documentary film. Beaconsfield, UK: National Film and Television School, 2015. DVD.

Joensen, Jóan Pauli. *Pilot Whaling in the Faroe Islands: History, Ethnography, Symbol.* Tórshavn: Faroe University Press, 2009.

Kerins, Seán P. *A Thousand Years of Whaling: A Faroese Common Property Regime.* Edmonton: CCI Press, 2010.

Lindquist, Ole. *Peasant Fisherman Whaling in the Northeast Atlantic Area: ca 900–1900 AD.* Akureyri, Iceland: Háskólinn á Akureyri, 1997.

Sanderson, Kate. "Grindadráp: The Discourse of Drama." *North Atlantic Studies* 2, no. 1–2 (1990): 196–204.

——. "Grindadráp: A Textual History of Whaling Traditions in the Faroes to 1900." M.Ph. thesis, University of Sydney, 1992.

WHALING IN ST. VINCENT & THE GRENADINES

Abrahams, Roger D. *Deep the Water, Shallow the Shore: Three Essays on Shantying in the West Indies.* Austin: University of Texas Press, 1974.

Adams, John E. "Last of the Caribbean Whalemen." *Natural History* 103 (1994): 64–72.

Junger, Sebastian. "The Whale Hunters." Chap. 3 in *Fire.* New York: W.W. Norton, 2001.

Romero, Aldemaro. "Yankee Whaling in the Caribbean Basin: Its Impact in a Historical Context." In *New Approaches to the Study of Marine Mammals,* edited by Aldemaro Romero and Edward O. Keith, 223–232. Vienna: InTech, 2012.

Ward, Nathalie. *Blows, Mon, Blows! A History of Bequia Whaling.* Woods Hole, MA: Gecko Productions, 1995.

Weston, Tom. *The Wind that Blows: A Portrait of the Last Yankee Whalers.* Documentary film. Bequia, St. Vincent & the Grenadines: The Grenadines Motion Picture Company, 2014. DVD.

WHALES AND WHALING AROUND THE WORLD

Barnes, Richard H. *Sea Hunters of Indonesia: Fishers and Weavers of Lamalera.* Oxford: Clarendon Press, 1996.

Basilio, Aurelio. *Caza y Pesca en Annobon.* Madrid: Instituto de Estudios Africanos, 1957.

Brydon, Anne. *The Eye of the Guest: Icelandic Nationalist Discourse and the Whaling Issue.* Ottawa: National Library of Canada, 1992.

Burnett, D. Graham. *Trying Leviathan: The Nineteenth-Century New York Court Case that Put the Whale on Trial and Challenged the Order of Nature.* Princeton: Princeton University Press, 2007.

Chase, Owen. *The Wreck of the Whaleship Essex.* San Diego: Harcourt Brace and Company, 1993.

Clapham, Phillip J. "Managing Leviathan: Conservation Challenges for the Great Whales in a Post-Whaling World." *Oceanography* 29, no. 3 (2016). http://dx.doi.org/10.5670/oceanog.2016.70.

Clode, Danielle. *Killers in Eden: the Story of a Rare Partnership between Men and Killer Whales.* Sydney: Allen & Unwin, 2002.

Culik, Boris. *Review of Small Cetaceans: Distribution, Behaviour, Migration and Threats.* Bonn: UNEP, 2004.

Day, David. *The Whale War.* London: Routledge, 1987.

Dickinson, Anthony B., and Chesley W. Sanger. *Twentieth-Century Shore-Station Whaling in Newfoundland and Labrador.* Montréal: McGill-Queen's University Press, 2005.

Dorsey, Kurkpatrick. *Whales and Nations: Environmental Diplomacy on the High Seas.* Seattle: University of Washington Press, 2013.

Elliott, Wendy, Heather Sohl, and Valerie Burgener. *Small Cetaceans: The Forgotten Whales.* Gland, Switzerland: World Wildlife Fund, 2009.

Epstein, Charlotte. *The Power of Words in International Relations: Birth of an Anti-Whaling Discourse.* Cambridge, MA: MIT Press, 2008.

Estes, James A., Douglas P. DeMaster, Daniel F. Doak, Terrie M. Williams, and Robert L. Brownell, Jr., eds. *Whales, Whaling, and Ocean Ecosystems.* Berkeley: University of California Press, 2006.

Fielding, Russell. "The Whale Drivers of Newfoundland." *Focus on Geography* 52, no. 3 (2009): 1–8.

Freeman, Milton, and Urs P. Kreuter, eds. *Elephants and Whales: Resources for Whom?* Basel: Gordon and Breach, 1994.

Gambell, Robert. "International Management of Whales and Whaling: An Historical Review of the Regulation of Commercial and Aboriginal Subsistence Whaling." *Arctic* 46, no. 2 (1993): 97–107.

Gillespie, Alexander. *Whaling Diplomacy: Defining Issues in International Environmental Law.* Cheltenham, UK: Edward Elgar, 2005.

Hoare, Phillip. *The Whale: In Search of the Giants of the Sea.* New York: Ecco, 2010.

International Whaling Commission, website. https://iwc.int/

Jefferson, Thomas, Marc Webber, and Robert Pitman. *Marine Mammals of the World: A Comprehensive Guide to their Identification.* London: Elsevier, 2015.

Kalland, Arne. *Unveiling the Whale: Discourses on Whales and Whaling.* New York: Berghahn Books, 2009.

Kraus, Scott D., and Rosalind M. Rolland. *The Urban Whale: North Atlantic Right Whales at the Crossroads.* Cambridge, MA: Harvard University Press, 2007.

Melville, Herman. *Moby-Dick, or the Whale.* New York: Harper & Brothers, 1851.

Mitchell, Edward. *Porpoise, Dolphin, and Small Whale Fisheries of the World.* Morges, Switzerland: IUCN, 1975.

Mowat, Farley. *A Whale for the Killing.* Boston: Little, Brown, 1972.

———. *Sea of Slaughter.* Toronto: McClelland & Stewart, 1984.

Payne, Roger. *Among Whales.* New York: Scribner, 1995.

Psihoyos, Louie. *The Cove.* Documentary film. Santa Monica: Lionsgate, 2001. DVD.

Reeves, Randall R. "The Origins and Character of 'Aboriginal Subsistence' Whaling: A Global Review," *Mammal Review* 32, no. 2 (2002): 71–106.

Robards, Martin D., and Randall R. Reeves, "The Global Extent and Character of Marine Mammal Consumption by Humans: 1970–2009." *Biological Conservation* 144 (2011): 2770–2786.

Robertson, Robert B. *Of Whales and Men.* New York: Knopf, 1954.

Roman, Joe. *Whale.* London: Reaktion, 2006.

Sakakibara, Chie. "Kiavallakkikput Agviq (Into the Whaling Cycle): Cetaceousness and Climate Change among the Iñupiat of Arctic Alaska." *Annals of the Association of American Geographers* 100, no. 4 (2010): 1003–1012.

Severin, Tim. *In Search of Moby Dick: The Quest for the White Whale.* New York: Basic Books, 2000.

Shoemaker, Nancy. "Whale Meat in American History." *Environmental History* 10, no. 2 (2005): 269–294.

Sullivan, Robert. *A Whale Hunt: How a Native-American Village Did What No One Thought It Could.* New York: Simon & Schuster, 2000.

Szabo, Vicki E. *Monstrous Fishes and the Mead-Dark Sea: Whaling in the Medieval North Atlantic.* Leiden: Brill, 2008.

Tønnessen, Johan Nicolay, and Arne Odd Johnsen. *The History of Modern Whaling.* Berkeley: University of California Press, 1982.

Würsig, Bernd, J. G. M. Thewissen, and Kit M. Kovacs, eds. *Encyclopedia of Marine Mammals.* London: Elsevier, 2017.

THE OCEAN

Bates, Marston. *The Forest and the Sea.* New York: Random House, 1960.

Carson, Rachel. *The Sea Around Us.* Oxford: Oxford University Press, 1951.

Earle, Sylvia. *Sea Change: A Message of the Oceans.* New York: Putnam, 1995.

Hugill, Stan. *Shanties from the Seven Seas: Shipboard Work-Songs and Songs Used as Work-Songs from the Great Days of Sail.* London: Routledge, 1961.

Safina, Carl. *Song for the Blue Ocean: Encounters Along the World's Coasts and Beneath the Seas.* New York: Holt, 1998.

Winchester, Simon. *Atlantic.* New York: Harper, 2010.

MERCURY AND OTHER POLLUTION

AMAP. *AMAP Assessment Report: Arctic Pollution Issues.* Oslo: Arctic Monitoring and Assessment Program, 1998.

Carson, Rachel. *Silent Spring.* Boston: Houghton Mifflin, 1962.

Evers, David C., D. G. Buck, S.M. Johnson, and M. Burton. *Mercury in the Global Environment: Understanding spatial patterns for biomonitoring needs of the Minamata Convention on Mercury.* Portland, ME: Biodiversity Research Institute, 2017.

George, Timothy S. *Minamata: Pollution and the Struggle for Democracy in Postwar Japan.* Cambridge, MA: Harvard University Press, 2001.

National Research Council of the United States. *Toxicological Effects of Methylmercury.* Washington, DC: National Academy Press, 2000.

United Nations Environment Programme. *Minimata Convention on Mercury.* Nairobi: UNEP, 2013.

World Health Organization. *Exposure to Mercury: A Major Public Health Concern.* Geneva: WHO, 2007.

Acknowledgments

Many authors start these sections with something along the lines of "This book couldn't have been written without . . ." I had always read that sort of thing as hyperbole until I finished this project. Now I can sincerely say, without exaggeration, that were it not for the assistance, guidance, and patience of two individuals—Vincent Reid in St. Vincent and the late Dorete Bloch in the Faroe Islands—this book simply would not exist. So much of what I learned and experienced is traceable to them. Vincent and Dorete each served as a mentor, teacher, liaison, and friend. I'm honored to know them both.

Vincent Reid's day job is supervising the Solid Waste Management Unit for St. Vincent & the Grenadines. His passion, though—and his expertise—is the cultural and environmental heritage of his namesake island. He is a combination fixer, amateur anthropologist and historian, tour guide, photographer, performer, and ambassador. He knows everyone on the island and can work anything out. Since we met in 2008, Vincent's charm and persuasiveness have worked countless times on my behalf with whalers, fisheries officers, and all manner of gatekeepers. I wish every academic fieldworker had a local contact like Vincent Reid wherever they work.

Dorete Bloch was one of the world's foremost experts on pilot whale biology. I first met her in 2005, during the initial season of my Faroe Islands research. I had just been awarded—much to my astonishment—a "traveling scholarship" from Fróðskaparsetur Føroya (the University of the Faroe Islands) that would pay for my fieldwork that year. Seeing something I did not yet see myself, Dorete believed in my ability as a researcher. She guided me along the way as I began the study that would eventually lead to this book. Dorete offered me free lodging at her research station, put me in touch with key interviewees, allowed me access to her vast library of whaling literature and data, and trusted me with the keys to the grind-mobile. (This last favor was ill-advised, it would turn out, as both the grind-mobile's front bumper and the bridge railing in Gjógv would attest—if they could.) More than these, though, she served as a mentor to my work at a time when I needed to learn a lot about how international environmental research is conducted. When Dorete died in 2015, we lost a great scientist and a wonderful person.

In St. Vincent, the following people also deserve heartfelt thanks: Samuel Hazelwood, who invited me onto his whaling boat and taught me his trade; Samuel's crewmembers, especially Papas and Limb, who accepted their boss's decision and welcomed me onboard; Diallo Boyea, whose interest in my research and willingness to contribute went far beyond what I was able to pay him for his time; the Honourable Saboto Caesar, Minister of Agriculture, Forestry, Fisheries and Rural Transformation, whose accessibility to me, my students, and my colleagues gave this research the government-approved legitimacy that it needed; Jennifer Cruickshank-Howard and Kris Isaacs at the Fisheries Division, who worked hard to facilitate all the paperwork my research required, especially the dreadful (but necessary) CITES permits; Adam Gravel and Tori Woodward of Salvage Blue, whose uncompromising commitment to both the people and the environment of the Caribbean should serve as a model to conservation organizations everywhere; and the John family—Darwin, Clare, Simeon, and Mirella—who welcomed me into their "Vincy Home" and showed me true Caribbean hospitality.

In the Faroe Islands, I owe more than can be expressed with a simple *takk fyri* to Kate Sanderson, with whom I corresponded long before ever docking in Tórshavn harbor and walking ashore for the first day of research that led to this book. Kate wrote such perceptive and well-researched prose about the grindadráp that I view my own work as merely filling in what Kate already knows but simply hasn't gotten around to writing down yet. More thanks are due to

Ólavur Sjúrðarberg, who transmitted his knowledge and experience to me gradually, speaking softly over many dinners of grind og spik in his Leirvík home; Bjarki Gyldenkærne Dalsgarð and Matthew Workman, who both always seem to be available to answer random questions about Faroese culture, nature, linguistics, or politics; Bjarni Mikkelsen, Janus Hansen, and Høgni Arnbjarnarson of Føroya Náttúrugripasavn (the Faroese Museum of Natural History) for their mentorship; Sarita Heinesen, Bjørki Geyti, and Astrid Andreasen, for their warmth and hospitality; David Geyti, for being a partner in adventure-seeking; Hannes Lesch and Eleonora Flach, for their sharing of food and labor; and Joen Remmer and Katja Dhyr Remmer, for their hospitality, food, and friendship.

Research funding for fieldwork that contributed to this book was granted by the Faculty Development Program at the University of the South, the Faculty Research Fund at the University of Denver, the West-Russell Fund at Louisiana State University, the Instructional Development Grant program at the University of Prince Edward Island, the dean's discretionary research fund at the University of Montana, the PhD grant program at Granskingarráðið (the Faroese Research Council), the traveling scholarship program at Fróðskaparsetur Føroya, the Bowman Expedition Fund and the McColl Family Fellowship at the American Geographical Society, and the Research Support Fund at the Viking Society for Northern Research. Without this support I would have, at best, had to resort to more Dumpster-diving and undocumented capoeira instruction. At worst, the project never would have been completed.

My approach to this kind of human-environmental research was developed under the guidance of my academic mentors—Kent Mathewson, Godfrey Baldacchino, and Jeffrey Gritzner—and I hope this book makes them proud. My work is buoyed by the support of my colleagues at Sewanee, especially Stephanie Batkie, John Gatta, David Haskell, Mark Hopwood, Eric Keen, Deb McGrath, Matthew Mitchell, Terry Papillon, Bran Potter, Sarah Sherwood, Clint Smith, Ken Smith, Scott Torreano, Jordan Troisi, and Chris Van de Ven, among others. Colleagues at other institutions—including Don Berg-felt and Fortune Sithole at Ross University, Adam Dahl at the University of Massachusetts Amherst, Jess Dutton at Texas State, Geoff Hill at Auburn, Jeremy Kiszka at Florida International, Angela Loder at the International Well Building Institute, Amy Potter at Georgia Southern, Benedict Singleton at the Swedish University of Agricultural Sciences, and Emma Smith at the University of the West Indies-Cave Hill—offered valuable advice and assistance during the research, writing, and publication processes. Special thanks are due to the Interlibrary Loan staff members at the University of the South and the University of Denver, who gladly accepted the challenge of tracking down ancient, obscure, and often non-English references to whaling activities in remote corners of the world.

The students who work with me in the lab and in the field are indispensable for their contributions to this project: Ellie Clark, Caroline Crews, Niko Darby, Stephen Fowler, Hannah-Marie Garcia, Michael Jacobs, Grey Jones, Helena Kilburn, Isabel Kirby, Komal Kunwar, Lauren Newman, Connor Peach, Suzanne Skinner, Luke Stallings, Leia Thompson, and Haley Tucker.

Thank you to the photographers who contributed their work to this book, allowing me to more fully tell this story with pictures as well as words: Høgni Arnbjarnarson, Andy Fielding, Bergur Hanusson, Terji Johansen, Tracy Ostrofsky, Joen Remmer, and Katja Dyhr Remmer. Special thanks to this book's cartographer, Alison Ollivierre, whose maps blend art and science in as effective and beautiful a way as I've ever seen.

It was an honor and a pleasure to work with Harvard University Press on this project. I want to especially thank Janice Audet for her expert editorial guidance through the entire process, as well as Esther Blanco-Benmaman, Kate Brick, Stephanie Vyce, and Rebekah White at Harvard and Angela Piliouras and Sue Warga at Westchester Publishing Services. This book was greatly improved through the effort of those who read and commented on early drafts of the manuscript: Sara Aparício, Bjarki Gyldenkærne Dalsgarð, Diane

Fielding, Catherine Macdonald, Aly Ollivierre, Will Winton, and the two anonymous readers whose peer reviews were secured by the publisher. Any of the book's faults that result either from errors that eluded the notice of these readers or from my own stubbornness in ignoring their advice are, of course, all mine.

Finally, to my family—parents Mark and Pat Fielding, brothers Andy and Cory, and most of all, Diane, Conrad, and Margaux at home—thank you sincerely for your love and support.

Index

Note: Figures are indexed in italic.